SO-CUH-918

REGIS COLLEGE LIBRARY
100 Wellesley Street West
Toronto, Ontario
Canada M5S 2Z5

THE SECOND VATICAN COUNCIL
ON OTHER RELIGIONS

THE SECOND VATICAN COUNCIL ON OTHER RELIGIONS

GERALD O'COLLINS, S.J.

REGIS COLLEGE LIBRARY
100 Wellesley Street West
Toronto, Ontario
Canada M5S 2Z5

OXFORD
UNIVERSITY PRESS

BX
1784
O26
2013

OXFORD
UNIVERSITY PRESS

Great Clarendon Street, Oxford, OX2 6DP,
United Kingdom

Oxford University Press is a department of the University of Oxford.
It furthers the University's objective of excellence in research, scholarship,
and education by publishing worldwide. Oxford is a registered trade mark of
Oxford University Press in the UK and in certain other countries

© Gerald O'Collins, S.J. 2013

The moral rights of the author have been asserted

First Edition published 2013

Impression: 1

All rights reserved. No part of this publication may be reproduced, stored in
a retrieval system, or transmitted, in any form or by any means, without the
prior permission in writing of Oxford University Press, or as expressly permitted
by law, by licence or under terms agreed with the appropriate reprographics
rights organization. Enquiries concerning reproduction outside the scope of the
above should be sent to the Rights Department, Oxford University Press, at the
address above

You must not circulate this work in any other form
and you must impose this same condition on any acquirer

British Library Cataloging in Publication Data
Data available

ISBN 978-0-19-967259-2

Printed in Great Britain by
the MPG Printgroup, UK

Preface

Publications, conferences, and other events are currently celebrating the fiftieth anniversary of the Second Vatican Council (1962–5). The task of interpreting and implementing the Council's teaching has now moved well into the twenty-first century. As Cardinal Franz König wrote in the London *Tablet* at Christmas 2002, 'the crucial process of reception, that all-important part of any church council, can take several generations. It continues today.' In his 'Spiritual Testament', dated 17 March 2000 and published after his death in April 2005, Pope John Paul II also wrote of the 'generations' involved in receiving and living Vatican II: 'For a long time to come it will be granted to new generations to draw on the riches which this Council of the twentieth century has blessed us with.'

At least three reasons encourage the ongoing reception of Vatican II. First, more diaries, personal archives, letters, and memoirs of those who shaped the Council and other new sources have become available: for instance, the council diary of a leading theological advisor at the Council, Yves Congar (1904–95). His two volumes in French, first published in 2002 and now translated into English (2012), record his contributions to eight of the sixteen texts promulgated by Vatican II. In 2001 Massimo Faggioli (with Giovanni Turbanti) listed and described the personal documentation then available (*Il Concilio inedito: Fonti del Vaticano II*). In a bibliographical survey published in the March 2008 issue of *Cristianesimo nella storia*, Turbanti could report a further batch of personal documents that had come to light. The passage of fifty years has continued to yield more and more historical and theological information about the Council's work and achievements.

Second, the sixteen documents of Vatican II amount to 30 per cent of the written texts coming from the twenty-one general councils of Catholic Christianity. Earlier councils often had a limited scope, frequently one dictated by the need to confront a specific crisis or heresy. The Second Vatican Council, called by Pope John XXIII to 'update' the life of the Catholic Church, offered a rich range of teaching. The first document to be promulgated, the Constitution on the Sacred Liturgy (*Sacrosanctum Concilium*) set the stage for the inner renewal of the Church. The last and longest, the Pastoral Constitution on the Church in the Modern World (*Gaudium et Spes*), spelled out the desire to live in solidarity with men and women everywhere, sharing their joys, hopes, and sufferings. Without having planned this in advance, the nearly 3,000 bishops who attended Vatican II moved from approving in 1963 a constitution aimed at revitalizing the worship of Roman Catholics to approving, in 1965 and at the very end of the Council, a constitution directed towards promoting the dignity and ultimate well-being of the whole human community. From start to finish, the Council had much to say about significant themes both 'within' and 'beyond' the Church (*ad intra* and *ad extra*).

Soon after Vatican II closed, some long and notable commentaries appeared: the twenty-four volumes of translation and commentary in French edited by Congar and others (1966–70); and five volumes in German edited by Herbert Vorgrimler and published in English as *Commentary on the Documents of Vatican II* (1967–9). Between 1970 and 1980, the acts of the Council appeared in twenty-eight volumes. René Latourelle organized a three-volume work, *Vatican II: Assessments and Perspectives* (1988–9). More recently, Giuseppe Alberigo and his group of international collaborators produced the five-volume *History of Vatican II*, which has appeared in seven languages and was edited in English by Joseph Komonchak (1995–2006). Peter Hünermann and Bernd Jochen Hilberath edited the five-volume *Herders Theologischer Kommentar zum Zweiten Vatikanischen Konzil* (2004–6). Many valuable monographs and innumerable articles have treated specific documents of Vatican II, particular themes it expounded, and its reception (e.g. Ormond Rush's landmark study, *Still Interpreting Vatican II: Some Hermeneutical Principles*, 2004). In an appendix to *Retrieving Fundamental Theology* (1993) I provided (with the help of Joseph Cassar) a forty-page bibliography on the Dogmatic Constitution on Divine Revelation (*Dei Verbum*). Four numbers of *Cristianesimo nella storia* (in 2003, 2005, 2008, and 2011) carried long annotated bibliographies on the Council, which amount to 132 pages and were prepared by Massimo Faggioli and his colleagues. But much more research still remains to be done—not only about the history, teaching, and ongoing reception of the Council but also about its theological background. The volume edited by Gabriel Flynn and Paul Murray, *Ressourcement: A Movement for Renewal in Twentieth-Century Catholic Theology* (2012), opens the way for further research into that background.

Third, interpreting, receiving, and implementing the teaching of Vatican II continues, and some of that work goes beyond what the bishops explicitly intended to convey through the sixteen texts they approved. Unquestionably, we should do our historical best to reconstruct what that body of authors had in mind when voting for the documents and addressing their audiences in the 1960s. But we should also allow for a plus value that goes beyond original meanings but without opposing them. In new and often greatly changed contexts, conciliar texts can communicate to their later readers more than their original authors ever consciously knew or meant.

In Chapter 10 of *Fundamental Theology* (1981) and later in Chapter 10 of *Rethinking Fundamental Theology* (2011), I joined others in maintaining that biblical texts gain a life of their own as they distance themselves from their original authors and addressees, enter new contexts, and find later readers. Here, in the terminology I first developed in 1981, the intention of the reader (*intentio legentis*) comes into play in activating potential meanings of texts produced by the sacred writers (*intentio auctoris*) and interpreted during 2,000 years of reception history (*intentio textus ipsius*). If this principle holds true of the Scriptures, it surely applies also to the sixteen documents of Vatican II.

Over the decades since the Council closed, the context in which we read those texts has changed enormously, both within and beyond the Church. Dramatic changes have affected the story of modern Catholicism. Let me mention only three such changes. First, in 1900 almost two-thirds of the world's Catholics lived in Europe and North America. A century later at least three quarters of them lived in Latin America, Africa, and Asia. When the Council ended in 1965 the world population had already crossed the three billion mark; by late 2011 it had moved beyond seven billion. Second, perhaps the most dramatic and surprising event in the twentieth century was the destruction of the Berlin Wall in November 1989, which signalled the collapse of the Soviet Union and the official end of Communism, at least in Europe. Third, both before and even more after 1989, new modes of communication and other hitherto unimaginable technological advances have promoted a globalized world economy, which, one must add, has done little to check the devastation of the human environment and the proliferation of ugly wars.

With an eye on the theme of this book, let me offer one example of reading texts in new contexts. The Second Vatican Council did not explicitly raise and answer the question: are other religions to be considered ways of salvation (and revelation)? But, as we will see below, the texts of the Council help us put and respond to this question in the global village of the twenty-first century.

In his serious and usually well documented *The Catholic Doctrine of Non-Christian Religions According to the Second Vatican Council* (1992), Miikka Ruokanen anticipated the theme of the present study. But he failed to include some important background items: for instance, the work of St Francis of Assisi, Blessed Ramon Llull, and Cardinal Nicholas of Cusa that marked the earlier history of Catholic Christianity's relations with 'the others'. Apropos of some relevant conciliar texts, more can be said and not least in the light of new information now available: for instance, it was Congar (as we know from an entry in his diary for 7 December 1965), who helped to shape two key articles in the Dogmatic Constitution on the Church, *Lumen Gentium* (nos. 16–17), and the first chapter of the Decree on the Church's Missionary Activity, *Ad Gentes.*

Moreover, Ruokanen's study also includes the relationship of the Catholic Church with Judaism, a massive and immensely important topic that involves studying the history of anti-Semitism and presents us with the fundamental question: how might Christians relate (a) Israel's ongoing covenantal life with God to (b) Christianity's belief in the universal revealing and saving significance of the crucified and risen Jesus? My book will have enough and more than enough to do by limiting itself to Vatican II's teaching on Buddhism, Hinduism, Islam, and other religions.

With that teaching, Catholics, for the first time in the history of Christianity, enjoyed some official guidelines on how they should view and then act towards the followers of other faiths. Since 1965 the Church's teaching in this area has assumed a fresh and more pressing importance. Huge population shifts that have brought Christians and 'others' into even closer proximity, the emergence of fanatical fundamentalism and terrorism, and a ruthless violence often practised by powerful governments have put interfaith relations at the top of the agenda for those who want to follow the injunction of

Christ to 'love your neighbour as yourself' (Mark 12: 31). The five articles of the Declaration on the Relation of the Church to Non-Christian Religions (*Nostra Aetate*) make it the shortest document approved by Vatican II, but in the post-9/11 world its prophetic value continues to grow.

The world situation supplies a 'political' urgency for any project aimed at presenting Vatican II's teaching on other faiths. Nevertheless, my primary purpose is that of 'setting the record straight'. Too often this teaching has been left unappreciated, played down, or in other ways misrepresented. After fifty years the task still remains of expounding critically the full scope of what the Council taught about the followers of other religions.

Chapters 1 and 2 of this book will summarize the historical background to the teaching of Vatican II on other faiths. That will take us from the New Testament, through the patristic period and the Middle Ages, and on to modern times—in particular, the teaching of Pope Pius XII and the thinking of such theologians as Jean Daniélou and Karl Rahner who helped to form and fashion what could and should be said about world religions.

Chapter 3 will examine what *Sacrosanctum Concilium* and *Lumen Gentium* said or at least implied about 'the religious others'. Chapter 4 will explore the teaching of the Declaration on the Relation of the Church to Non-Christian Religions, *Nostra Aetate* (in particular, nos. 1–3, 5).

Chapter 5 will take up the contribution of *Ad Gentes* (in particular, nos. 1–9). In Chapter 6, I will turn to some relevant teaching from the Pastoral Constitution on the Church in the Modern World, *Gaudium et Spes*. Chapter 7 will bring together the different strands of teaching gleaned from the five documents of Vatican II examined in Chapters 3 to 6.

The Council launched certain trajectories that belong very much to the story of its teaching on other religions. Hence Chapters 8 and 9 will examine some central features in the reception and development of this teaching by Vatican II, which came both in official (papal) teaching (John Paul II) and in theological reflection (Jacques Dupuis).

Chapter 10 will sketch the lasting challenges that confront the Catholic Church's teaching about and relationship to people of other living faiths.

The translation of biblical texts will normally follow the New Revised Standard Version; very occasionally I prefer my own rendering. In the case of the Vatican II documents, rather than use the translations edited by Walter Abbott, Austin Flannery, or Norman Tanner, I prefer to translate myself directly from the Latin original.

Right at the outset clarity demands that I briefly address (a) the nature of divine revelation, (b) its mediation, and (c) something introduced by Ruokanen, a traditional distinction between the supernatural and natural orders. Those who wish more information on (a) and (b) might consult the extensive treatment provided by my *Rethinking Fundamental Theology* (2011).

(a) With many others I understand revelation to be primarily the self-revelation *of God* and only secondarily a revelation (of knowledge) *about God*. To be sure, one should clarify what knowledge about God has been revealed—that is to say, the *content* of revelation. But, primarily and as an *event* or series of *events*, revelation means God's personal self-disclosure. Hence the primary question becomes: does or did God reveal himself to those who follow other religious traditions? And if so, what then, in a secondary place, might be the 'content' or knowledge about God conveyed through such events of revelation? Both within Christianity and beyond, it is essential to distinguish between knowing God (through events of personal divine self-disclosure) and what is then known about God (or the 'content' communicated through such events).

This distinction can also be expressed by contrasting 'Mystery' (in upper case) with 'mysteries' (in lower case)—a contrast that will be taken up in Chapter 4 below. Primarily revelation means the self-revelation of God who is Mystery (in upper case and in the singular). Secondarily and a consequence, revelation brings a knowledge of mysteries (in lower case and in the plural). Hitherto unknown and inaccessible mysteries about God are now disclosed. But, in the first instance, revelation involves the mysterious God, the Mystery, taking the initiative to encounter personally human beings.

(b) On the human side, such encounters are mediated through private prayer, public worship, and all manner of personal experiences of God, as well as through inherited religious beliefs and practices. Any attempts to limit the mediation of divine self-revelation through, for instance, the channel of human reason alone simply cannot account for what adherents of different faiths report about their encounters with the self-manifesting God.

Finally (c), some still want to maintain a distinction between 'supernature' and 'nature'—in this case between a supernatural revelation granted by God and a merely natural knowledge of God resulting from a human search. Such a distinction would have seemed strange to someone whom we will discuss in Chapter 1, St Justin Martyr (d. around AD 165). His view of the 'seeds of the Word' being scattered everywhere seemed, to speak anachronistically, to recognize everything as supernatural or coming through the gracious initiative of God. The supernature/nature distinction emerged in the Middle Ages, was taken up by the First Vatican Council (1869/70), but was not followed by Vatican II. God freely calls all to a supernatural destiny. Hence all divine self-revelation, wherever and whenever it occurs, must accordingly be deemed supernatural in its purpose and nature. In the world in which we live, all events of God's self-disclosure are supernatural or aimed to gift human beings with unmerited grace here and with glory hereafter. As is the case with (a) and (b) above, this theme (c) will emerge later in this book, especially when discussing Karl Rahner (end of Chapter 2) and *Lumen Gentium* 16 (Chapter 3). But to avoid misunderstanding, it seems important to clarify the three issues from the beginning.

In writing this book, I received considerable help and encouragement from Stephen Connelly, Bronwyn Wallace, and other staff members of the Dalton McCaughey Library (Melbourne), Siobhain Dib and Margaret Watts at the Veech Library (Sydney), John Borelli, David Burrell, Robert Gribben, Anne Hunt, Daniel Madigan, Danielle Mann, Thomas Michel, Randall Prior, Herman Roborgh, and Jared Wicks, as well as from Tom Perridge and two anonymous readers for Oxford University Press. For all that assistance, I am most grateful. I also wish to express my warm thanks to the community and staff at Jesuit Theological College, Parkville (Australia) where I wrote this work. With much gratitude and affection I dedicate this book to George Carey, Eileen Carey, John Batt, and Margaret Batt, who have for years proved such inspiring and encouraging friends.

Australian Catholic University and MCD University of Divinity,
Pentecost 2012.

Contents

REGIS COLLEGE LIBRARY
100 Wellesley Street West
Toronto, Ontario
Canada M5S 2Z5

Abbreviations

AAS	*Acta Apostolicae Sedis*
AG	Vatican II, *Ad Gentes*
DH	Vatican II, *Dignitatis Humanae*
DV	Vatican II, *Dei Verbum*
DzH	H. Denzinger and P. Hünermann (eds), *Enchiridion symbolorum, definitionum et declarationum* (42nd edn., Freiburg im Breisgau: Herder, 2009)
GS	Vatican II, *Gaudium et Spes*
LG	Vatican II, *Lumen Gentium*
NA	Vatican II, *Nostra Aetate*
ND	J. Neuner and J. Dupuis (eds.), *The Christian Faith* (7th edn, Bangalore and New York: Theological Publications in India/Alba House, 2001)
ODCC	F. L. Cross and E. A. Livingstone (eds), *The Oxford Dictionary of the Christian Church* (3rd edn, Oxford: Oxford University Press, 2005)
SC	Vatican II, *Sacrosanctum Concilium*
TRE	H. Krause and G. Müller (eds), *Theologische Realenzyklopädie*, 36 vols (Berlin: Walter de Gruyter, 1977–2004)
UR	Vatican II, *Unitatis Redintegratio*

ONE

From the New Testament
to the Middle Ages

Through the Word, all his creatures learn that there is one God, the
Father, who controls all things and gives existence to all.

St Irenaeus, *Adversus Haereses*

For the first time in the history of the twenty-one general councils
recognized by Catholic Christianity, the Second Vatican Council
developed some teaching on other religions. While Vatican II broke
new ground, there were, nevertheless, scriptural and other ancient
texts on which the Council drew in developing this doctrine. Let me
recall some major items offered by the New Testament and later
writings and observe how some of this material entered what Vatican
II would say about other religions in *Sacrosanctum Concilium, Lumen
Gentium, Nostra Aetate, Ad Gentes,* and *Gaudium et Spes* (in chronological order).

The New Testament

In *Salvation for All: God's Other Peoples*,[1] I wrote at book length about
the scriptural testimony to God's active benevolence in reaching out to
redeem and save all people. Here let me limit myself to some of that
witness, coming from several of Paul's letters, the Acts of the Apostles,

1. G. O'Collins, *Salvation for All: God's Other Peoples* (Oxford: Oxford University Press,
2008).

and the prologue to John's Gospel. I begin with three themes from Paul: Christ as the agent of creation, as the reconciler of the world, and as the last Adam.

Three Themes from Paul

(1) First of all, the Christian redefining of Jewish monotheism meant recognizing Christ as the agent through whom the whole of creation has come into existence and remains in existence: 'For us there is one God, the Father, from whom are all things and for whom we exist, and one Lord, Jesus Christ, through whom are all things and through whom we exist' (1 Cor. 8: 6).[2] Presumably the repeated 'we exist', like the 'for us', points primarily to Paul and his fellow Christians. But 'from whom are all things' (said of the Father) and 'through whom are all things' (said of the one Lord, Jesus Christ) come across as all-embracing; everything and everyone exist through the power of the Father and his Son. As the One who creates all things and keeps all things in existence, the Lord Jesus Christ is intimately involved in the existence of all human beings. Even though Paul did not draw such a conclusion, his profession of faith implied the sovereign rule and profound presence of Christ in the life of every man and woman, including the non-evangelized and non-baptized. First Corinthians 8: 6 turns up only once in the five Vatican II documents we will consider: in a footnote to *Ad Gentes* (3, n. 11), along with three similar texts from the New Testament (John 1: 3, 10; Col. 1: 16; Heb. 1: 2), in support of the statement that it was through the Son that God 'made the world' (*AG* 3). The Council might have used this Pauline teaching about Christ being powerfully present in all creation as a platform from which to reflect on the relationship of all human beings to him. But, as we shall see, it was the language of Acts 17 and the prologue to John's Gospel that *Ad Gentes, Lumen Gentium,* and *Nostra Aetate* privileged in presenting this relationship.

(2) Secondly, in two letters Paul introduced new terminology by using *reconciliation* to describe the redeeming work of Christ.[3] The

---

2. See Joseph A. Fitzmyer, *First Corinthians* (New Haven, CT: Yale University Press, 2008), 342–4; Anthony C. Thiselton, *The First Epistle to the Corinthians* (Grand Rapids, MI: Eerdmans, 2000), 635–8.
3. See O'Collins, *Salvation for All*, 122–3; O'Collins, *Jesus Our Redeemer: A Christian Approach to Salvation* (Oxford: Oxford University Press, 2007), 10–15.

reconciliation proclaimed by Paul embraces all humanity and may even enjoy a cosmic dimension. The earliest passage that deployed the language of reconciliation stated: 'through Christ, God reconciled us [all humanity] to himself and gave us [Paul] the ministry of reconciliation; that is, God was in Christ reconciling the world to himself' (2 Cor. 5: 18–19). The first 'us' denotes all human beings, Jews and Gentiles alike, whom God reconciled to himself through Christ. God took the initiative to reconcile to himself 'the world', that is to say, all sinful humanity and perhaps also (in the light of the 'new creation' in 2 Cor. 5: 17) the whole created universe.[4]

The second classic passage in which Paul writes of this reconciling action of God comes in Romans: 'while we were yet enemies, we were reconciled to God through the death of his Son' (Rom. 5: 10). The 'we' embraces both Jews and Gentiles. A few chapters later in the same letter, Paul employs the language of reconciliation to expound the universal impact of Christ's death and resurrection. With a view to Gentiles embracing Christian faith and so drawing more Jews to Christ, he writes of Christ effecting 'the reconciliation of the world' (Rom. 11: 15). Here 'world' denotes the human race, or at least the Gentiles who make up the overwhelming majority of human beings. 'World' may also point beyond the reconciliation of humanity and indicate a 'cosmic extension of that effect' to 'the whole universe'.[5] In these terms, the reconciliation with God achieved by Christ would touch both humanity and the entire created world. One is encouraged to interpret cosmically the 'reconciliation of the world' by what Paul has expounded three chapters earlier. Created nature, he expects, will be liberated from decay and share with human beings in the final freedom and glory (Rom. 8: 18–25).

A letter that may not have been written directly by Paul is clear about the cosmic dimension of the reconciliation brought by the crucified and risen Jesus: 'in him [Christ] all the fullness of God was pleased to dwell, and through him [God was pleased] to reconcile to

---

4. See Murray J. Harris, *The Second Epistle to the Corinthians* (Grand Rapids, MI: Eerdmans, 2005), 424–63; Thomas Stegman, *The Character of Jesus: The Linchpin of Paul's Argument in 2 Corinthians* (Rome: Pontificio Istituto Biblico, 2005), 181–3, 271–82; Margaret E. Thrall, *A Critical and Exegetical Commentary on the Second Epistle to the Corinthians* (Edinburgh: T. & T. Clark, 1994), 407–49.

5. Joseph A. Fitzmyer, *Romans* (New York: Doubleday, 1993), 612; see also 119–20, 400–1; Arland J. Hultgren, *Paul's Letter to the Romans* (Grand Rapids, MI: Eerdmans, 2011), 212–15, 408–9.

himself all things, whether on earth or in the heavens, making peace by the blood of his cross' (Col. 1: 19–20). However we interpret the nuances of 'all the fullness', only conscious agents can, properly speaking, be alienated and then reconciled with each other in a new, peaceful situation. 'All things' include here such agents (whether Jews or Gentiles), but evidently refer to more than them. It makes better sense to think of this 'reconciliation' not merely as establishing friendly relations between personal agents (God and sinners),[6] but also as Christ making all created things peacefully conform, at least in principle, to the wise plan of God.[7]

These two verses complete a hymn which depicts the supremacy and universal relevance of Christ not only in the order of redemption but also in that of creation. He is 'the firstborn over all creation', since every created thing has its origin 'through him', exists 'for him', and 'holds together in him' (Col. 1: 15–17). 'New creation' and the total created order define a further perspective when recognizing Christ's universal dominion and universal reconciling impact.

Many people feel themselves drawn to the warm, relational language of reconciliation. Such language continues to communicate well, and could have been taken up by the Second Vatican Council to express and develop a positive mindset towards the adherents of other religions. Once again the Council gave only a minor role to this Pauline terminology. Referring to 2 Corinthians 5: 18–19, *Nostra Aetate* confessed that in Christ, 'in whom God reconciled all things to himself', human beings 'find the fullness of [their] religious life' (*NA* 2). A footnote in *Ad Gentes* quoted a commentary on St John's Gospel by St Cyril of Alexandria. He linked (a) Paul's teaching on all people being 'reconciled to the Father' with (b) 'the Word' who dwells 'in all' (presumably here all the baptized) and forms 'one temple' and 'one body' (*AG* 7, n. 45) *Gaudium et Spes* appealed to the same verses in 2 Corinthians when confirming the statement that in Christ 'God reconciled us to himself and among ourselves' (*GS* 22, n. 25). Clearly the powerful presence of Christ as universal 'Reconciler'

---

6. Even if the hymn in Col. 1: 15–20 does not refer explicitly to human sin, the verses that follow make it clear that the divine work of reconciliation involves those who were formerly 'enemies' of God (Col. 1: 21–2).

7. On this hymn, see Markus Barth and Helmut Blanke, *Colossians* (New York: Doubleday, 1994), 193–251, esp. 213–24.

might have supplied a theology and terminology for the Council to deploy in its texts concerned with 'the others'. But Paul's attractive language received only a passing nod.

(3) A third contribution by the Apostle did somewhat better. To express the blessings of grace and eternal life that Christ has brought for all human beings, Paul introduced another 'corporate' figure, the first Adam, who was pictured as triggering the whole story of human sin. The Apostle drew on Jewish traditions and scriptures to develop in his own striking way a contrast between the original Adam and the 'New' or 'Last' Adam to be found first in 1 Corinthians and later in Romans. Joseph Fitzmyer has gathered the evidence to show that 'the incorporation of all human beings in Adam' is an idea which 'seems to appear for the first time in 1 Corinthians 15: 22'. He likewise offers evidence that allows him to qualify as 'novel teaching' Paul's argument in Romans about the 'maleficent influence that Adam's sin had 'on all human beings'.[8]

Here Paul's contribution proved very successful in the history of Christianity. St Irenaeus (d. around 200) and other notable teachers, writers, and artists enriched Christian theology by reflecting on Jesus as the New/Second/Last Adam. Liturgical texts (e.g. the *Exultet* or Easter Proclamation), official teaching (e.g. the Council of Trent on justification [DzH 1524; ND 1928]), poets (e.g. John Donne in 'Hymn to God my God in my Sickness' and John Milton in *Paradise Regained*), painters (e.g. Masaccio and Michelangelo), icons of Eastern Christianity, and enduring legends (see the *Golden Legend* by Blessed James of Voragine [d.1298]) have linked the images of Adam and Christ to illustrate the universal scope of the redemption effected by the Second Adam. Just as all humanity was harmed by the sin of Adam and Eve, so the redemption brought by Christ, the Last Adam, has an even more radical impact on the entire human race and on the whole created order.[9]

When elaborating some teaching on other religions, Vatican II contributed to this ongoing reception of Paul's theme. *Ad Gentes* linked Paul with John to observe that 'as man' Jesus Christ is 'the new Adam, full of grace and truth (John 1: 14)' (*AG* 3). A footnote in the same document quoted St Cyril of Alexandria who calls Christ 'the last Adam', but moved at once to speak about 'the Word' who 'dwells

---

8. Fitzmyer, *Romans*, 136, 406, 412.
9. See O'Collins, *Jesus Our Redeemer*, 37–42, 107–8, 113.

in all' (*AG* 7, n. 45)—another indication, incidentally, of how the Council privileged Johannine language in its vision of 'the others'.

While pursuing at greater length the Pauline theme of the new Adam, *Gaudium et Spes*, nevertheless, also associates it with John 1: 14 and its sublime statement that 'the Word became flesh': 'it is only in the mystery of the incarnate Word that the human mystery truly becomes clear. For Adam, the first man, was a type of the future [Adam]: namely, Christ the Lord, the last Adam'. The two 'mysteries', that of the Word made flesh and that of human beings, match each. By revealing 'the mystery of the Father and of his love', the new Adam simultaneously reveals human beings to themselves and 'discloses' their 'most high calling'. The revelation of the two mysteries also has its redemptive impact: as 'the perfect man', Christ 'has restored to the children of Adam [presumably all people] the likeness to God which had been disfigured ever since the first sin', and raised our human nature 'to a sublime dignity'. Then the document at once makes an affirmation that enjoys vast implications for those who reflect on the situation for followers of other religions: 'by his incarnation, the Son of God, in a certain way, united himself with every human being' (*GS* 22).[10]

Unquestionably, in this paragraph *Gaudium et Spes* appeals to the Pauline theme of the New/Last Adam but, one must add, without making it central to its argument about Christ being united with all human beings. To support that affirmation, the document twice introduces the Johannine theme of 'the Word becoming flesh' or the 'incarnation of the Son of God'. A citation from the Second Council of Constantinople about what happened at the incarnation cements further the connection with the prologue of John's Gospel and its language about the Word becoming flesh: 'neither was God the Word changed into the nature of flesh, nor his flesh converted into the nature of the Word' (*GS* 22, n. 22).

---

10. This theme from the Fathers of the Church is found e.g. in St Hilary of Poitiers (d.367): 'He [Christ] was made man of a virgin so that he might receive into himself the nature of flesh; that the body of mankind as a whole might be sanctified by association with this mixture ... He who is God co-existed with us in the flesh, and thus we have been restored from the flesh to the divine nature' (*De Trinitate*, 2. 24. 25; trans. taken from Henry Bettenson, *The Later Christian Fathers* (Oxford: Oxford University Press, 1970), 53). For the same theme, see also (later in this chapter) St Athanasius of Alexandria (d.373).

At the end, the same paragraph of *Gaudium et Spes* will return to the religious status of all human beings. But it does so, not in the light of the New/Last Adam, but in terms of the resurrection of the crucified Christ and the Holy Spirit offering to all people the possibility of sharing in the Easter mystery: 'we must hold that the Holy Spirit offers to all the possibility of being joined, in a way known to God, to this paschal mystery'. In a later chapter we take up this statement which offers a firm basis for Christians to understand and interpret the situation of 'the others'.

Once again Paul's contribution, in this case about Christ as the New/Last Adam, played only a minor role in what Vatican II retrieved from the Scriptures when developing some teaching about the adherents of other religions. What Paul wrote about this and several other themes implied an intimate connection of Christ with the lives of all human beings. The Council might have pressed Paul much more into service to elucidate the existence of those millions who have not heard and accepted the gospel.[11] Let me turn to another New Testament author, in this case Luke and his presentation of Paul in dialogue with Epicurean and Stoic philosophers in Athens (Acts 17: 16–34).[12]

Luke on the Situation of the Others

Luke has a generous view of the religious life that 'outsiders' can enjoy. As the story of Cornelius, a Roman centurion who came to embrace the Christian faith (Acts 10: 1–11: 18), classically illustrates, outsiders can be favoured with divine visions and the manifest presence of the Holy Spirit. Furthermore, their religious experience may have something very significant to teach not only Christians in general but also the leaders of the Church in particular. Those who treasure the authority of the Scriptures dare not take a less generous view of the religious experience of 'outsiders' and their possibilities. Jesus is 'Lord of all people' (Acts 10: 36). While his authority extends to all (Acts 10: 42), his benefits are open to all (Acts 10: 43).[13]

---

11. For a fuller treatment of what Paul has to offer for our theme, see O'Collins, *Salvation for All*, 121–41.
12. On Acts 17: 16–34, see J. A. Fitzmyer, *The Acts of the Apostles* (New York: Doubleday, 1998), 599–617; and Robert W. Wall, *The Acts of the Apostles*, in *The New Interpreter's Bible*, x (Nashville: Abingdon, 2002), 241–50.
13. On the whole Cornelius story, see O'Collins, *Salvation for All*, 149–52. In the course of that story, St Peter reflects on the universal benevolence of God (Acts 10:35)—a

When Paul speaks in Athens—either on the hill of the Areopagus or to the council of the Areopagus—his discourse appeals to the common ground he shares with his audience. The Apostle has already been preaching in the marketplace (the 'agora') the good news of Jesus and his resurrection, but hearers have grossly misunderstood the message. Paul must deliver his message in a fresh way that will communicate in the cultural and religious setting which now faces him. The discourse of Paul yields some useful pointers about the religious situation of those who have not yet heard or not yet accepted the gospel. Let us see first the details of Paul's approach and how he introduces his message.

The basic cultural value familiar to Paul's audience concerns knowledge. They ask him: 'May we *know* what this new teaching is that you are proposing? It sounds rather strange to us, so we would like to *know* what it means?' (Acts 17: 19–20; italics mine). In his reply Paul takes up the value of knowledge: 'Athenians, I see how extremely religious you are in every way. For as I went through the city and looked carefully at the objects of your worship, I found among them an altar with the inscription "To a God *Unknown*"' (Acts 17: 22–3; italics mine). The Apostle takes this as a sign of their worshipping, yet without their really knowing, the one, true God. At the end Paul returns to the theme of knowledge and its absence, ignorance: 'God has overlooked the times of human *ignorance*'. 'All people everywhere'. can know the divine command to repent and prepare themselves for the day of judgement (Acts 17: 30–1). A wonderful 'inclusion' begins with the Athenians' worship of 'a God Unknown' and ends with the times of 'ignorance' that will come to a close for 'all people everywhere'. Paul has engaged a fundamental value of his audience, their desire for knowledge.

What all people can know is a relationship that transcends every racial and religious difference, the fundamental relationship of every creature to the Creator. God has 'made the world and everything in it'. In particular, 'from one [ancestor, Adam, to whom Luke 3: 38 has traced the human ancestry of Jesus], he [God] made all nations to inhabit the whole earth'. God is close not merely to every nation but also to every individual: 'God is not far from each of us. For in him we live and move and have our being'. Everyone is called to repent and

statement that would be echoed by *LG* 9: 'at all times and in every race, anyone who fears God and does what is just has been acceptable to him'.

prepare for the 'day on which he [God] will have the world judged in righteousness' (Acts 17: 24, 27–8, 30–1). Thus all human beings share the same basic relationship to God as creator and final judge. Together they make up God's 'offspring' (Acts 17: 28–9) or family. They are all God's people and God's children. It is in the created status shared by every human being that Paul finds the basis for the divine call to the whole of humanity.

Human beings are created by God and preserved in existence by God, 'so that they would grope' and 'search for God' (Acts 17: 26–7). Their life comes from God and exists in God. Hence their search for God belongs to a radical relationship with God, which determines their total existence. God remains constantly present as the all-determining One, even (or especially?) when human beings search and blindly grope for him.

In the strategy of his speech, Paul shows himself very tactful. Readers have been told that he 'was deeply distressed to see that the city [Athens] was full of idols' (Acts 17: 18). But when Paul recalls his tour of the places and objects of worship, he does not express that feeling. Rather he congratulates the Athenians on being 'extremely religious in every way', and finds a specific point of contact through an altar with an inscription 'to a God Unknown'. That inscription, he suggests, testifies to the implicit awareness that the Athenians already had of the God whom Paul now wishes to proclaim (Acts 17: 22–3). The Apostle is not going to introduce a 'foreign' or alien deity, who hitherto had nothing to do with the people of Athens (Acts 17: 18). Rather he will speak of the God already implicitly worshipped by them, even if hitherto not explicitly known. Paul presses on to find common ground with Greek poets and philosophers. He draws from 'your own poets'—specifically, a remark about God ('for we too are his offspring') taken from the opening lines of a poem by Aratus of Soli or Tarsus (d. before 270 BC).[14]

At the end Paul speaks of a new time that requires all people to repent and prepare for the world's judgement which will come through 'a man [Jesus] whom he [God] has appointed' and authorized 'by raising him from the dead' (Acts 17: 30–1). Thus at the close of a

---

14. Since Aratus was a Stoic, quoting him is a courteous gesture to the Stoic philosophers in Paul's audience.

tactful speech which respects the Graeco-Roman culture of his audience, Paul makes his own faith clear: he views world history and its finale from only one perspective, that of the crucified and risen Jesus.

Clearly idolatry is a serious problem for Paul. Yet even here his approach is gentle: 'we ought not to think that the deity is like a statue of gold, or silver, or stone, a work of human art and imagination' (Acts 17: 20). The 'we ought not' puts things delicately. There is no 'I' denouncing what 'you' do. It is almost as if Paul himself feels inclined to fashion idols, but holds back, realizing that this is something 'we should not do'.

The skilful and respectful strategy of the speech provides a model of dialogue with those who have had no contact with Jewish monotheism and Scriptures. Does the speech yield any pointers for Christian thinking about the religious situation of those who have not or have not yet been evangelized?

Paul's address in Athens pictures *the* major Christian missionary in the second half of Acts seriously confronting and being confronted by Graeco-Roman culture for the first time. In preaching to the Gentiles of the city, he faces pagan idolatry, Greek philosophy, and Athenian intellectual curiosity. And yet, as Joseph Fitzmyer helpfully points out, such 'speeches are addressed to the readers of Acts rather than to the individual audiences named in the narratives'.[15] Through the figure of Paul, Luke is preaching to his readers. Since that includes readers nearly 2,000 years later, we can apply his texts to the question of those who either have never heard of Christ or have not (yet) accepted the message about him. Luke does not explicitly raise this issue. But the text that he directs to his readers provides some hints and suggestions for those who do ask about 'the religious others'.

(1) First of all, what Luke writes inculcates a respectful appreciation for the cultures and religions of 'others'. The relatively brief speech in Athens shows such respect for the Greek poets and philosophers. Paul quotes a line from Aratus, who was both a poet and a (Stoic) philosopher. At least some of the philosophers in the audience would be in substantial agreement with the belief that it is God who 'has made the world and everything in it' (Acts 17: 24). Instead of launching at once into a denunciation of idol worship, Paul congratulates the Athenians

---

15. Fitzmyer, *The Acts of the Apostles*, 106.

on being 'extremely religious in every way'. In particular, he thought-
fully appreciates what is implied by an altar with the inscription 'to a
God Unknown' (Acts 17: 22–3). In other words, Luke pictures the
Apostle as looking for what is true, valuable, and worthwhile in the
culture and religion of these 'others'.

This attitude of positive appreciation is theologically well based.
God shows providential benevolence towards all human beings and
supplies what is good and necessary for their existence. Christian
readers of an earlier speech (in Lystra) cannot ignore how nature
testifies to the divine concern for all people everywhere (Acts
14: 17). Since God acts with such positive goodness towards everyone,
Christians should share something of that generous attitude when they
reflect on the religious status of the 'others'. In fact, they are not truly
'others'. All human beings are God's 'offspring' (Acts 17: 28–9) and
make up one family of God.

(2) This brings us to a second guideline to be drawn from the
Areopagus meeting. Luke recognizes a most significant factor in the
common ground shared by Paul and those whom he addresses: their
basic orientation to God. The whole of humanity is united in its origin
from one and the same Creator, who 'made the world and everything
in it'. All created beings come from God, who 'made all nations to
inhabit the whole earth, and allotted the times of their existence and
the boundaries of the places where they should live' (Acts 17: 24, 26).
All human beings, both collectively and individually, are intimately
close to the Creator God: in him they 'live and move and have their
being'. Their lives are always enveloped by God, on whom they
remain utterly dependent—physically, spiritually, and intellectually.
God sustains them constantly in the ultimate purpose of their human
existence, that of 'groping' and searching for God. When Christians
reflect on and approach 'others', they should never forget how all
human beings share alike the same radical closeness and orientation
to God.

(3) Third, the way in which Paul engages the Athenians' desire for
knowledge hints at a feature of human orientation to God that has been
appreciated and expressed in various ways by great Christian thinkers,
ancient and modern. Karl Rahner (1904–84), for instance, understood
the human spirit to be dynamically open to the fullness of being. Our

mind is born with a primordial desire to know the Infinite One.[16] We might adapt what St Augustine of Hippo (354–430) wrote at the start of his *Confessions* and say: 'our minds were made for you, O Lord, and will not rest until they rest in you, O Lord'. Whether they realize this or not, all people share the same deep hunger to know (and love) God. Whenever we meet each other, we meet people with a radical hunger in their minds and hearts—a deep desire for God.

(4) Finally, there are many ways in which God continues to be misunderstood everywhere. But whatever the situation, God is no 'stranger'. As Luke portrays matters, Paul does not aim at introducing into the cultural and religious context of Athens a 'foreign' or alien deity. Even if hitherto not explicitly known, 'the God Unknown' has already been present among the Athenians. Paul gives a face and a name to the divine Anonymous One: it is the man Jesus whom God has raised from the dead and authorized to be the judge of everyone at the end of world history.

Vatican II and the Areopagus Speech

Paul's Areopagus speech provides much food for thought, and several passages in Vatican II documents appeal to it when elaborating some teaching on other religions.

(1) First of all, a passage in *Lumen Gentium* echoes three themes from Paul: (a) his language about the 'God Unknown', who (b) 'gives to all people life and breath and all things', and (c) is 'not far from each one of us' (Acts 17: 23–8).[17] This passage in *Lumen Gentium* reads: 'nor is God [c] remote from those who in shadows and images seek [a] the unknown God, since [b] he gives to all people life and breath and all things' (*LG* 16).

Glossing Luke's text and placing the search for the unknown God 'within shadows and images (*in umbris et imaginibus*)' might have come from (a) Plato, (b) the New Testament, (c) St Thomas Aquinas, or (d) Blessed John Henry Newman (or from more than one of these sources

---

16. See K. Rahner, *Foundations of Christian Faith*, trans. William V. Dych (New York: Seabury Press, 1978), 31–5, 51–5; Rahner, *Hearer of the Word: Laying the Foundation for a Philosophy of Religion,* trans. Joseph Donceel (New York: Continuum, 1994), *passim.*
17. *LG* refers the reader to Acts 17: 25–8, but the reference should be Acts 17: 23–8.

and even from all four of them). Let me explain. (a) The text could be intended to recall an allegory introduced at the start of Book 7 in Plato's *Republic,* and concerned with the 'shadowy' knowledge of reality that affects all human beings as long as they are imprisoned in the 'cave' of this world. (b) The gloss in *Lumen Gentium* 16 might have aimed at evoking the language about light coming to those who 'sit in darkness and the shadow of death' that Luke 1: 79 and Matthew 4: 16 have drawn from the Jewish Scriptures. Another New Testament source is possible here. As a major contributor to this article, Yves Congar[18] (not to mention those he was collaborating with) could have thought of the 'foreshadowing' theme found in the Letter to the Hebrews, when it speaks of the Levitical priesthood offering 'worship in a sanctuary that is a sketch and shadow of the heavenly one' (Heb. 8: 5), and of the Old Testament law itself being 'only a shadow of the good things to come and not the true form of these realities' (Heb. 10: 1). (c) What favours identifying Thomas Aquinas as the source of the gloss is the reference to his *Summa Theologiae* 3. 8. 3 ('Is Christ the head of all human beings?') attached (as n. 18) only a few lines earlier in *Lumen Gentium* 16. In that article Thomas argues that 'the holy Fathers [= the saintly figures of the Old Testament] did not rely on the sacraments of the law as certain things [or things in their own right] but as images and shadows (*imaginibus et umbris*) of future things' (ad 3). The order of *Lumen Gentium* (*umbris et imaginibus*) reverses that of Thomas (*imaginibus et umbris*). But the terminology remains the same.

There is an obvious objection to suggesting a scriptural background for the phrase '*in umbris et imaginibus*' from *Lumen Gentium* 16: 'nor is God remote from those who *in shadows and images* seek the unknown God, since he gives to all people life and breath and all things'. When speaking of those still coping with 'shadows' (Matthew, Luke, and Hebrews) or with 'shadows and images' (Thomas Aquinas), the three New Testament authors and Thomas think of Jewish people. But, in our passage from *Lumen Gentium*, the focus has moved beyond Jews (and Muslims), who know the God of Abraham, to a wider group that

18. In the diary he wrote during Vatican II and, specifically in the entry for 7 December 1965, Yves Congar lists *Lumen Gentium* 16 and 17 among his contributions to the Council's documents: *My Journal of the Council*, trans. Mary John Ronayne and Mary Cecily Boulding (Collegeville, MN: Liturgical Press, 2012), 871.

resembles Paul's audience in Athens who continue to seek 'a God Unknown'. Yet one might argue that, if the language of 'shadows and images' describes the situation of Jewish (and Muslim) believers, all the more does it apply to those who follow other religions.

When crafting *Lumen Gentium* 16, Congar may also have had in mind (d) the motto that Blessed John Henry Newman chose for his memorial: '*ex umbris et imaginibus in veritatem* (from shadows and images into the truth)'. Congar knew something of the work and life of Newman, and, being a Dominican and so sharing the motto '*Veritas* (Truth)', could have been attracted by the last word on Newman's memorial (*veritatem*).[19] As for Newman himself and the reasons for his choice, he could have intended to echo Plato's allegory of the cave, the language of Matthew, Luke, and Hebrews, or even that of Thomas Aquinas.

(2) When thinking about what all human beings have in common, *Nostra Aetate* begins by declaring that 'all peoples are one community [and] have one origin, since God made the entire human race dwell on the whole face of the earth' (*NA* 1). The document supports this statement by referring in a footnote (*NA* 1, n. 1) to Acts 17: 26: 'from one [ancestor], he [God] made all nations to inhabit the whole earth, and he allotted the times of their existence and the boundaries of the places where they would live'. The document might also have cited explicitly the words of Acts 17: 28–9 about all people being God's 'offspring'. It could also have followed *Lumen Gentium* in recognizing how, through the activity of creating and sustaining all people in existence, God remains intimately close to everyone. At all events, a common origin in God provides *Nostra Aetate* with a strong starting point for acknowledging the solidarity of all human beings.

(3) Finally, when expounding the universal divine plan for salvation, *Ad Gentes* cites Acts 17: 27 about human beings seeking God in many ways, 'so that they would perhaps touch and find him, although he is not far from each one of us' (*AG* 3). Human beings engage in their religious search because God is constantly and intimately near them and so has already 'found' them.

19. As regards Congar's contacts with Newman, see G. O'Collins and Michael Keenan Jones, *Jesus Our Priest: A Christian Approach to the Priesthood of Christ* (Oxford: Oxford University Press, 2010), 230. Apropos of Newman himself, his choice of words may have been affected by Cicero, *De Officiis,* which uses the language of '*umbra et imaginibus* (shadow/shaded outline and images)' (3. 69).

Augustine and others over 2,000 years of Christianity have elaborated this thought. Let me cite St Anselm of Canterbury's prayer to God: 'Teach me to seek you, and reveal yourself to me as I seek, because I can never seek you if you do not teach me how, or find you unless you reveal yourself' (*Proslogion*, 1).

Through the Areopagus speech in Acts 17, Luke gave shape and biblical backing to Vatican II's teaching on the followers of other religions. But a trajectory initiated by John's Gospel endured over the centuries and carried through to affect that teaching more than any other biblical witness.

The Prologue of John and Other Religions

What the prologue to John's Gospel proposed about the Word (1: 1–18) fed into *Nostra Aetate*. Here Vatican II stated that 'the Catholic Church rejects nothing of those things that are *true and holy*' in the other religions. She has a sincere respect for those [other] manners of acting and living, those precepts and doctrines, which, although differing in many ways from what she herself holds and proposes, nevertheless, often reflect a ray of that Truth, which enlightens all human beings' (*NA* 2). Even if the text included no explicit reference, it obviously echoed the language of the Johannine prologue about the Word being 'the light of human beings' (John 1: 4), 'the true light that enlightens everyone' (John 1: 9).[20]

When recognizing what is 'true and holy' in other religions (*NA* 2), the Council introduces a pair of similar blessings that recalls an earlier conciliar statement about those who, without any fault of their own, have not yet reached an explicit faith in God: 'whatever *good or truth* is found among them is considered by the Church to be a preparation for the gospel' (*LG* 16). 'True and holy', as well as 'good or truth', echo the Johannine language about the Word being 'full of grace and truth' and about 'grace and truth' coming through Jesus Christ (John 1: 14, 17). The two conciliar statements and the prologue all speak of 'truth'.

---

20. Here Vatican II respects the universal scope of John 1: 9, unlike the Council of Trent which in its second session (7 January 1546) appealed to this verse in the cause of 'the light of catholic truth' dispelling 'the darkness of heresies' (N. P. Tanner [ed.], *Decrees of the Ecumenical Councils*, ii (London: Sheed & Ward, 1990), 661).

What is 'holy' (*NA* 2) or 'good' (*LG* 16) overlaps with 'grace' (John), without their being strict equivalents. *Ad Gentes* 9 maintains the Johannine pair unchanged when referring to the elements of 'truth and grace' found among various peoples. We will return later to the 'paired' terminology, which John's prologue encouraged.

Ad Gentes borrows from the prologue to characterize Christ, 'the new Adam', as being 'full of grace and truth' (*AG* 3). The same document then quotes Irenaeus and calls the divine Word the one 'through whom all things were made and who was always present to the human race' (*AG* 3, n. 8; John 1: 3, 10). A later footnote, which cites Origen, adds that those who come to know God are 'led by the Word who is with God' (John 1: 1). The same footnote also quotes Cyril of Alexandria, who combines the prologue's language of 'the Word' with John 2: 21 (which speaks of 'the temple' of Christ's risen body): 'the Word dwells in all in one temple, that is to say [in that temple] which he assumed for us and from us, so that having all people in himself, he might reconcile all in one body to the Father' (*AG* 7, n. 45).

For such Johannine language to take its place in Christian discourse, we did not have to wait for Irenaeus, Origen, and Cyril of Alexandria. Justin Martyr had already developed a 'Logos/Word Christology'. He wrote of the Word being 'with God' when 'in the beginning God created and ordered all things' (*Second Apology*, 5). Justin had his eye on the revelatory and saving role of Christ for those who were not (or were not yet) Christians.

Justin and Other Fathers of the Church

(1) In his *First Apology*, a work addressed to Roman authorities who were persecuting Christians, Justin wrote: 'we have been taught that Christ is the first begotten of God and that he is the Word (Logos) of whom the whole human race partakes. *Those who have lived according to the Word are Christians*, even though they have been considered athe- ists: such as, among the Greeks, Socrates, Heraclitus, and others like them' (46; italics mine).[21] Probably the most important pre-Socratic

---

21. See *Writings of Saint Justin Martyr*, trans. Thomas B. Falls (Washington, DC: Catholic University of America, 1948).

philosopher, Heraclitus (d. around 475 BC) held that everything is in a state of eternal flux. Justin may have listed him here as a foil to Socrates, who was associated with Plato in arguing for a higher world of changeless ideas. Both philosophical extremes, Heraclitus and Socrates/Plato, had some share in the same divine Word. Turning his gaze from past philosophers to the present, Justin called 'Christians' not only 'those who lived then' but also those 'who live now according to reason' (ibid.).

In developing the Johannine theme of the pre-existent Logos as universal mediator of creation and revelation, Justin wrote of 'the seeds of the Word' that have been dropped everywhere and, at least to some extent, in every person (*Second Apology*, 8, 10, 13)—a theme that, as we shall see, makes a notable appearance at Vatican II in *Lumen Gentium* and, even more, *Ad Gentes*. Justin argues that, in one way or another, the whole human race shares in the Logos (*First Apology*, 46). Many people live only 'according to a fragment of the Logos'. Christians live 'according to the knowledge and contemplation of the whole Logos, who is Christ' (*Second Apology*, 8).

Justin applies the mediation of the Logos to Greek history, interpreting it as a prelude and preliminary to Christ and Christianity:

Plato's teachings are not contrary to Christ's but they are not in all respects identical with them, as is the case with the doctrines of others—the Stoics, the poets and the prose authors. For each, through his share in the divine generative Logos, spoke well, seeing what was suited to his capacity... whatever has been spoken aright by anyone belongs to us Christians; for we worship and love, next to God, the Logos who is from the unbegotten and ineffable God... All those writers were able, through the seed of the Logos implanted in them, to see reality darkly. For it is one thing to have the seed of a thing and to imitate it up to one's capacity; far different is the thing itself, shared and imitated in virtue of its own grace (ibid., 13).

While claiming to know 'in virtue of its own grace' the incarnate Logos 'who is from the unbegotten and ineffable God', Justin and other Christians do not deny some presence and impact ('the seeds') of the Logos in the life and thought of Plato, the Stoics, poets, and various prose authors—an impact that makes their teachings in certain respects identical with those of Christ.

We might sum up Justin's argument. Wherever the Logos is present, there is some true light and genuine knowledge of God. But we face a universal presence. 'The whole human race' shares in the Logos, who is present everywhere and to everyone brings 'true light and genuine knowledge of God'. Justin was even ready to give the name of 'Christians' to all those who respond by living 'according to the Word'—an early intimation of what Karl Rahner would popularize on the eve of Vatican II as 'anonymous Christians'.

A younger contemporary of Justin, St Irenaeus of Lyons (d. around 200), maintained the universal role of the Word in the work of revelation: 'The Word of God, present with his handiwork from the beginning, reveals the Father to all, to whom he wills, when he wills and how the Father wills' (*Adversus Haereses*, 4. 6. 7). A little later, Irenaeus added: 'Through the Word all his creatures learn that there is one God, the Father, who controls all things, and gives existence to all . . . the Son makes the Father known from the beginning. For he has been with the Father from the beginning' (ibid., 4. 20. 6–7).

No human being has ever remained 'outside' or excluded from this omnipresent, mediatorial role of the Word/Son. In revealing to them the one God and Father, the Word 'is always present to the human race' (ibid., 3. 18. 1) and not merely to some chosen groups of men and women. At the same time, only the Word could play this role: 'No other being had the power of revealing to us the things of the Father, except his own proper Word' (ibid., 5. 1. 1). This universal presence of the Son/Word retains enduring significance for those who reflect on the divine self-revelation and salvation available for all, as we shall see in a chapter on *Ad Gentes*.

Clement of Alexandria (d. around 215) continued such reflections on the Logos; Clement's *Protrepticus* ('Exhortation to the Greeks/Heathen') and *Stromateis* ('Miscellanies') would be cited immediately after Irenaeus by Vatican II (*AG* 3, n. 2). In the first work, an exhortation to non-believers, Clement developed a Logocentric theology: the Logos, already at work in Judaism and in the best Greek philosophers and poets (who partially perceived the truth of God), became incarnate in Jesus Christ who fully revealed God and life in God to human beings. Clement found in John 1: 9 ('the true Light that enlightens everyone coming into the world') the biblical warrant for speaking of 'the common Light' who 'is not hidden to anyone' but 'shines on all human beings' (*Protrepticus*, 9. 25). This 'Light of human beings' is 'the Word, by whom we behold God' (ibid.). Having 'received certain flashes of the divine Word', the Greeks could 'give forth some utterances of truth' (ibid., 7. 22).[22]

Even more than Justin, Clement attributed much to the practice of philosophy: 'by reflection and direct vision, those among the Greeks who have philosophized accurately discern God' (*Stromateis*, 1. 19). God 'gave the commandments' to the Jews and 'philosophy' to 'the others'; 'by two different processes of advancement', he 'leads [them] to perfection' which comes with Christ and faith in Christ (ibid., 7. 2). Thus the partial knowledge through the philosophy which God gave to the Greeks 'was a preparation, paving the way' for what would be 'perfected' through Christ (ibid., 1. 5). Hence Clement was ready to call the philosophy of the Greeks a 'covenant' made by God with them and a 'stepping stone' to the philosophy of Christ: 'all things necessary and profitable for life came to us from God, and philosophy more especially was given to the Greeks, as a covenant (*diathēkē*) peculiar to them—being, as it is, a stepping stone (*hupobathra*) to the philosophy which is according to Christ' (ibid., 6. 8). Like the Jewish law, philosophy had a transitional role in the 'preparation of the Gospel' (see below).

Famously, Clement recognized in Asia even greater leaders ('non-Greek philosophers'), who were inspired by God, taught divine truths, and oriented people towards Christ—in particular, Indian sages: 'of these there are two classes, some of them called Sarmanae and others Brahmins'. Clement added: 'Some of the Indians obey the precepts of Buddha, whom, on account of his extraordinary sanctity, they have raised to divine honour' (ibid., 1. 15). In effect, Clement recognized some religious truth in the Hindu and Buddhist traditions and hence a positive role in the history of revelation and salvation. Without explicitly citing Clement, Vatican II was to share such positive sentiments towards Hinduism and Buddhism (*NA* 2).

Shortly after Clement, Origen[23] endorsed a similar vision of the universal light made available by the divine Logos: 'it is not true that [God's] rays were enclosed in that man [Jesus] alone ... or that the Light which is the divine Logos that causes these rays existed nowhere

---

22. *Clement of Alexandria, Exhortation to the Heathen*, trans. William Wilson, Ante-Nicene Christian Library, iv (Edinburgh: T. & T. Clark, 1867), 74, 82, 84.
23. Like Irenaeus and Clement, Origen would also be cited by Vatican II's *AG* (4, n. 6; 7, n. 19).

else' (*Contra Celsum*, 7. 17). Hence Origen was ready to detect rays of divine light in Greek philosophy and elsewhere.

The Logos Christology espoused by Justin, Irenaeus, Clement, and Origen opened the way for Christians not only to acknowledge the pervasive influence of the Logos beyond Christianity but also to enter into dialogue with non-Christian thinkers, at least in the Mediterranean world. Those who endorsed Jewish, Platonic, and Stoic forms of thought about the Logos could find a measure of common ground with Christians, who, nevertheless, remained distinctive with their faith that 'the Logos was made flesh'. But, in general, the notion of 'the Logos' offered a bridge to contemporary culture.[24]

(2) In the fourth century, other writers were to develop more 'sophisticated' versions of a Logos Christology—notably Athanasius of Alexandria in his *Contra Gentes, De Incarnatione,* and other works. He argued that, since human beings are 'rational (*logikoi*)', they all share somehow in the Logos; they have in themselves at least 'some shadows of the Word' (*De Incarnatione*, 3).[25]

Encouraged by the Stoic idea of the world as one body (*De Incarnatione*, 41), Athanasius understood the Word to fill the universe (*Contra Gentes,* 42), to guide it (ibid., 40, 41), and thus to make God the Father known to all (*Contra Arianos*, 3. 14). Athanasius maintained the theme of the Word, who is 'the image and true glory of God', dwelling within all human beings (ibid., 3. 10).

This view belonged with Athanasius' vision of the whole world existing by partaking of the Word; creatures exist only because they share in the creative Word of God. It is 'through his own eternal Word' that God makes everything, and constantly keeps everything in existence (*Contra Gentes,* 41).[26] This theology involved maintaining that the entire created world is deified, since it participates in the Word who becomes flesh; 'he [the Word] deified what he put on, and, what's more, he gave this to the human race' (*Orations,* 1. 42).[27]

---

24. On the four authors, see, respectively, 'Justin Martyr, St', *ODCC*, 620–1; 'Irenaeus, St', *ODCC*, 951–2; 'Clement of Alexandria', *ODCC*, 367; 'Origen', *ODCC*, 1200–2.

25. Robert Thomson, *Contra Gentes and De Incarnatione* (Oxford: Clarendon Press, 1971), 141.

26. Ibid. 115.

27. Khaled Anatolios, *Athanasius* (London: Routledge, 2004), 99.

Thus creating all things through the Word entailed deifying all things through the Word: 'the whole of creation participates in the Word', and so 'the Word glorifies creation and presents it to the Father by deifying it and granting it adoption'. Since 'the Word deifies the things that have come into being' (*Letter to Serapion*, 1. 23, 25), this Athanasian vision of the universe necessarily implies that followers of other religions partake in the Word and are somehow deified by the Word. Athanasius himself did not draw the conclusion, but his teaching on the Christological face of all creation applies to the millions who belong to religions other than Christianity.[28]

Yet, when reflecting on other religions, Vatican II, as later chapters will illustrate, drew on Justin and Irenaeus rather than on Athanasius and, for that matter, retrieved John's prologue directly rather than citing anything from St Augustine of Hippo (354–430). According to Augustine, it is not only as the Word creating everything but also as the divine Light illuminating the human mind that Christ is involved with all human beings. Augustine unpacks John 1: 4: 'our illumination is a participation in the Word, namely, in that life which is the light of human beings' (*De Trinitate*, 4. 4). Whoever they are and whether or not they are aware of this, the intellectual activity of all men and women, in tending towards the truth, involves the light of the Word. Hence Platonist philosophers, even though they are not baptized Christians, can perceive 'the light of the unchangeable Truth' (ibid., 4. 20). Augustine cannot renounce John's teaching about 'the true Light that enlightens every human being' (John 1: 9), and that includes all those who have not or have not yet accepted Christianity.

Here Augustine makes his thinking more specific by recognizing the presence not only of 'hidden saints' but also of 'prophets' among the Gentiles (*Contra Faustum*, 19. 2; *De catechizandis rudibus*, 22. 40). Echoing Origen,[29] he even declares roundly that the divine gift of 'prophecy was extended to all nations' (*In Ioannem*, 9. 9). But once again Vatican II did not follow Augustine by speaking specifically of sanctity and prophecy to be found among the followers of other religions. In the next chapter

---

28. On the relation between God and creation in Athanasius' thought, see Khaled Anatolios, *Athanasius: The Coherence of his Thought* (London: Routledge, 1998).
29. In *Contra Celsum* Origen wrote: 'In every generation the Wisdom of God descended into those souls which he found holy, and made them to be prophets and friends of God' (4. 7).

we will recall a pessimistic view about the salvation of many people that shadowed the later years of Augustine's life.

To complete this sampling of the patristic period, we should add something about Eusebius of Caesarea (d. around 339), a prolific writer who is recalled for various things but not least for being the earliest Church historian. The fifteen books of his *Praeparatio Evangelica* cover many items, and develop, for instance, implausible suggestions already made by Origen and Clement of Alexandria about Greek philosophers plagiarizing texts of the Old Testament. Nevertheless, calling much of what came before and beyond Christianity a 'preparation for the Gospel' enjoyed a long impact, right down to the documents of Vatican II which cited the work of Eusebius (e.g. *LG* 16; *AG* 3).

Let us leap ahead now to the second thousand years of Christianity. Do we find any early intimations of Vatican II's teaching on other religions? Was there anything that set the stage for what *Lumen Gentium, Nostra Aetate*, and the other documents had to say about the theory and practice of relations with 'the religious others'?

After the generous Christian openness of Justin, Irenaeus, Clement of Alexandria, and other early writers, sadly much of what we find from the Middle Ages down to the sixteenth century and beyond suffered from ignorance and was shaped by fear about maintaining Christian identity. The followers of Jesus came to base their identity partly on the repudiation of the Jews (who lived among them) and the Muslims (who lived beyond their frontiers). Given the union of altar and throne that stretched back to Constantine, being 'outside the Church' and being 'outside the nation' (or dangerously opposed to the king, emperor, or other ruler) were often understood to be more or less the same. In particular, the immense success of Islam, both militarily and, for centuries, intellectually, prompted many followers of Jesus to indulge in hostility and mindless rant against these dangerous 'outsiders', the Muslims and their prophet Muhammad.[30] Christians met Muslims very rarely for anything like interreligious dialogue; if they met, it was normally on the battlefield or, as in the case of the Venetian Republic, for trade. But, as we shall see at once, not all Christians shared such negative views.

---

30. See Jeremy Johns, 'Christianity and Islam', in John McManners (ed.), *The Oxford Illustrated History of Christianity* (Oxford: Oxford University Press, 1990), 163–95, 673; Richard W. Southern, *Western Views of Islam in the Middle Ages* (Cambridge, MA: Harvard University Press, 1962).

TWO

From Gregory VII to the Twentieth Century

> God, who knows completely the minds and souls, the thoughts and habits of all persons, will not permit, in accord with his infinite goodness and mercy, anyone who is not guilty of a [grave] voluntary fault to suffer eternal punishment.
>
> Blessed Pius IX, *Quanto conficiamur moerore*

> Human beings can never even begin to have anything to do with God or to approach God without already being borne by God's grace.
>
> Karl Rahner, *Foundations of Christian Faith*

To complete the run-up to the Second Vatican Council and the teaching and figures in the Christian tradition that affected, positively or negatively, thinking about other religions, we can begin with St Gregory VII (pope 1073–85), St Francis of Assisi (1181/2–1226), and St Thomas Aquinas (c.1225–74).

From Gregory VII to Thomas Aquinas

(1) Relations between Gregory VII and those 'beyond' the Catholic Church featured a remarkable letter of 1076 (*Epistola*, 21) sent to Anzir, the Muslim king of Mauretania (in modern Algeria), whom the Pope thanked for freeing some Christian prisoners and promising to liberate some more.[1] Anzir had even proposed a candidate to be ordained a

---

1. J.-P. Migne, *Patrologia Latina*, 148, coll. 450–2; H. E. J. Cowdrey, *The Register of Pope Gregory VII 1073–1085: An English Translation* (Oxford: Oxford University Press, 2002), 204–5.

bishop and so take care of his Christian subjects. Nearly 900 years later, in *Nostra Aetate* (3, n.1) Vatican II recalled this letter, which recognized how Christians and Muslims honour Abraham and worship one and the same God. It was referenced in the only footnote for the entire section dealing with other religions and, specifically, with Buddhism, Hinduism, and Islam (*NA* 1–3).

In his letter Gregory put the king's action in the context of universal revelation and salvation. He first declared that 'he who enlightens all people coming into the world' (see John 1: 9) had enlightened the mind of the king, and then cited the words of 1 Timothy 2: 4 about God 'who wishes all people to be saved'. The Pope expressed the faith he shared with the king by saying: 'we and you must show in a special way to the other nations [Christian and non-Christian alike] an example of charity, for we believe and confess one God, although in different ways, and praise and worship him daily as the creator of all ages and the ruler of this world'. The Pope ended by praying, 'in our heart and with our lips, that God may lead you to the abode of happiness, to the bosom of the holy patriarch Abraham, after long years of life here on earth' (ND 1002).

In *Salvation Outside the Church?*, Frank Sullivan expounds the response to this question that came from a Flemish theologian Albert Pigge (1490–1542), and praises him for having 'drawn a conclusion that, as far as I know, no Christian had drawn before him: that Moslems, too, could . . . find salvation through their sincere faith in God'.[2] What Gregory VII wrote over 400 years before Pigge, however, shows a pope clearly endorsing that conclusion.

Notoriously, however, the pontificate of Gregory VII featured conflicts with secular rulers and, in particular, with the German ruler, Henry IV (emperor 1065–1106). Apropos of non-Christian rulers, the Pope's positive attitude to the faith of Muslims and resolution to give 'an example of charity' did not stand in the way of hostile moves against them in the political power-struggles in which he was engaged. Two years before writing to King Anzir, Gregory VII had planned (unsuccessfully, as it turned out) a military campaign against the Turks.[3]

2. Francis A. Sullivan, *Salvation Outside the Church? Tracing the History of the Catholic Response* (Mahwah, NJ: Paulist Press, 1992), 81.
3. On Gregory VII, see H. E. J. Cowdrey, *Pope Gregory VII* (Oxford: Clarendon Press, 1998).

(2) A century later the foundation of the mendicant ('living by beg-
ging') orders of Franciscans and Dominicans helped to revitalize medieval Catholicism. St Dominic (c.1174–1221) founded the Order of
Preachers (commonly called the Dominicans); his followers were to
include St Thomas Aquinas, to whom we return below. Dominic's
contemporary and friend, St Francis of Assisi, inspired numerous
Franciscan mystics and missionaries. He espoused a peaceful approach
to Muslims, who for centuries had been condemned by many Christians as the archetypal enemies of their faith.

For the first time in the history of 'rules' for religious orders, Francis
inserted a particular section about relations with Muslims. Chapter 16
of what came to be called the 'Early Rule' (the *Regula non bullata* of
1221) called for understanding and peaceful relations between Christian friars and their Muslim 'brothers' and other 'non-believers'. In a
chapter added later (Ch. 22), Francis reiterated his eirenic, Jesus-
inspired attitude towards Muslims and other 'infidels'; they were to
be considered 'brothers' and 'friends'. Francis himself put into practice
what he preached by cultivating friendly relations with Muslims,
notably with a sultan whom he visited in Egypt.[4]

Jacques Dupuis remarks that the 'prophetic' voice of Francis in
'calling for mutual understanding and reconciliation between Christians and their "Muslim brothers" would bear fruit later', not least in
Vatican II's *Nostra Aetate*.[5] Beyond question, Franciscan bishops and
advisers who attended the Council were predisposed to remember the
shining example of Francis back in the thirteenth century; and so too
were other bishops and advisers who, while not themselves Franciscans, knew and esteemed the work of Francis. Yet he was never cited
either in *Nostra Aetate* (1–3) or in further sections of the Council's texts
that dealt with 'other' believers. Vis-à-vis those who, from the Middle
Ages down to the nineteenth century (inclusive), reflected on and
wrote about 'outsiders', the Second Vatican Council referred only to
Gregory VII's letter and, as we shall see, to one passage from Thomas

---

4. For details and bibliography, see 'Francis of Assisi, St', *ODCC*, 635–6; Jacques
   Dupuis, *Toward a Christian Theology of Religious Pluralism* (Maryknoll, NY: Orbis
   Books, 1997), 104–5. See also Andrea Di Maio, 'Cristianesimo in dialogo con i non
   cristiani: L'approccio "testimoniale" di Francesco e Bonaventura', *Gregorianum* 87
   (2006), 762–80.
5. Dupuis, *Toward a Christian Theology of Religious Pluralism*, 104.

Aquinas. Earlier teaching from the New Testament and the Church Fathers proved much richer sources to be retrieved apropos of the religious situation of 'other' believers.

(3) When examining the spiritual situation and future destiny of 'outsiders', the thinking of Thomas Aquinas was affected by an axiom inherited from St Cyprian of Carthage (d.258): 'outside the Church no salvation (*extra ecclesiam nulla salus*)'. Following on from some earlier Christian writers (St Ignatius of Antioch, St Irenaeus, and Origen), Cyprian developed and repeatedly invoked the principle of 'outside the Church no salvation'. However, he had in mind Christians who had culpably put their salvation in jeopardy by separating themselves from the Church through heresy or schism. It was not an axiom that he applied to others: that is to say, to those who were not (or who were not yet) Christians.[6]

However, after the time of Cyprian, such writers as St Ambrose of Milan, St Gregory of Nyssa, and St John Chrysostom began applying the axiom to everyone who had not accepted Christian faith. These writers assumed that the Christian message had been proclaimed more or less everywhere, and that those who had failed to accept it were guilty. The 'outsiders' had shut their eyes to the truth, refused baptism and entry into the Church, and so had left themselves in the situation of being 'beyond' salvation.[7]

Augustine, in particular, took a pessimistic view of the prospects not only for those who (through heresy or schism) had separated themselves from the community of the Church but also for all children and adults who died without baptism. Naturally he tried (but failed) to reconcile a view that involved the eternal damnation of countless people with the divine desire to save all, which 1 Timothy 2: 3–4 classically expressed: 'God our Saviour desires everyone to be saved and to come to the knowledge of the truth.' This text encouraged St Prosper of Aquitaine (d. *c.*463) to declare that divine grace could bring outsiders to salvation, even though the light of the gospel had not reached them. But most of Augustine's other followers endorsed his extreme position on 'no salvation outside the Church'.[8] The classic

---

6. For details, see Sullivan, *Salvation Outside the Church?*, 18–21.
7. Ibid., 24–8.
8. Ibid., 28–43.

text from 1 Timothy would form a key scriptural warrant for Vatican II's positive statement of God's will to save all people (e.g. *LG* 16; *NA* 1, n. 2).

In the thirteenth century, Thomas Aquinas exercised his teaching ministry less than a century after Innocent III had firmly endorsed the principle of *extra ecclesiam nulla salus*. First, the Pope prescribed in 1208 a profession of faith to be made by Waldensians who wanted to return to the unity of the Catholic Church: 'We believe in our hearts and confess with our lips that there is one church, not that of the heretics, but the holy Roman Catholic and Apostolic Church, outside of which we believe that no one is saved' (DzH 792). In 1215 the Fourth Lateran Council met under Innocent III, and against Albigensian heretics issued a definition of Catholic faith that included the statement: 'There is one universal church of the faithful, outside of which nobody at all is saved' (DzH 802; ND 21). The Council echoed here a letter of Cyprian (*Ad Iubaianum*, 21), but could not recognize how he limited his dictum to Christian heretics or schismatics who separated themselves from the Church, and did not consider the situation of 'anyone at all'.

Thomas commented on the statement of Lateran IV and in various other passages returned to the question of salvation 'outside the Church'.[9] By his time it was becoming steadily clearer that the question concerned innumerable people living outside the Mediterranean world. Dominican and Franciscan missionaries had gone into Asia, and Marco Polo (*c.*1254–*c.*1324) would soon bring back news of China.[10]

---

9. On the relevant passages in Thomas Aquinas, see ibid., 47–62. On elements in Thomas's thinking that could be developed into a theology of religions, see Roman A. Siebenrock, 'Theologischer Kommentar zur Erklärung über die Haltung der Kirche zu den nichtchristlichen Religionen: *Nostra Aetate*', in Peter Hünermann and Bernd Jochen Hilberath (eds), *Herders Theologischer Kommentar zum Zweiten Vatikanischen Konzil*, iii (2005), 591–677, at 602–6. Siebenrock also has valuable things to say about *De pace fidei* by Nicholas of Cusa, to which we come later in this chapter (ibid., 606–11).

10. Sullivan, apropos of what Marco Polo reported about central Asia and China, states that 'St Thomas makes no reference to this in his writings' (*Salvation Outside the Church?*, 55). But, since Thomas died in 1274 and so before Marco Polo returned from China in 1295 (after which he dictated what became known as *The Travels of Marco Polo*), Thomas could not be expected to refer to what the Venetian traveller had discovered. But there is one surprising 'silence' on the part of Thomas. It concerns the Crusades, five major expeditions which began in 1096 and ended in 1270, which might have encouraged him to think more about Muslims and Muslim-Christian

Thomas knew and respected the work of Islamic and Jewish philosophical theologians, like Avicenna, Averroes, and Maimonides, and engaged with them in his *Summa Contra Gentiles*.[11] He presupposed common ground in debating with them questions about God. Yet he never explicitly took up the question, for example, of divine revelation and salvation reaching the innumerable Muslims who lived not that far away from Southern Italy, where he was born, grew up, and later taught for a time (in Naples).

For Thomas, faith in Christ and receiving the sacraments, above all, baptism and the Eucharist, were necessary for salvation. What then, for instance, of someone who had never heard of Christ and the Christian message? Thomas suggested that God would provide such a person with an 'exposition of what must be believed for salvation' either 'by a preacher of the faith, as in the case of Cornelius, or by a revelation, so that it would then be in the power of the free will to make an act of faith'.[12] Elsewhere he put this solution even more vigorously: provided a person in that situation 'followed his natural reason in seeking the good and avoiding evil, we must most certainly hold that God would either reveal to him, by an inner inspiration, what must be believed, or would send a preacher to him, as he sent Peter to Cornelius'.[13]

This solution calls for two comments. First, Thomas cheerfully envisaged divine 'revelation' (his word) being granted to those who have never had the chance of hearing the Christian message. When we reach the Second Vatican Council, we will need to face the question of divine self-revelation reaching 'outsiders'. Here we can at least pause to recall the authority of Thomas. He had no difficulty about such revelation being available for 'outsiders' and prompting their faith. Second, Thomas invoked the episode of Cornelius (Acts

relations; yet Thomas never mentions the Crusades. As regards Marco Polo's account of China, some have queried whether he actually reached China and allege that what he reports is largely hearsay. But their arguments, which depend upon noting things that he does not say about China (e.g. the use of chopsticks and the custom of binding feet), have not prevailed.

11. See David B. Burrell, 'Aquinas and Jewish and Islamic Authors', in Brian Davies and Eleonore Stump (eds), *Oxford Handbook of Aquinas* (Oxford: Oxford University Press, 2012), 65–73.
12. *In III Sententias,* distinctio 25. 2. 1, solutio 1 ad 1.
13. *De Veritate,* 14. 11 ad 1.

10: 1–11: 18) to illustrate how God might act in a special way to send a preacher to someone who 'seeks good and avoids evil', but who knows nothing yet about the Christian message. The Second Vatican Council, however, took up the case of the Cornelius differently, by remarking that the Holy Spirit 'sometimes visibly anticipates apostolic action' (AG 4). This theme of the Spirit active 'outside' the visible Church and her missionary activity was to be developed by Pope John Paul II, as we will see in Chapter 8.

Being one of the few Christian scholars ever to write a commentary on the Letter to the Hebrews, Thomas was well aware of the account of faith in 11: 1–3 and of the further statement in 11: 6: 'without faith it is impossible to please God; for those who would approach him must believe that he exists and that he rewards those who seek him'. What Hebrews 11 says about faith involves basic attitudes towards God and does *not* include the explicit faith in Christ that we find, for instance, in Romans 10: 8–10.[14] Yet Thomas insisted on the present necessity of 'explicit faith in the mysteries of Christ'.[15] In the case of those who lived before the coming of Christ, he recognized how implicit faith in Christ could suffice for their salvation, and he held such implicit faith to be expressed by what Hebrews 11: 6 proposed about the existence and providence of God.[16] But *after the coming of Christ*, the one mediator of salvation, explicit faith in him was necessary. Yet, as we saw above, according to Thomas such faith could be triggered by the divine revelation coming through a 'revelation' or an 'inner inspiration'.

As regards the necessity of being incorporated into Christ through baptism, Thomas clearly held that no one could be saved without baptism. And yet baptism might take the form of 'baptism of desire'. A 'person can obtain salvation without actually being baptized, on account of the person's desire for baptism'. In such a case, 'God, whose power is not tied to visible sacraments, sanctifies a person inwardly'.[17] This desire for baptism need not be explicit but could be implicit. Thomas cited Cornelius as an example of someone whose desire for

---

14. On the possibilities offered by Hebrews when interpreting the faith of 'outsiders', see G. O'Collins, *Salvation for All: God's Other Peoples* (Oxford: Oxford University Press, 2008), 252–9.

15. *Summa Theologiae*, 2a. 2ae. 2. 7.

16. Ibid., 2a. 2ae. 1. 7 resp.

17. Ibid., 3a. 68. 2 resp. On the necessity of baptism for salvation, see ibid., 3a. 68. 1.

baptism was implicit.[18] Thomas mounted a similar argument about the Eucharist and its necessity for salvation: 'a person can be saved through the desire to receive this sacrament', just as one can be saved through a desire for baptism, before actually receiving baptism.[19]

The notion of an 'implicit faith' in Christ and 'implicit baptism of desire' would be followed by notable successors of Thomas and, in part, by the Council of Trent (1545–63). But such language from Thomas about the 'implicit' or 'explicit' religious attitudes of people was hardly taken up in the documents of the Second Vatican Council, and only in the case of those who 'not without divine grace strive to lead an upright life' but who 'without fault of their own have not yet reached an explicit recognition (*expressam agnitionem*) of God'. 'Divine Providence does not deny them the helps necessary for salvation' (*LG* 16).

When reflecting on the situation of 'outsiders', Vatican II drew only once on Thomas—to support the statement that 'those who have not yet received the Gospel are ordered (*ordinantur*) to the People of God for different reasons (*diversis rationibus*)' (*LG* 16).[20] When discussing the grace of Christ as head of the Church, Thomas had raised the question: 'is Christ the head of all human beings?' Maintaining that Christ is the head not only of the Church but also of all human beings, albeit 'in different degrees', Thomas replied to the first objection by stating: 'unbelievers, although they are actually not part of the Church, nevertheless, belong to it potentially. This potentiality is based on two things: first, and principally, on the power (*virtute*) of Christ, which is sufficient for the salvation of the whole human race; and, second, on freedom of choice.' This all-inclusive view has the advantage of clearly attributing the salvation of human beings primarily to the risen Christ and to Christ not as the head of the Church but as the head of all humanity. This universal headship *also means* that all human beings, while they are not 'actually part of the Church' and so are literally '*extra ecclesiam* [outside the Church]', are, nevertheless, 'ordered' in 'different degrees' to Christ's Church and belong to it at least

18. Ibid., 3a. 69. 3 ad 2.
19. Ibid., 3a. 73. 3 resp.
20. *LG* 16, n. 18 refers to the *Summa Theologiae*, 3a. 8. 3. ad 1. Without referencing Aquinas, the closing sentence of *LG* 17 also follows him in calling Christ 'the head of all'.

'potentially'. But principally it is not the Church but the 'power of Christ' that will bring them salvation and the means for salvation.

Without saying so, Thomas moved here towards a new axiom: '*extra Christum nulla salus* (outside Christ no salvation)', and made it clear that there is no way of being 'outside Christ'. Jesus Christ remains the head of the entire human race. This being 'in different degrees' under his headship involves, to be sure, being 'ordered' to his Church in various ways. But the universal headship of the risen Christ is the primary factor. This passage in Thomas's *Summa Theologiae* signalled a teaching that would flourish at Vatican II, not least in its two constitutions on the Church.

From Boniface VIII to the Nineteenth Century

(1) Shortly after the death of Thomas, Pope Boniface VIII reacted to a hostile French king, Philip the Fair, by issuing in 1302 a 'bull' or papal letter sealed with a *bulla* or special seal regularly attached to important documents, *Unam Sanctam* ('One Holy [Church]'). This 'bull' highlighted, more than any previous teaching, the authority that the Pope exercised under Christ and in the 'One, Holy, Catholic Church'. When emphasizing the role of the Pope as visible head of the Church, Boniface drew the conclusion that, if they were to be members of Christ's flock, people needed to be subject to its visible shepherd, the Pope (DzH 872; ND 804). He then developed a theory of his spiritual power being supreme and therefore giving him temporal authority over kings and emperors. The closing sentence of *Unam Sanctam* read: 'we declare, state, and pronounce that it is altogether necessary to salvation for every human creature to be subject to the Roman pontiff' (DzH 875; ND 804).[21]

While much of this 'bull' obviously proposed a now long abandoned view of the relationship between spiritual and temporal authority, what of the final sentence? Many theologians understand the necessity of submission to the Roman pontiff as no more than another way—in Boniface's situation a defiant and challenging way—of expressing the

21. For the text of *Unam Sanctam*, see Henry Bettenson and Chris Maunder (eds), *Documents of the Christian Church* (Oxford: Oxford University Press, 2011), 121–2.

need of being in communion with the Catholic Church in order to be saved. In other words, Boniface, albeit in papal-centred terms, simply reiterated the traditional teaching of 'outside the Church no salvation'.[22] The question raised by Thomas Aquinas and his successors remained on the table: what is entailed by being 'outside the Church'?

(2) More than a century after Boniface VIII, what is commonly called the Council of Florence (lasting from 1431 to 1445, and meeting not only in Florence but also in three other cities) went beyond what was taught by Innocent III in the 1208 profession of faith for the Waldensians and by the Fourth Lateran Council in 1215 (see above). When confessing the principle of 'outside the Church no salvation', the 1208 profession of faith explicitly mentioned 'heretics' being outside the one Catholic Church. Otherwise it refrained from specifying any other group affected adversely by the axiom. Lateran IV did not specify even heretics but left matters quite general: 'outside' the one Church 'no one at all is saved'. In its *Decree for the Copts* of 1442, however, the Council of Florence turned specific: 'The holy Roman Church . . . firmly believes, professes, and preaches that "no one remaining outside the Church, not only pagans" but also Jews, heretics, or schismatics, can become partakers of eternal life, but they will go to the "eternal fire prepared for the devil and his angels" [Matt. 25: 41].' The Council quoted here a North African bishop, St Fulgentius of Ruspe (468–533), a vigorous critic of Arians and Pelagians, whose *De Fide ad Petrum* followed the pessimistic views of the later Augustine about the damnation not only of many 'within' the Church but also of everyone 'outside' the Church. The conclusion for this section of the *Decree for the Copts* also quoted Fulgentius verbatim: 'no one can be saved, no matter how much he has given in alms, even if he sheds his blood for the name of Christ, unless he remains in the bosom and unity of the Catholic Church' (DzH 1351; ND 810; *De Fide ad Petrum*, 81, 82).[23]

Other notable bishops during the first millennium of Christianity also presumed the guilt of separated Christians and of those who had not accepted the Christian faith, and consigned them all to damnation. John Chrysostom, for instance, passed such a judgement on 'pagans'

22. See Sullivan, *Salvation Outside the Church?*, 63–6.
23. See Fulgentius, *De fide ad Petrum, Corpus Christianorum: Series Latina*, 91A, 757; *Fulgentius: Selected Works*, trans. Robert B. Eno (Washington, DC: Catholic University of America Press, 1997), 104.

and 'Jews'.[24] Augustine presumed the guilt not only of 'heretics' and 'schismatics' who remained 'outside' the Church but also of 'pagans' and 'Jews' who did not accept the Christian message.[25] But the Council of Florence's *Decree for the Copts* contains for the first (and only) time a list from a general council of the Church making such a harsh judgement on four groups: 'pagans', 'Jews', 'heretics', and 'schismatics'. This council met after the Crusades and at a time when in 1453 Muslim forces were about to capture Constantinople, the last Christian stronghold in the East. It might seem surprising then that the Council did not also name and condemn Muslims explicitly. It may have intended them to be included under 'pagans'. Or was the Council being politically discreet by not naming Muslims in a decree for Coptic Christians, who lived in Egypt, a country overrun by Islam centuries before? Or did commercial considerations play a role? After all the Venetians, in particular, persistently traded with Muslim countries, as well as being intermittently at war with them?

Apart from this particular question about Islam, Frank Sullivan draws attention to the fact that those at the Council of Florence shared a mindset with the overwhelming majority of Christians in the Middle Ages: whoever did not accept the message of Christ was presumably guilty and, therefore, excluded from eternal salvation. Historical circumstances made such a severe judgement understandable but never acceptable.[26]

The Second Vatican Council was to avoid ever speaking of 'pagans', 'heretics', and 'schismatics'. As regards 'Jews' and 'Muslims', the Council's language remained courteous in *Nostra Aetate* and *Lumen Gentium*. In later chapters we will examine the positive judgements Vatican II would pass on various groups of 'outsiders'. On 7 May 2000, an ecumenical service, led by Pope John Paul II at the Colosseum, celebrated martyrs and other outstanding witnesses of faith from the twentieth century. Since those honoured that afternoon included Anglican, Orthodox, and Protestant lay persons and leaders (e.g. Paul Schneider, a Lutheran pastor who was killed in Buchenwald concentration camp in 1939), the ceremony in fact disowned the teaching that the Council of Florence had drawn from Fulgentius of Ruspe. John

---

24. For details, see Sullivan, *Outside the Church?*, 24–7.
25. Ibid., 28–39.
26. Ibid., 66–9.

Paul II joined his brothers and sisters from other Christian communities in praising courageous witnesses who 'shed their blood for the
name of Christ' without being 'in the bosom and unity of the Catholic
Church'.

But both before and after the Council of Florence, a few Christians
questioned the 'outside the Church no salvation' principle and its
harsh application: notably the mystic and missionary Ramon Llull
(c.1233–c.1315) and someone on whom Llull exercised considerable
influence, Cardinal Nicholas of Cusa (1401–64).[27]

(3) Llull wrote various works defending Christian faith against Jews,
Muslims, and Christian heretics. But the only book in which he
presented together and in detail Christianity, Judaism, and Islam was
The Book of the Gentile and the Three Wise Men.[28] The gentile, an
agnostic, discusses with the three wise men (each representing one of
the three monotheistic religions) the arguments with which they
expound and defend their beliefs. A striking courtesy and humanity
characterize the whole work, which Llull may have intended to serve
as a model for such interfaith dialogue. The gentile finds himself
convinced by the arguments made by the three wise men for the
existence and the infinite goodness of God. But before he can state
which religion he wishes to join, the wise men depart and leave him to
his choice, pledging themselves to carry further their discussion.

Especially in the last section, the wise men express the wish that
there could exist among them a common faith in God and a common
religion. As one of them says, 'just as we have one God, one Creator,
one Lord, we should also have one faith, one religion, one sect, one
manner of loving and honouring God, and we should love and help
one another, and make it so that between us there be no difference or
contrariety of faith or customs'. As the three wise men depart, one asks
the others: 'Would you like to meet once a day, and . . . have our
discussions last until all three of us have only one faith and one religion,
and until we can find some way to honour and serve one another, so
that we can be in agreement? For war, turmoil, ill will, injury, and
shame prevent people from agreeing on one belief.'[29]

---

27. On Llull see *ODCC* 996, and on Nicholas of Cusa see ibid., 1156–8.
28. Anthony Bonner (ed. and trans.), *Selected Works of Ramon Llull*, i (Princeton, NJ:
    Princeton University Press, 1985), 91–304.
29. Ibid., 301, 303.

Even more than Llull, Nicholas of Cusa had an impact with his work, *De pace fidei* (On the peace of faith). It appeared in 1454, twelve years after the extreme statement by the *Decree for the Copts* about 'no salvation outside the Church' and just one year after Constantinople was conquered by the Turks. In 1437, Nicholas himself had visited Constantinople and collected some Greek manuscripts that could be used for the deliberations on unity with Eastern Christians at the Council of Florence. With all Western Christendom, he was shaken by the fall of Constantinople, but reacted not by calling for a renewal of the Crusades but by arguing for peace between the different religious faiths.[30]

Nicholas of Cusa chose the form of vision to develop a brief dialogue in which he himself is the visionary or dreamer.[31] He imagines himself taken up into heaven, where angels plead with God that the people on earth, who invoke him by different names and worship him in different ceremonies, may be reconciled in one universal religion, albeit with a variety of rites. Christ himself suggests a dialogue to overcome errors and establish one orthodox faith. Called to the presence of Christ, St Peter, and St Paul, those who represent various religions and seemingly irreconcilable teachings discuss their differences. At the end Paul announces that different people may keep their own ceremonies, provided they preserve faith and peace. God then sends the representatives back to earth where they should lead their people in true worship. They are then to meet again in Jerusalem, profess the one, true faith, and build upon it a lasting peace.

In his pioneering study, Nicholas wanted to show how the faith of all believers converges, at least implicitly. Differences come from the mystery of God that at best can be known only imperfectly. Various rites can be maintained, provided faith and peace are preserved. At a time of great hostility, Nicholas of Cusa's work stood out by suggesting how the religions of the world converge on Christ. But, like Francis of Assisi and Ramon Llull, he was not even briefly

---

30. See James E. Biechler and H. Lawrence Bond, *Nicholas of Cusa on Interreligious Harmony: Text, Concordance, and Translation of 'De pace fidei'* (Lewiston, NY: Edwin Mellen Press, 1990); and Pio Gaia, 'L'ecumenismo religioso di Nicolò Cusano nel "De pace fidei"', in Romano Penna (ed.), *Vangelo, religioni e cultura* (Cinisello Balsamo: San Paolo, 1995), 233–61.

31. For the text of *De pace fidei*, see Nicholas Cusanus, *Opera Omnia*, vii, Raymond Klibansky and Hildebrand Bascour (eds) (Hamburg: Meiner Verlag, 1970).

acknowledged in the documents of Vatican II. In his case, the negative views expressed about his work by Hans Urs von Balthasar, Henri de Lubac, and some other twentieth-century scholars stood in the way.[32]

(4) Almost fifty years after Nicholas of Cusa published *On the Peace of Faith*, the discoveries initiated by Columbus in 1492 revealed the existence of millions of human beings in societies that had gone on for many centuries without the slightest chance of hearing about Jesus Christ and joining the Church. The arrival of Europeans in the Americas raised with new rigour the issue of universal participation in the benefits of Christ's redemption. How could he have been the Saviour for the indigenous peoples of the Americas? How could they have shared in his redemptive grace without ever having heard his name?

While the discovery of the New World came as a complete surprise, Europeans had not completely lost a sense of many people living in Africa and Asia—beyond the borders of their 'Christendom'. When Genghis Khan was elected chief of the Mongol tribes in 1206, his election triggered a series of events that led to the world becoming one. He created an empire that overran northern China, devoured central Asia, and penetrated into the Europe. At the same time, routes opened up in the opposite direction. Marco Polo visited China in 1271–5 and knew the courts of Kublai Khan, the grandson and successor of Genghis Khan. Marco Polo's account of his travels provided the first European description of the Far East. His tales of the wealth of 'Cathay' fascinated later generations, including a Genovese navigator, Christopher Columbus, who thought he could reach Asia by sailing westward. Without the events Genghis Khan set in train, the New World might have remained undiscovered by the West for longer, perhaps much longer.

The start of the Western age of discovery pre-dates, however, Columbus's crossing of the Atlantic. Portuguese explorers such as Prince Henry the Navigator (1394–1460) promoted the exploration and colonization of the Canaries and the Azores. Under his patronage, Portuguese seamen sailed well down the west coast of Africa. In 1487 the Portuguese Bartolomeu Dias (d. 1500) became the first European captain in modern times to round the Cape of Good Hope and so open

---

32. See Dupuis, *Toward a Christian Theology of Religious Pluralism*, 108–9.

up new sea routes to India and beyond.[33] Within a few years of these Portuguese voyages and Columbus's discoveries, Europeans began to circumnavigate the world, to name it with European names ('Africa', 'America', 'Asia', and 'Australia'), and to map it. Western and Christian domination was on the way.

European conquerors, merchants, and missionaries found to their astonishment pockets of Christians in India and memories of a Christian presence in China. In the first century, St Thomas the Apostle seems to have spread Christianity in Southern India before being martyred near Chennai. Missionaries from the Church of the East had reached China in the seventh century, and Syriac Christianity survived there until the fourteenth century. The memory of this earlier Christian presence was still alive when Jesuit missionaries arrived in the sixteenth century.[34] But, in general, when they went west, south, or east, Europeans discovered vast populations of people who had lived for centuries without contact with Christianity and without any chance of hearing the message of Jesus Christ. What could be said about their chances of salvation? In the sixteenth century this question was being widely raised by theologians.[35]

But, given its concern with inner-Church reform and with meeting the challenges of the Protestant Reformers, the Council of Trent did not take up this issue. When, for instance, in 1562 it addressed the question of 'the most holy sacrifice of the Mass' (DzH 1738–59; ND 1545–63), its focus remained fixed on the institution of the Eucharist, its sacrificial nature, its value for the faithful, and other 'internal' issues that concerned the Church at worship. But Christ's sacrificial self-giving took place for the whole world. Risen from the dead, he now lives forever to make intercession for all humanity. As perfect priest and victim he continues to offer himself for everyone. When at the

---

33. Herodotus, a Greek historian who died before 420 bc, tells of travellers sailing around Africa (*History*, 4. 42).
34. For a brief account of Christianity in China, see Peter C. Phan, 'Catholicism and Confucianism: An Intercultural and Interreligious Dialogue', in James L. Heft, *Catholicism and Interreligious Dialogue* (New York/Oxford: Oxford University Press, 2012), 169–91, at 178–81.
35. Sullivan (*Salvation Outside the Church?*, 69–76, 78–81) presents the replies that came from such theologians as Francisco de Vitoria (1493–1546), Melchior Cano (1505–1560), Domingo Soto (1524–60), and Albert Pigge, and then those that came from a post-Trent group of theologians: St Robert Bellarmine (1542–1621), Francisco Suarez (1548–1619), and Juan de Lugo (1583–1660) (ibid., 88–99).

Eucharist the faithful intercede for others, they do so in, with, and through Christ—a mediatorial activity for the salvation of 'others' expressed by 'the General Intercessions' that reach out in prayer to the whole world during the Eucharistic celebration.

First Timothy contains the classic passage about the divine desire to save all people: 'God our Saviour wishes everyone to be saved and to come to the knowledge of the truth. For there is ... one mediator between God and humankind, Christ Jesus, himself human, who gave himself as a ransom for all' (1 Tim. 2: 3–6). Immediately before this passage the same letter calls for prayers to be made for all people and, in particular, for political leaders (1 Tim. 2: 1–2). In the second century, St Justin Martyr witnessed to the practice of praying for everyone in need, and by the fourth century the Roman Rite included nine solemn Prayers of Intercession. In the Roman Rite such prayers dropped out of general use at the liturgy, being preserved in the Good Friday celebration alone, only to be restored by the Second Vatican Council. Citing the passage in 1 Timothy, *Sacrosanctum Concilium* decreed the reintroduction at the Eucharist of prayers of intercession for 'the holy Church, for those who rule us politically, for those weighed down by various needs, for all human beings, and for the salvation of the entire world' (*SC* 53). We will return later to the function of baptized believers praying, at the Eucharist and in other settings, for other human beings everywhere.

But in three ways the teaching of Trent did contribute to reflection on the religious situation of 'others'. First, when dealing with the necessity of faith for justification, the Council cited Hebrews 11: 6, which simply maintains the need to believe that God exists and rewards those who seek him (DzH 1532; ND 1935). The Council's decree did not go on to say that explicit faith in Christ was always necessary. For those who knew nothing of Christ, the kind of faith in God presented by Hebrews would seemingly be sufficient for their justification. Second, while insisting on the necessity of baptism for justification and salvation, Trent allowed either for 'the bath of regeneration' or for the desire of baptism (DzH 1524; ND 1924). This left open the question: could such a desire for baptism be implicit and not clearly formulated?

Third, unwittingly in its 1562 session on the sacrificial nature of the Mass, Trent taught something very positive about cultic and sacrificial activity among 'outsiders'. It cited the classical oracle from Malachi

1: 11, where 'the Lord of hosts' says: 'from the rising of the sun to its
setting my name is great among the nations, and in every place incense
is offered to my name, and a pure offering; for my name is great among
the nations'. As many had done since the early centuries of the
Church, the Council understood this 'oracle' to predict 'the clean
oblation/offering' of the Eucharist, the Council then spoke of the
Eucharistic offering being 'prefigured by various types of sacrifices
under the regime of nature and of the law. For it includes all the
good that was signified by those former sacrifices; it is their fulfilment
and perfection' (DzH 1742; ND 1547). This was a generous evaluation
not only of the Jewish sacrifices (under 'the law') but also of sacrifices
offered in other religions ('under the regime of nature'). These latter
sacrifices included (and include) various 'good' elements, which in the
divine plan 'prefigured' the Eucharist and reached their 'fulfilment and
perfection' in the Eucharist.

(5) In the aftermath of Trent, Juan de Lugo joined Francisco Suarez
and other (Jesuit) theological predecessors in holding that those who
never had the chance of hearing the gospel but, with the help of divine
grace, kept the natural law and believed in God would be saved.
Implicitly their faith in God involved Christian faith, the desire for
baptism, and membership in the Church. De Lugo went even further
than other Roman Catholic theologians in proposing the possibility of
salvation for those 'outsiders' who, while learning about Christ, found
the message insufficient or unconvincing and with sincere faith continued their existing religious practice. They could not recognize the
truth of the gospel, and should not be considered guilty of sinful
unbelief.

Perfectly aware that the teaching of Innocent III and Boniface VIII,
not to mention the Council of Florence, ruled out salvation for those
'outside the Church' (see above), de Lugo argued that the sincere
outsiders he had in mind should not be called 'non-Christians'. While
not visibly joined to the Church, 'interiorly' they share the faith of the
Church and will be reckoned by God with Christians.[36]

---

36. J. de Lugo, *Tractatus de virtute fidei divinae*, disp. 12, 18, and 20; in his *Disputationes Scholasticae et Morales*, ed. J. B. Fournials, i (Paris: Vivès, 1868), 385–437, 657–75, 751–76; ii, 1–50.

attitudes towards those of other faiths.[40] The Reign of Terror in France (1793–4) targeted clergy and religious along with aristocrats, while the revolutionary government slaughtered devout peasants in the Vendée. When Napoleon had Pius VI (pope 1775–99) carried off as a prisoner to France, he took the Catholic Church to the edge. But in France, Germany, Italy, and elsewhere the aftermath of the Napoleonic wars witnessed a spiritual revival and, in particular, a new enthusiasm to promote foreign missions in Africa, the Americas, Asia, and Oceania. Such religious congregations with specifically African focus as the Holy Ghost Fathers, the Society of African Missions, the White Fathers, and the Verona Fathers came into existence. Many missionaries learned to appreciate the religious teachings, moral values, and customs that they encountered, for instance, among Hindus, Buddhists, and followers of traditional African religions. Some would set themselves to use those teachings, values, and customs as means for expressing the Christian message. From the early nineteenth century, Anglican and Protestant missionary societies, led and inspired by figures like David Livingstone (1813–73), became very active. Where Christians in medieval Europe had enjoyed little or no first-hand contact with 'others' apart from Jews and Muslims, missionaries in China and India, for example, now lived and worked surrounded by millions of those who practised religiously different ways of life.

Such contacts 'on the ground' prompted and encouraged serious academic study. Some missionaries committed themselves to studying Sanskrit and other ancient languages, so that they might understand and interpret more intelligently the classic texts of Hinduism, Buddhism, and further Asian religions. Missionaries in Muslim countries knew that their work demanded a truly professional knowledge of Arabic and the Koran. In the Middle Ages, Ramon Llull had been a shining example in showing how such knowledge facilitates dialogue with Muslims. From the nineteenth into the twentieth century thousands followed his lead. Universities and colleges in Europe and around the world were also to play their part by initiating studies in the languages and literature of religions other than Christianity.

---

40. On developments in papal teaching and theological reflection that led up to Vatican II, see Siebenock, 'Nostra Aetate', 612–33.

Both academic developments and contacts 'on the ground' facilitated a knowledge of other religions, without which the teaching developed at Vatican II would have been unimaginable. These developments and contacts took place within the wider matrix of the political and economic expansion of Europe—a colonial history that included many such horrors as the slave trade (that continued in West Africa up to the 1860s), the Opium Wars in China, and wars by European powers over colonies and spheres of influence that culminated in the enormous tragedy of the First World War. Yet that colonial history—often inspired by greed and fear and following the law of force rather than the force of law—had its role in bringing people together and making possible a new knowledge of other religions.

And so too did the revolution in science and technology that gathered pace through the nineteenth century and into the twentieth century. Communications grew faster and easier, as steamships replaced sail and trains took over from horse transport. The advent of wireless, the telephone, motorcars, air travel, and television brought the whole world even closer together. The Second Vatican Council would be the first general council to which many bishops travelled by air. By the 1960s the world of Christians and all 'the others' had become a global village.

Even before the French Revolution arrived, Catholics and other Christians faced serious challenges from the Enlightenment, the first major intellectual movement in the Western world to develop outside the control of the Catholic Church (and of Christianity, in general) for well over 1,000 years. Some of these intellectuals and, in particular, Jean-Jacques Rousseau (1712–78) pushed Catholics and Protestants, who had insisted on explicit Christian faith being necessary for salvation, into reconsidering their position. Was faith in God (and what it implied) sufficient to save those who were inculpably ignorant of Christ and the Christian message?

In *Émile* and, specifically, in the section entitled *The Creed of a Priest of Savoy*, Rousseau objected to the prevailing view that eternal salvation was available only to those who professed Christian faith. Such a view was incompatible with the justice of God. Rousseau put words into the mouth of someone living in a distant part of the world and hearing from a missionary the Christian message for the first time: 'You proclaim to me a God, born and dead two thousand years ago at the other end of the world in some little town, and you tell me that whoever has not believed in this mystery will be damned.' The man continues to challenge the missionary: 'you say that you come to teach this to me. But why did you not come to teach it to my father, or why do you damn this good old man for never having known anything about it? Ought he to be eternally punished for your laziness, he who was so good and beneficent, and who sought only the truth?'[41]

How could Catholics and Protestants claim that God was utterly just in condemning to eternal punishment those who had no chance of embracing explicit Christian faith? Were non-Christians all guilty of grave sins that made them unworthy of being enlightened about that faith by missionaries? Rousseau deftly uses the case of the local person's own kindly and truth-seeking father to remind his readers of something Vatican II would amply acknowledge two centuries later: much holiness and truth can characterize the lives of those who have never become Christians or have never had the chance of becoming Christians. Many centuries earlier the Jewish Scriptures had also recognized numerous 'holy outsiders', such as Melchizedek, Job, and Ruth.[42] As Rousseau realized, a theory that consigned to hell such 'holy outsiders' could not be reconciled with the justice of God and, one should add, with the love of God. Those who followed Rousseau in putting this case also helped to bring Catholic thinking and teaching beyond the dreary pessimism of Jansenism.

Two influential teachers at the Roman College (later the Gregorian University) took part in that change: Giovanni Perrone (1794–1876) and Johann Baptist Franzelin (1816–86).[43] Both (and, especially, Perrone) shaped the climate of opinion that led Blessed Pius IX (pope 1846–78) to adopt a more inclusive interpretation of the principle 'no salvation outside the Church'. Yet one should point out that it was not merely current theological teaching but also the new missionary expansion in Africa, the Americas, Asia, Australia, and Oceania that influenced the thinking of Pius IX.[44] This expansion brought abundant contacts 'on the ground' with the followers of other religions, and by a process of osmosis 'from below', affected the way popes and

41. *Émile or On Education*, trans. Allan Bloom (New York: Basic Books, 1979), 305.
42. See O'Collins, *Salvation for All*, 25–7, 199–206.
43. See 'Perrone, Giovanni', *ODCC*, 1265; 'Franzelin, Johann Baptist', ibid., 640.
44. See Giacomo Martina, *Pius IX*, 3 vols. (Rome: Gregorian University Press, 1974–90), esp. vol. 2, where Martina illustrates the need to situate this long pontificate within the context of the Catholic Church around the world.

various leaders in the Catholic Church thought about the religious reality of 'others'.

Perrone proposed a theme that would be taken up in the following century by Karl Rahner: the 'gospel law (*lex evangelica*)' or obligation to hear and accept the Christian message came into existence only when and where it was and is (eventually) preached. As long as such promulgation had not taken place, people who remained in a pre-Christian situation could be saved without baptism and adherence to Christianity. Perrone argued that the axiom 'outside the Church no salvation' applied only to those who through their own fault remained in the state of heresy, schism, or unbelief. In the case of those to whom the gospel had not (or had not yet) been preached and whose faith could not therefore come 'from hearing' (Rom. 10: 17), God brings about their faith through 'an internal supernatural illumination or revelation'.[45] The prestige of Perrone led to his view being widely adopted among Catholics, and his solution was confirmed in 1854 by Pius IX.

The day after he solemnly defined the Immaculate Conception of the Blessed Virgin Mary, Pius IX spoke to the cardinals and many bishops who had come to Rome for the extraordinary event of such a dogmatic definition. In this address, *Singulari Quadam*, the Pope expressed himself on two fronts. On one front, he argued against those like Rousseau (not mentioned by name) that the principle of 'no salvation outside the Church' did not 'set limits' to the 'mercy and justice' of God. Yet, on another front, he recognized how 'invincible' and inculpable 'ignorance' excused many people from belonging to the Church. They could not be considered 'guilty' in 'the eyes of the Lord'. Pius IX clearly envisaged an indefinitely large number of people who came into this category. He put his teaching in the form of a rhetorical question: 'who could presume for oneself the ability to set the boundaries of such ignorance, taking into consideration the natural differences of peoples, lands, talents, and so many other factors?' (ND 813, 1009–10). For the first time in the history of Catholic Christianity, a pope or general council mitigated the necessity of belonging to the Church as a condition for salvation. Pius IX tempered the unqualified

---

45. G. Perrone, *Praelectiones theologicae de virtutibus fidei, spei et caritatis* (Regensburg: Pustet, 1865), in *De Fide*, n. 321, p. 115. On Perrone, see further Sullivan, *Salvation Outside the Church?*, 108–12.

harshness of the way in which Innocent III, Boniface VIII, and the Council of Florence had expressed the axiom of 'no salvation outside the Church'.

In an encyclical letter of 1863, *Quanto conficiamur moerore,* Pius IX returned to the same two themes. He warned against the 'liberal' error that denied the necessity of the Church for salvation. But, at the same time, he put even more strongly what he had said nine years earlier. Once again, while insisting on the necessity of the Church for 'eternal life', he rebutted Rousseau (again not mentioned by name) for claiming that this necessity impugned the divine justice: 'God, who knows completely the minds and souls, the thoughts and habits of all persons, will not permit, in accord with his infinite goodness and mercy, anyone who is not guilty of a [grave] voluntary fault to suffer eternal punishment'. Hence those who are without such serious guilt in not embracing Catholic Christianity ('invincibly ignorant' in the technical jargon), 'if they carefully keep the precepts of the natural law which have been written by God in the hearts of all persons, if they are prepared to obey God, and if they lead a virtuous and dutiful life, can by the power of divine light and grace, attain eternal life' (DzH 2865–7; ND 814). While speaking of 'the natural law', the Pope envisaged a supernatural situation (affecting, in fact, 'the hearts of all persons'), that of those who 'by the power of divine light and grace' attain eternal life. In the same encyclical he encouraged Catholics everywhere to foster friendly relations with the followers of other religions. In particular, they should 'help with all the services of Christian love' those who were 'poor, sick, or afflicted by any other evils'. (Here Pius IX encouraged what very many missionaries were already doing in Africa, Asia, and elsewhere by providing, for instance, educational services and health care.) The Pope also called on Catholics to 'try to lead' those of other faiths 'from the shadows of error in which they lie to the Catholic truth' (ND 1012).

In effect, Pius IX had qualified the classic axiom and now made it read: 'no salvation for those *culpably* outside the Church'. He also presupposed that 'the power of divine light and grace' was universally present and available, not only in supporting a truly moral life but also in bringing people everywhere to eternal salvation. Furthermore, for the first time official teaching encouraged Roman Catholics to develop friendly relations with those 'outside' and not merely look upon them as people whose salvation was jeopardized. At the same time, the Pope did not mention anything about the faith (e.g. a merely implicit faith in Christ) of those who remained inculpably 'outside', about their baptism of desire, or about any role of the Church in furthering their salvation. Finally, the unqualified talk of being led from the 'shadows of error' to 'the truth' is scarcely compatible with the attitude of Justin Martyr and Vatican II in acknowledging the 'seeds of the Word' and elements of 'truth and holiness' found everywhere.

The brief remarks of Pius IX might be taken to imply that people of other faiths could be saved *despite* their religion and not *through* their religion. Certainly, when he speaks of those 'outside' who 'carefully keep the precepts of the natural law', 'obey God', and 'lead a virtuous and dutiful life', he does not say a word about their being helped to do so through practising their faith (e.g. Hindu or Muslim faith). In that sense the Pope's vision remained narrow, and simply did not encompass the possibility of another faith enriching and vitalizing the moral life of those who 'carefully keep the precepts of the natural law'.

Where Perrone and Pius IX remained silent about the Church being involved in the salvation of those who were not numbered among her visible members, Johann Baptist Franzelin reflected on this question in his posthumous *Theses de Ecclesia Christi*, and did so, specifically, in the twenty-fourth thesis: 'on union with the Church as a necessary means for justification and salvation'.[46] He argued that those who do not visibly belong to the Church are, nevertheless, saved only 'through the Church' and 'in the Church'—in other words, 'by virtue of their relationship with the Church'.

Insisting that salvation was not possible without the gift of faith, Franzelin argued that such faith comes (a) either from hearing the Christian message (*fides ex auditu*), or (b) from an interior illumination (*interna illuminatio*) provided by God for those who had no other way of receiving the revealed truth. If (a), the message is derived, immediately or at least ultimately, from the Church, which is the community that originally received the revealed 'deposit of faith', preserved it, and continues to proclaim it. If (b), the grace of such an interior illumination comes 'through the Church' in the sense of orienting those who receive it towards the Church.

46. J. B. Franzelin, *Theses de Ecclesia Christi* (2nd edn.; Rome: Polyglot Press, 1907), 413–25.

Thus 'no salvation outside the Church' amounts to 'no salvation without a relationship with the visible Church on earth', which means, in the case of those who know nothing about the need to be members of the Church, an implicit desire of belonging to the Church (*votum ecclesiae*). In the eyes of God such people are united with the Catholic Church.[47]

Vatican II would not use Franzelin's language of being saved 'through the Church' and 'in the Church'. But, as we will see in the next chapter, it did introduce the terminology of being 'ordained' or related to the Church, and so too did Pius XII.

The Twentieth Century before Vatican II

En route to the broader religious horizons of Vatican II, we will engage ourselves with two official documents and two theologians. To be sure, many more official texts and theologians could be cited to illustrate developments in Catholic thinking about 'the religious other'. But these four examples suffice to plot major lines in the progress of such thinking.

(1) A 1943 encyclical by Pope Pius XII, *Mystici Corporis* (the Mystical Body), touched on our question, even though the document had a somewhat different central theme: only the Roman Catholic Church is the mystical body of Christ, and 'only those' who have received baptism and 'profess the true faith' are 'in reality (*reapse*) members of the Church' (*Mystici Corporis*, 21; DzH 3802; ND 849). If that constituted membership in the Church, how did the Pope envisage the situation and prospects of followers of non-Christian religions and others who, for no fault of their own, had never received baptism?

First of all, Pius XII went beyond what Pius IX had written in 1863 (see above) by exhorting the faithful to pray for those 'others': 'it is our further and earnest desire that the common prayer of the faithful should reach out with burning charity to those who have not yet received light from the truth of the Gospel' (*Mystici Corporis*, 101).[48]

47. Ibid., 414–16.
48. I use the translation from the original Latin made by George D. Smith (London: Catholic Truth Society, 1958).

For the first time in the story of Catholic Christianity, official teaching enjoined the practice of such prayer. We return to this theme in the next chapter.

Second, the Pope addressed his heartfelt desire to all 'outside the Catholic Church', whether other Christians or non-Christians: 'with a most loving heart we invite them all, each and every one, to yield their free consent to the inner stirrings of God's grace and strive to extricate themselves from a state in which they cannot be sure of their own eternal salvation'. He explained what he meant by not being 'sure' of salvation: 'although they may be ordered (*ordinentur*) to the mystical Body of the Redeemer by some unconscious yearning and desire (*inscio quodam voto ac desiderio*), yet they are deprived of those many great heavenly gifts and aids which can be enjoyed only in the Catholic Church' (DzH 3821; *Mystici Corporis*, 102). This teaching gave papal authority to what Robert Bellarmine had proposed centuries earlier: those people who do not actually belong to the Church can be saved by their desire of belonging to it.[49] Pius XII also confirmed the view of Francisco Suarez: even an implicit desire would be enough.[50]

Thus a pope finally taught authoritatively a theological opinion that had been developed centuries before: an 'unconscious' or implicit wish or desire to belong to the Church sufficed for salvation. But Pius XII also introduced something new: such people could be saved by being 'ordered' or related to the Church, and not precisely by being, through their unconscious desire, already members of the Church (as Franzelin had proposed). The term 'ordered' would win its place in Vatican II's teaching.

(2) Pius XII's encyclical appeared in 1943. But before the 1940s ended, a group in the archdiocese of Boston, led by Leonard Feeney, insisted that it was only through actual membership of the Catholic Church that anyone could be saved. The one exception Feeney and his followers admitted was the case of catechumens who explicitly desire

---

49. Sebastian Tromp, who drafted *Mystici Corporis* for Pius XII, was an expert on the teaching of Bellarmine and edited eleven volumes of his works; for details of these works, see 'Bellarmine, St Robert', *ODCC*, 182–3.

50. On *Mystici Corporis*, see Dupuis, *Toward A Christian Theology of Religious Pluralism*, 126–9; K. Rahner, 'Membership of the Church according to the Teaching of Pope Pius XII's Encyclical *Mystici Corporis*', trans. Karl-Heinz Weger, in *Theological Investigations*, ii (London: Darton, Longman & Todd, 1963), 1–88; Sullivan, *Salvation Outside the Church?*, 131–4.

baptism, are preparing to enter the Catholic Church, but die unexpectedly before being baptized. Through a letter from the Holy Office addressed to the Archbishop of Boston, Pius XII responded to Feeney's rigid interpretation of 'outside the Church no salvation'. While repeating in substance what *Mystici Corporis* had already said, the letter added a reference to what the Council of Trent taught about baptism 'of desire' (see above) and filled out what belonging to the Church 'at least in desire and longing (*voto et desiderio*)' means: 'it is not always necessary that this desire be explicit, as it is with catechumens. When one is invincibly ignorant, God also accepts an implicit desire, so called because it is contained in the good disposition of soul by which a person wants his or her will to be conformed to God's will' (DzH 3869–70; ND 855).

The official endorsement of belonging to the Church either *in re* or *in voto* reached back through the Council of Trent to Thomas Aquinas (see above). But it was not the language that would be adopted by the Second Vatican Council, which, in any case, did not explicitly introduce or discuss the axiom *extra ecclesiam nulla salus*. In various texts (above all, *Lumen Gentium* and *Unitatis Redintegratio*) the Council also made a distinction that Augustin Bea (1881–1968), Yves Congar,[51] and other ecumenically minded theologians failed to find either in *Mystici Corporis* or in the Holy Office letter of 1949. Those two documents did not distinguish between non-Catholic Christians and non-Christians. In the case of the former group, one cannot talk about baptism of desire; they are already incorporated in Christ through faith and baptism. But our focus in this book remains on members of world religions and other non-Christians and what Vatican II taught about their religious situation.

(3) On the eve of Vatican II and during the four years it met, notable theologians, who exercised considerable influence inside and outside the Council, offered their reflections on those whom they normally named as 'non-Christians'. To complete the picture before moving to the conciliar texts, let me take two examples: Karl Rahner (1904–84) and Jean Daniélou (1905–74). What did they say, and can we hear echoes of their views in the relevant Vatican II texts? We begin with two essays by Rahner: the first is a lecture given in April 1961, and the

---

51. 'Congar, Georges-Yves', *ODCC*, 401.

second is a radio broadcast that went on air in the summer of 1964 (i.e. some months before Vatican II promulgated *Lumen Gentium* and well over a year before the promulgation of *Nostra Aetate* and then *Ad Gentes*). Some footnotes and three pages (at the end) were to be added to the text of the broadcast before it was originally published in German in 1969.[52]

First of all, we sketched above the global matrix in which new thinking about the 'religious others' developed. Rahner remarked that 'today everybody is the next-door neighbour and spiritual neighbour of every one else in the world.' Hence 'every religion which exists in the world is—just like all cultural possibilities and actualities of other people—a question posed, and a possibility offered, to every person'. He saw the Western world 'opening out into a universal world-history in which every people and every cultural sector become an inner factor of every other people and every other cultural sector'. This meant that there is now '*one* history of the world, and in this *one* history both the Christians and the non-Christians' live in 'one and the same situation and face each other in dialogue'.[53] In a sense, Vatican II's Constitution on the Church in the Modern World, *Gaudium et Spes*, embodied this vision of the new global village and what it involved religiously and interreligiously.

Second, without mentioning him by name, Rahner picked up and developed Perrone's notion that the 'gospel law' did not start everywhere at the same time. Rahner queried whether the 'demand' made by Christianity as 'the absolute religion' takes place 'really at the same chronological moment for all human beings'; for 'the occurrence of this moment has itself a history, and thus is not chronologically simultaneous for all people, cultures, and spaces of history'. As Rahner pointed out, 'normally the beginning of the objective obligation of the Christian message for all people' has been 'thought to occur in the

52. K. Rahner, 'Christianity and the Non-Christian Religions', trans. Karl-Heinz Kruger, *Theological Investigations*, v (London: Darton, Longman & Todd, 1966), 115–34; id., 'Anonymous Christians', trans. Karl-Heinz Kruger and Boniface Kruger, *Theological Investigations*, vi (London: Darton, Longman & Todd, 1969), 390–8. The material added to the broadcast was inserted after the Council ended, and rebutted objections to Rahner's notion of 'anonymous Christians'; he argued that some passages in *Lumen Gentium* and *Ad Gentes* vindicated his position. We will come to that when analysing the conciliar texts themselves.
53. Rahner, 'Christianity and the Non-Christian Religions', 117, 121.

apostolic age'. He proposed 'a different opinion in this matter': the 'beginning of Christianity for actual periods of history' could be 'postponed to those moments in time when Christianity became a real historical factor in an individual history and culture'. Thus in different places, 'the absolute obligation of the Christian religion has in fact come into effect' at different times. Hence 'the absence of any sufficient historical encounter with Christianity' meant that 'the Christian religion' was not really present 'in the history of the people concerned'.[54] Here Rahner neatly met some of the questions raised by Columbus's discovery in 1492, but by the mid twentieth century and the arrival of the global village, this view enjoyed more historical than actual interest.

Third, the 'old' denigrating terminology, used by the Council of Florence and countless Christians when speaking of 'pagans' as outside the Church, lingered on with Rahner. He wrote not only of 'non-Christians' but also of 'pagan religions', adding at once that he was taking 'pagan' here 'as a theological concept without any disparaging content'. He noted how 'the pious, God-pleasing pagan' was 'a theme of the Old Testament'.[55] Daniélou was also not averse to using the language of 'pagan'.[56]

Recently, for the sake of 'brevity' and 'clarity' and its 'many advantages', Paul Griffiths has proposed dividing the world into three categories: 'Jewish, Christian, and pagan, where the last term means simply neither-Jewish-nor-Christian'. He proceeded to write twenty times of 'pagan(s)' in less than five pages.[57] But I doubt whether colleagues in theology will find 'many advantages' in this proposal. Whatever its origins, 'pagan' now carries too many unpleasant connotations (e.g. of 'pagans' being 'unenlightened' and even 'perverse'). Hindus, Buddhists, and followers of other world religions would not be happy about being categorized as 'pagans'. Should one or can one 'simply' assign a personal meaning to 'pagan' and ignore common usage, in which the word suffers from an ugly history? Even though Rahner and Daniélou were ready to maintain the language of 'pagan',

54. Ibid., 119, 120, 121.
55. Ibid., 120, 122.
56. See J. Daniélou, *Holy Pagans of the Old Testament*, trans. Felix Faber (London: Longmans, Green & Co., 1957).
57. P. J. Griffiths, 'Review Symposium' on O'Collins, *Salvation for All*, in *Horizons* 36 (2009), 133–8.

Vatican II never used the word '*paganus*', even if occasionally a few vernacular translations from the original Latin have carelessly introduced that term when rendering the conciliar language of 'nations (*gentes*)' and 'peoples (*populi*)'.

Griffiths, while reinstating the terminology of 'pagan', wanted to exclude the language of 'religions' and various 'religious traditions'; that language, he argued, would wrongly presuppose that Christianity and Judaism are to be called 'religions'.[58] Unquestionably, 'religion' can be and has at times been a misused term. But this did not stop Rahner from inserting 'religion' not only in the title of his lecture ('Christianity and the Non-Christian Religions') but also using 'religion' (e.g. 'the Catholic religion', 'the Christian religion', 'institutional religion', and 'the religions') throughout that lecture. The Second Vatican Council was to use the term 'religion (*religio*)' seventy-one times, speaking of 'different religions' and 'other religions' (*NA* 1, 2), 'the Christian religion' (*LG* 11, 26, 35, 50; *AG* 16; *GS* 19), and so forth. The Council had no quibbles about the language used by Rahner and others, and called *Nostra Aetate* a 'Declaration on the Relation of the Church to Non-Christian Religions'.

A fourth theme of Rahner's lecture went beyond matters of terminology and highlighted a Christocentric vision firmly endorsed by the Council (e.g. *Gaudium et Spes*, 22): 'God desires the salvation of everyone', and 'this salvation willed by God is the salvation won by Christ, the salvation of supernatural grace which divinizes the human person, the salvation of the beatific vision'. Like Henri de Lubac (1896–1991),[59] Rahner moved beyond the First Vatican Council and

58. Ibid., 134.
59. H. de Lubac, *The Mystery of the Supernatural*, trans. Rosemary Sheed (London; Geoffrey Chapman, 1967); French original, *Le Mystère du surnaturel* (Paris: Aubier, 1965); see also *Surnaturel. Études historiques* (Paris: Aubier, 1946), a work never translated into English. Neo-scholastic theology separated 'nature' and 'grace' extrinsically, with 'nature' enjoying no intrinsic desire for the supernatural and with 'grace' a layer added to the already complete nature. De Lubac rejected the notion of 'pure nature'; it is a merely hypothetical state. Human persons are created with a single, supernatural, final goal, which is intrinsic to human nature as it exists, even if the fulfilment of this goal comes from God. Rahner agreed that, from the moment of their conception, human beings have a supernatural 'finality' inscribed in their very being. On de Lubac, see Brigitte Cholvy, 'Une controverse majeure: Henri de Lubac et le surnaturel', *Gregorianum* 92 (2011), 797–827; through opposing the extrinsic quality of 'nature/supernature' schemes, de Lubac, Rahner, and others helped to make Vatican II somewhat inhibited about using 'supernatural' and related terms; for

the scheme it inherited and endorsed about the 'natural' and 'supernatural' orders, a scheme in which 'the natural light of human reason' preceded and was distinguished from 'another, supernatural way' (DzH 3004; ND 113). There is only one world of (freely given) grace, in which 'every human being is really and truly exposed to the influence of divine, supernatural grace', by means of which 'God communicates himself, whether the individual takes up an attitude of acceptance or of refusal towards this grace'. Rahner added: 'we have every right to suppose' that grace has not only been offered outside the Church, 'but also that, in a great many cases at least, grace gains the victory in the human being's free acceptance of it, this being again the result of grace'.[60]

Three years later in a radio broadcast, Rahner introduced the term 'supernatural existential' to describe the situation created for human freedom by the redemptive work of Christ. Even before they accept (or reject) grace, human beings are positively preconditioned from 'within' by the self-communication which, in and through Christ, God offers to all. Hence 'the expressly Christian revelation' is 'the explicit statement of the revelation of grace', which all human beings already experience 'implicitly in the depths' of their being.[61] As we will see, *Gaudium et Spes* (no. 22) and the first encyclical of Pope John Paul II, *Redemptor Hominis* (nos. 8, 13) have similar things to say, and could easily evoke Rahner's 'supernatural existential'. But the term itself, adapted from the philosophy of Martin Heidegger (1889–1976), while suitable as theological jargon, was hardly appropriate for the public teaching of a council or a pope.[62] In any case, as we have seen, Vatican II made minimal use of the terminology of 'supernatural' and related terms'.[63]

Fifth, this primordial 'revelation of grace' means that 'it would be wrong to regard the pagan [!]' who hears the Christian message for the first time 'as someone who has not yet been touched in any way by

details, see ibid., 816. See also Hans Boersma, 'Nature and the Supernatural in *la nouvelle théologie*: The Recovery of a Sacramental Mindset', *New Blackfriars* 93 (2012), 34–46, at 36–8.

60. Rahner, 'Christianity and the Non-Christian Religions', 122–3, 124.
61. Rahner, 'Anonymous Christians', 393–4.
62. Heidegger, in coining the term *existential*, intended it to describe a situation that as a matter of fact preconditions the way human freedom is exercised.
63. See Cholvy, 'Une controverse majeure', 816.

God's grace and truth'. From within 'he has already been given *revelation in a true sense* even before he has been affected by missionary preaching from without'. Since the human correlate of God's self-revelation is human faith, implicit faith can, therefore, 'occur in a so-called pagan'.[64] Unlike some or even many others, as we will see when examining *Nostra Aetate* and *Ad Gentes*, Rahner acknowledged that God's self-revelation 'in the true sense' comes to all people and that, through divine grace, they can respond with genuine faith, albeit of an implicit kind. Centuries earlier Thomas Aquinas (see above) proposed that those who could never hear the Christian message but tried to seek good and avoid evil could be blessed with a divine revelation, and so come to the faith they needed for salvation. That divine revelation with the human response of faith can occur 'outside' the missionary proclamation of the Church, while acceptable to Aquinas and Rahner, still remains unimaginable to some. As we shall see, they contrast the situation of 'theological faith' (with which Christians respond to 'revelation') with that of the mere 'belief' or 'beliefs' of those who follow other religions and who still search for the self-revealing God.

Sixth, Rahner showed, as we saw above, a robust confidence that, 'in a great many cases at least, grace gains the victory in the human being's free acceptance of it, this being again the result of grace'. Hence, when missionaries meet members of extra-Christian religions, they meet people 'who can and must already be regarded in this or that respect as an anonymous Christian'. These anonymous Christians have already been touched by 'God's grace and truth', and their situation is 'Christianity of an anonymous kind'.[65] Hence 'the proclamation of the gospel' turns 'anonymous Christians' into those who now explicitly know the 'Christian belief' that was already there 'in the depths' of their 'grace-endowed being'.[66]

Rahner anticipated two objections that would be brought against his language of 'anonymous Christians'. (a) It could give rise to the false conclusion that the 'explicit preaching of Christianity' was 'super-fluous'. He agreed that his proposal should affect the way missionaries conceive and practise their work; they deal with people 'living by an anonymous Christianity not as yet fully conscious of itself'. But he insisted on the need to proclaim the gospel: 'the individual who grasps

64. Rahner, 'Christianity and the Non-Christian Religions', 131–2; italics mine.
65. Ibid., 131, 133.   66. Ibid., 132.

Christianity in a clearer, purer and more reflective way has, other things being equal, a still greater chance of salvation than someone who is merely an anonymous Christian'.[67] (b) Rahner also recognized that non-Christians could dismiss his proposal about anonymous Christianity as 'presumptuous', since it judged everything holy found in any human being to be the 'fruit' of Christ's grace. Yet Rahner considered his claim not only to be humbling, in that it recognized the kingdom of God to be 'greater' than the Church, but also based on the example of St Paul when he said: 'What you do not know and yet worship that I proclaim to you' (Acts 17: 23).[68]

Nevertheless, Rahner had to defend his talk about 'anonymous Christianity' against the charge of lessening 'the importance' of preaching the Word of God and receiving new members of the Church through baptism. Those who interpreted his remarks that way, he replied, had not read them 'with sufficient attention'. He agreed that 'the name itself is unimportant', but it pointed to a reality recognized by Vatican II's teaching on the situation of non-Christians.[69] In the event, the Council did not adopt the language of 'anonymous Christians' or 'anonymous Christianity'. *Ad Gentes*, *Lumen Gentium*, and *Nostra Aetate* did, however, all follow Rahner (and others) in speaking of the elements of 'grace and truth' to be found in those who had not or had not yet heard and accepted the gospel. As for Rahner himself, in a lecture given in October 1967 on 'atheism and implicit Christianity', he began by remarking that 'implicit Christianity' could also be called 'anonymous Christianity' but admitted that such names are 'of secondary importance'.[70] A few years later in a hitherto unpublished chapter he allowed that 'anonymous Christian' and 'anonymous Christianity' are 'not essential' and 'merely a terminological question'.[71] In his magisterial *Foundations of*

67. Ibid.
68. Ibid., 134; see my reflections on Acts 17 in Chapter 1 above.
69. 'Anonymous Christians', 397, 398. See Anita Röper, *The Anonymous Christian*, trans. Joseph Donceel (New York: Sheed & Ward, 1966). For the debate on Rahner's 'anonymous Christian/Christianity', see Dupuis, *Toward a Christian Theology of Religious Pluralism*, 143–9; Sullivan, *Salvation Outside the Church?*, 162–81.
70. K. Rahner, 'Atheism and Implicit Christianity', trans. Graham Harrison, *Theological Investigations*, ix (London: Darton, Longman & Todd, 1972), 145–64, at 145.
71. K. Rahner, 'Anonymous Christianity and the Missionary Task of the Church', trans. David Bourke, *Theological Investigations*, xii (London: Darton, Longman & Todd, 1974), 161–78, at 164, 165.

Christian Faith Rahner devoted a section to God's self-communication to every human being as 'supernatural existential', but did not introduce the language of 'anonymous Christianity' when treating the history of salvation and revelation.[72]

Seventh and finally, what did Rahner say on the eve of Vatican II about non-Christian religions and their possible role as ways of salvation for their followers? While acknowledging the presence of some 'religious, ethical and metaphysical aberrations', he recognized in such extra-Christian religions 'supernatural, grace-filled elements'.[73] Here he saw a comparison to be made (not an identity to be admitted) between such religions and 'the Old Testament religion'. The former belong to 'general salvation-history', whereas the latter forms the 'immediate pre-history' for the New Testament. Yet in both cases we observe 'a morality that is never pure but is always also corrupted'. Hence Rahner argued: for a religion to be 'intended by God', it does not have to be 'pure and positively willed by God *in all its elements*'.[74]

As regards the followers of other religions, Rahner agreed that if human beings, given their social nature and radical solidarity with each other, are going to 'have a positive, saving relationship to God, they are going to have it within *that religion*' which is at their disposal. Indeed, Rahner maintained that they have 'the right and indeed the duty' to live their 'relationship to God within the religious and social realities' offered by their 'particular, historical situation'.[75]

The bishops at Vatican II were to align themselves with Rahner in recognizing the 'grace-filled elements' in world religions, presumably understanding such elements to be 'supernatural'. But they remained silent, at least explicitly, about whether such religions were in some sense 'positively willed by God' and hence part of the one, overall divine plan of salvation. The texts they approved also remained silent (again, at least explicitly) about whether the followers of these religions might, in their particular situation, have a right and even a duty to live

72. K. Rahner, *Foundations of Christian Faith: An Introduction to the Idea of Christianity*, trans. William V. Dych (New York: Seabury Press, 1978), 126–33, 138–75; German original 1976. A few years later, however, Rahner returned to his 'anonymous' language in 'Anonymous and Explicit Faith', trans. David Morland, *Theological Investigations*, xvi (London: Darton, Longman & Todd, 1979), 52–9.
73. 'Christianity and Non-Christian Religions', 121, 122, 130.
74. Ibid., 129, 130–1; italics mine.
75. Ibid., 128, 131; italics his.

out their relationship to God through these religions. *Nostra Aetate* cited in a footnote a letter from Pope Gregory VII to a Muslim king, which went further than the teaching of Vatican II. The Pope understood the practice of Islam to be the effective way of salvation for King Anzir (see above).

(4) After examining in detail a groundbreaking lecture delivered by Rahner in 1961 and partly echoed in Vatican II, we can be much more brief about a less 'generous' view of extra-Christian religions developed by someone who was also a leading *peritus* (expert) at Vatican II. In an article that appeared in 1964 and so a year before the Council promulgated *Ad Gentes* and *Nostra Aetate*, Jean Daniélou wrote: 'Religions are a gesture of man towards God; revelation is the witness of a gesture of God towards man'. He explained what this had involved historically: 'the religions are creations of human genius; they witness to the value of exalted religious personalities, such as Buddha, Zoroaster, Orpheus. But they also have the defects of what is human. Revelation is the work of God alone.' Daniélou added: 'religion expresses man's desire for God. Revelation witnesses that God has responded to that desire. Religion does not save. Jesus Christ grants salvation.'[76]

This interpretation of non-Christian religions (a) clearly excluded any notion of God intending the religions and involving them in the one divine plan of salvation for all people. The religions may be 'creations of human genius', but they are only that. (b) It seems that Daniélou's view ruled out revelation occurring anywhere but in the biblical history. The religions express the human desire to God, but only that human desire. They do not mediate any revelation. (c) Apropos of religions having 'the defects of what is human' and revelation being 'the work of God alone', one might comment that Christianity also has from the very beginning displayed 'the defects of what is human' and that the ways in which revelation (and salvation) are mediated through the Church are by definition not 'the work of God alone'. (d) Daniélou's scheme of human desire/divine response converges with the scheme of question/answer adopted by *Nostra Aetate* (no. 1) and *Gaudium et Spes* (e.g. no. 22). Here one might add that not only the religions but also Christianity itself expresses the human desire

---

76. 'Christianisme et religions non-chrétiennes', *Études* 321 (1964), 323–36, at 327.

for God, to which God has responded (see *GS* 21). (e) In the ultimate sense, neither Christianity nor any religion saves. As the Council of Trent put matters, God alone is 'efficient cause' of justification and salvation (DzH 1529; ND 1932).

Despite Daniélou's considerable influence at the Council, *Nostra Aetate* was to acknowledge, with a clear nod towards John 1: 9, that the religions often 'reflect a ray of that Truth which enlightens all people' (no. 2). Hence it is insufficient to say that they are merely 'creations of human genius', simply human attempts to know God and achieve salvation through one's own resources. They also express 'gestures' of God towards human beings. As we will see later, *Lumen Gentium* and, even more, *Nostra Aetate* also implied that divine revelation comes to those of extra-Christian religions, while *Ad Gentes* clearly presents revelation as a universal reality. Yet Daniélou's view of other religions doubtless helped to inhibit the Council from ever clearly stating (as Rahner did above) that the religions were in any way positively intended by God and were genuine, if imperfect, ways of salvation for their followers. Moreover, Daniélou's vision of the extra-Christian religions merely expressing a human search for God cast a long shadow over the reception of Vatican II's teaching on those religions and their followers.

One could critically evaluate what other theologians, such as Yves Congar, Henri de Lubac, Raimon Panikkar, and Gustave Thiels, had written about the situation of 'the religious others'. But enough has been said to sketch the major themes of official teaching and theological reflection in circulation as the Council met. We begin with two documents approved, respectively, in 1963 and 1964: *Sacrosanctum Concilium* and *Lumen Gentium*.

THREE

Sacrosanctum Concilium and *Lumen Gentium* on the Religious Others

> Jesus Christ, the High Priest of the New and Eternal Covenant,
> when he assumed a human nature, introduced into this land of exile
> the hymn that in heaven is sung throughout the ages.
>
> Vatican II, the Constitution on the Sacred Liturgy

When examining what Vatican II taught about 'the religious others', it may seem strange to cite the first document the Council approved. Nevertheless, at least for three reasons, as we shall see, the Constitution on the Sacred Liturgy (*Sacrosanctum Concilium*), promulgated by the Second Vatican Council on 4 December 1963, merits its place on the agenda for this chapter before we move to the Dogmatic Constitution on the Church (*Lumen Gentium*), promulgated on 21 November 1964. What *Sacrosanctum Concilium* envisaged about 'the others' differed dramatically from what happened in the sixteenth century at the Council of Trent (1545–63).

Trent aimed to clarify and defend Catholic doctrine and meet the challenges of the Protestant Reformers when it developed teaching on the sacraments in general and baptism and confirmation in particular (1547), the Eucharist (1551), penance and extreme unction (1551), communion under 'both kinds' and communion for children (1562), the Mass as sacrifice (1562), the sacrament of orders (1563), and the sacrament of matrimony (1563). Various Reformers had put into question the number of sacraments 'instituted' by Christ, the reality of the Eucharistic presence, the sacrificial character of the Eucharist, the nature of ministerial ordination, and other matters concerning the worship and sacramental life of the Church. The Council aimed 'to do away with errors and to root out heresies which in this our age are directed against the holy sacraments' (DzH 1600; ND 1310). In expounding 'the true and ancient doctrine on the faith and on the sacraments', Trent set itself 'to supply a remedy for all the heresies and other serious evils which now deeply trouble God's Church and divide it into so many different parts' (DzH 1635; ND 1512). Shaped by these historical circumstances, the Council had much to teach about the worship and sacramental life of the Church. But, as we already noted in the last chapter, its concerns remained 'ad intra' or within Christianity. It did not attend to the 'big picture' and how the liturgy is *also* concerned with the salvation of those who have not been baptized and never will be baptized.

When the bishops assembled for the Second Vatican Council in 1962, they did so in happier and, in the broadest sense, more 'ecumenical' days. In that climate, understanding and reforming the liturgy of the Roman Catholic Church inevitably brought up the question: where does God come into view for 'the others'? Right from the first document that it approved, the Council showed a mindset that encompassed the whole of humanity.

Sacrosanctum Concilium

Unlike some of the other texts of the Council (e.g. *Lumen Gentium* and *Nostra Aetate*), *Sacrosanctum Concilium* enjoyed a relatively untroubled passage to its final approval.[1] It emerged as the product of a well developed liturgical movement, which had long encouraged all the baptized to participate actively in official worship and let the Eucharist become the real centre of their community and personal lives. Initiated by Abbot Prosper Guéranger (1805–75) and the Benedictine Abbey of

---

1. On this conciliar text see Rita Ferrone, *Liturgy: Sacrosanctum Concilium* (Mahwah, NJ: Paulist Press, 2007); Josef A. Jungmann, 'Constitution on the Sacred Liturgy', trans. Lalit Adolphus, in Herbert Vorgrimler (ed.), *Commentary on the Documents of Vatican II*, i (London: Burns & Oates, 1967), 1–88; Reiner Kaczynksi, '*Sacrosanctum Concilium*', in Peter Hünermann and Bernd Jochen Hilberath (eds), *Herders Theologischer Kommentar zum Zweiten Vatikanischen Konzil*, ii (Freiburg im Breisgau: Herder, 2004), 1–210; Reiner Kaczynksi, 'Toward the Reform of the Liturgy', in Giuseppe Alberigo and Joseph Komonchak (eds), *History of Vatican II*, iii (Maryknoll, NY: Orbis, 2000), 189–256; Mathijs Lamberigts, 'The Liturgy Debate', in *History of Vatican II*, ii (1997), 107–66; Evangelista Vilanova, 'The Intersession 1963–1964', in *History of Vatican II*, iii, 347–490, at 471–86.

Solesmes, the movement received official encouragement in 1903 when St Pius X promulgated measures promoting frequent communion and the reform of church music. Across Europe and in the USA, such Benedictines as Lambert Beauduin (1873–1960), Odo Casel (1896–1948), and Godfrey Dieckman (1908–2002), along with such others as Pius Parsch (1884–1954), Romano Guardini (1885–1968), and Josef Jungmann (1889–1975), promoted not only scholarly studies of the liturgy but also its pastoral development. Pope Pius XII's 1947 encyclical on liturgical worship, *Mediator Dei* (Mediator of God), brought further encouragement and some reforms, which culminated in the restoration of the Holy Week ceremonies. The support of bishops, monasteries, and other centres in France, Germany, and elsewhere also laid the ground for what was to come through Vatican II: the introduction of the vernacular and the reform of the rites.

A passage from *Mediator Dei* on the Divine Office deserves to be quoted, in particular because it would be retrieved in *Sacrosanctum Concilium* and, as we will see, remains relevant to the question of Vatican II's teaching about other religions. The encyclical contained a vivid picture of the incarnate Word of God initiating his priestly work by leading off a worldwide hymn of praise to God: 'The Word of God, when he assumed a human nature, introduced into this land of exile the hymn that in heaven is sung throughout all ages. He unites the whole community of human kind with himself and associates it with him in singing this divine canticle of praise' (ND 1225; *Mediator Dei*, 144). These two sentences from the encyclical evoke something of the Book of Revelation's vision of earthly liturgy being matched (and surpassed) by heavenly liturgy (especially Rev. 4: 1–5: 14), and add a further picture. At the incarnation the Son of God led off a cosmic hymn, and that hymn of divine praise will never end. We return below to this passage.

The draft of what was to be promulgated as *Sacrosanctum Concilium* was the first 'schema' to be debated by Vatican II (in October and November 1962). Various amendments were proposed, and the relevant commission worked on them. When the bishops returned for the second session of the Council in the autumn of 1963, they discussed in detail the revised text, considered further amendments, and voted on the document, chapter by chapter. On 22 November 1963, the entire 'schema' was approved by 2,158 votes, with only 19 against it; on 4 December 1963, the Constitution on the Sacred Liturgy was solemnly proclaimed.

(1) From the opening paragraph, a worldwide mindset distinguished this constitution. It named the four related concerns that motivated the whole work of the Council: (a) supporting growth in 'the life' of Roman Catholics; (b) updating those institutions that are subject to changes; (c) promoting 'union' among all Christians; and (d) strengthening 'whatever can help to call all people into the fold of the Church'. These four concerns provided cogent reasons for 'the renewal and promotion of the liturgy' (SC 1). Unlike the Council of Trent, Vatican II presented its teaching on the liturgy within the context not only of all Christianity but also of the entire human race.

The second paragraph reflected the same mindset. Through the liturgy and especially through the Eucharist, 'the faithful express and *manifest to others* the mystery of Christ and the genuine nature of the true Church'. As well as feeding their spiritual lives and bringing them to 'the fullness of Christ', the Eucharist 'strengthens their power to *preach Christ*, and thus show forth, *to those who are outside,* the Church as a sign lifted up among the nations under which the scattered children of God may be gathered into one' (SC 2; italics mine).[2] From the outset, *Sacrosanctum Concilium* presented the Eucharist as *also* involving an open desire to 'preach Christ' and 'manifest' his mystery to the world. Rather than continuing to insist 'outside the Church no salvation', the first document of Vatican II signalled a commitment to 'those who are outside' and wish to share with them the life of Christ and the fellowship of the Church (in that order). The Council knew how the Eucharist calls for an outreach to all 'the religious others' around the world. A commitment to the liturgy necessarily involves an active openness to the whole human race.

Continuing in a similar vein, Chapter 1 of *Sacrosanctum Concilium* (on 'general principles for renewing and promoting the sacred Liturgy') opens by quoting the classic text about God wanting 'all human beings to be saved and to come to the knowledge of the truth' (1 Tim. 2: 4). It refers at once to Christ coming as 'the Mediator between God and human beings' (1 Tim. 2: 5 being footnoted rather than quoted). It sums up the work of Christ as 'redeeming human kind and giving perfect glory to God' (SC 5). Over and over again this opening chapter

---

2. Here SC evokes John 11: 52 (about Jesus 'gathering into the one the dispersed children of God'). This text recurs when the Council attends to all the 'outsiders' (LG 13).

reveals the same all-encompassing vision and desire that 'all human beings should know the one true God and Jesus Christ whom he has sent' (*SC* 9).

(2) Given the world-encompassing mindset of our document, we should not be surprised that in a second chapter (dedicated to the Eucharist) it restores the 'prayer of the faithful', 'an old tradition' which had never been given up in the East, but which had disappeared in the Roman liturgy, except on Good Friday.[3] This prayer was to be restored 'after the gospel and homily, especially on Sundays and holidays of obligation'. Recalling in a footnote 1 Timothy 2: 1–2 (which enjoins a similar form of prayer), *Sacrosanctum Concilium* explains: 'by this prayer in which the people are to take part, intercessions are to be made for the holy Church, for those who lead us politically, for those weighed down by various needs, *for all human beings, and for the salvation of the entire world*' (*SC* 53; italics mine).

Later in this book I will explore the question: what do such prayers made by the Eucharistic assembly for 'all human beings and for the salvation of the whole world' imply theologically? If the 'law of praying is the law of believing', what should Christians believe (and hope) about the divine plan of salvation for all human beings, including those who are not baptized? Here I wish only to flag the all-encompassing mindset shown by the Council in the first document it approved and promulgated. That text conveys a sense of Catholics worshipping in solidarity with the world and concerned about the salvation of all people.

The introduction of the 'prayer of the faithful' has resonated everywhere with Catholics and some other Christians. They, or at least those of the older generation, know that this feature of their worship is due to the Council, even if they remain unaware of the precise text that legislated for the change (or rather retrieval). But there is another paragraph in *Sacrosanctum Concilium* that has largely escaped even scholarly attention. Most, if not all, experts in Christianity and other religions seem to have remained unaware that an image with which the Council began its teaching on the Divine Office (Ch. 4) is

3. See Adolf Adam, *The Eucharistic Celebration: The Source and Summit of Faith*, trans. Robert C. Schultz (Collegeville, MN: Liturgical Press, 1994), 49–51; Jungmann, 'Constitution on the Sacred Liturgy', 38; Kaczynski, '*Sacrosanctum Concilium*', 130–1; Gerard Moore, *Lord, Hear Our Prayer: Praying the General Intercessions* (Strathfield, NSW: St Paul's Publications, 2008), 11–17; 'Bidding Prayer', *ODCC*, 208.

enormously significant for their special area. This is the third theme to be drawn from the constitution that will enhance our picture of Vatican II's attitude towards the innumerable 'religious others'.

(3) Without adding a reference (seemingly an oversight), *Sacrosanctum Concilium* quotes the passage from Pius XII's *Mediator Dei* that we cited above, significantly replacing 'the Word of God' by a title that evokes Hebrews, 'the High Priest of the New and Eternal Covenant': 'Jesus Christ, the High Priest of the New and Eternal Covenant, when he assumed a human nature, introduced into this land of exile the hymn that in heaven is sung throughout all ages. He unites the whole community of human kind with himself and associates it with him in singing the divine canticle of praise' (*SC* 83).[4] Earlier the same constitution had taught that the risen Christ is present 'when the Church prays and *sings*' (*SC* 7; italics mine). Now the document speaks of singing one 'divine canticle of praise', led by the incarnate 'Cantor' himself, who joins the whole human race in sharing this heavenly hymn that he has brought to earth. The High Priest of the New and Eternal Covenant continues his priestly work through the Church, which is 'ceaselessly engaged in praising the Lord [presumably understood here as God the Father] and interceding for the salvation of the whole world' (*SC* 83).[5]

What sources does *Sacrosanctum Concilium* retrieve when it pictures Christ as the incarnate Cantor and/or Choirmaster of a universal hymn of praise? Its immediate source are the lines that it silently quotes from *Mediator Dei*, which in turn cited Augustine's *Expositions of the Psalms*: 'it is the one Saviour of his [mystical] body, our Lord Jesus Christ, Son of God, who prays for us, who prays in us, and who is prayed to us by us. He prays for us as our priest; he prays in us as our head; he is prayed to by us as our God. Let us therefore recognize in him our voice and in us his voice' (85. 1). Augustine understood the Psalms, in particular, to be the voice of the whole Christ, head and body/members.[6] The text

---

4. For a chapter dedicated to the Divine Office that comes in a document on the liturgy, using a priestly title for Christ seems more appropriate than 'the Word of God', which readily evokes John's statement of the incarnation ('the Word was made flesh').
5. Kaczynski, '*Sacrosanctum Concilium*', 167–8.
6. On the psalms being 'the voice of Christ to the Father (*vox Christi ad Patrem*)', as well as 'the voice of the Church about Christ to the Father (*vox Ecclesiae ad Patrem de Christo*)' and 'the voice of the Church to Christ (*vox Ecclesiae ad Christum*)', see Balthasar Fischer, 'Le Christ dans les Psaulmes', *La Maison Dieu* 27 (1951), 86–113.

of *Mediator Dei*, crafted by Pope Pius XII and his ghost writer(s), explicitly took those who drafted *Sacrosanctum Concilium* back to this passage from Augustine. But the authors of the Constitution on the Sacred Liturgy might also have been inspired by such earlier writers as Clement of Alexandria and/or by Ignatius of Antioch (d. *c.*107).

In an early passage of his *Protrepticus* ('Exhortation to the Greeks/ Heathen'), Clement twice speaks of the Word, who was in the beginning and has now appeared on earth, as 'the New Song' (1. 3).[7] Later in the same work he pictures 'the eternal Jesus, the one, great high priest' who 'raises the hymn with us' as he invites us to 'join the choir' and cries aloud: 'I summon the whole human race...Come unto me and gather together as one well ordered unity under the one God and under the one Logos of God' (12. 33).[8] We could put together the two passages and speak of 'the New Song', who as the 'one, eternal high priest' gathers together 'the whole human race' into 'the well ordered unity' of an immense choir to sing the praises of the one God.

From the early second century such praising of God with Christ had been presented as *praying* or *singing* together. Thus Ignatius of Antioch, when using musical metaphors to depict the unity and harmony between a bishop and his clergy and/or congregation, wrote: 'and may each of you remain joined in chorus, so that being harmonious in concord, receiving God's variation in unity, you may sing with one voice through Jesus Christ in the Father, that he may both hear you and recognize you through what you do well, as members of his Son' (*Ephesians*, 4. 2).[9] In classical Greek literature and later, the image of the chorus was applied to the harmony of the cosmos, to the political concord of a city, to union within a family, and to similar situations where peace reigns.[10]

---

7. With this title for Christ, he echoed the language of the Psalms about 'singing a new song to the Lord' who comes to rule and bring salvation (Ps. 96: 1; 98: 1; 149: 1).
8. Clement of Alexandria, *Exhortation to the Heathen*, trans. William Wilson, Ante-Nicene Christian Library, iv (Edinburgh: T. & T. Clark, 1867), 22, 108.
9. Trans. from W. R. Schoedel, *Ignatius of Antioch* (Philadelphia: Fortress, 1985), 51; trans. corrected. As Schoedel points out, 'it is likely that the reference in this context to the Ephesians as "members" (μέλη) of God's Son is to be understood as play on words; they are also his "melodies" (μέλη)' (ibid., 53).
10. Ibid., 51–3.

Whatever its ancient source or sources, the opening words of Chapter 4 of the Constitution on the Sacred Liturgy offer no references, not even *Mediator Dei* (no. 144) which they quietly quote. The passage pictures 'a canticle of divine praise' directed to God and understood to be also a hymn sung by all creatures in heaven. Christ in his high-priestly role is represented as having inaugurated the singing of the divine praises on earth, by assuming the human condition in his incarnation. He is pictured as associating with himself not merely those who come to know and believe in him but also the whole human community. Together they all form a chorus, of which he is the leader.

This passage strikingly portrays Christ actively present to and for all human beings. The unity of the whole human race in him, which began with the incarnation, must be understood to be strengthened and perfected through the crucifixion, resurrection, and the outpouring of the Holy Spirit. Finally, it will be consummated when human beings reach 'the halls of heaven'. This picture of Christ the Cosmic Choirmaster serves brilliantly to symbolize the union in him of all the baptized and non-baptized alike. Long before they might become aware of this, even those who have never heard his name are mysteriously but, through grace, truly in the hands of Christ the Choirmaster of the world. The redemption may be depicted as a united musical engagement.

Though its powerful image of Christ the universal Choirmaster and/or Cantor, the Council encourages those who pray and/or sing the Divine Office to give themselves wholeheartedly to two projects: praising God and interceding for the salvation of the whole world. Through its first document, Vatican II shows its openness to the entire human race and leaves us once again with the question: what should Christians, and especially those devoted to the Divine Office, believe and think about the divine plan of salvation for all human beings?

As it happened, when the Council promulgated *Sacrosanctum Concilium* on 4 December 1963, it also promulgated its Decree on the Means of Social Communication (*Inter Mirifica*).[11] This short decree, if

---

11. See Joseph Famerée, 'Bishops and Dioceses and the Communications Media (5–25 November 1963)', in *History of Vatican II*, iii, 117–91, at 175–91; Lamberigts, 'The Discussion of the Modern Media', in *History of Vatican II*, ii, 267–79; Hans Joachim Sander, '*Inter Mirifica*', in *Herders Theologischer Kommentar*, ii, 233–59; Karlheinz

often judged the weakest text to come from Vatican II, shows, never-theless, a deep concern for 'the salvation of all people', which it also describes as 'the salvation and perfection of the entire human family' (no. 3). Here we glimpse again a frame of mind attentive to God's plan to save the whole human race, including the millions of non-Christians.

As for *Sacrosanctum Concilium* itself, the document was not as dra-matically challenging (and not as startlingly new) as what we read in the Declaration on the Relation of the Church to Non-Christian Religions. But right from the first important text promulgated by the Council, we can see how the salvation of all humanity stood high in the spiritual imagination and agenda of the bishops and their advisors at Vatican II.

Lumen Gentium

Before examining what *Lumen Gentium* contributed specifically to Catholic thinking and teaching about the 'religious others', we need to recall something of the embattled development of this dogmatic constitution. Among the nine drafts (or 'schemata') distributed (seven in August and two in November 1962) to the bishops attending Vatican II there was a 'schema' on the Church (*De Ecclesia*). It was delivered to the bishops only on 23 November and had been largely prepared by Marie-Rosaire Gagnebet and Sebastian Tromp, under the watchful eye of Cardinal Alfredo Ottaviani, the head of the Theo-logical Commission.[12] This 'schema' highlighted the Church as a hierarchical society rather than as being both a mystery and the whole people of God. Following the 1943 encyclical of Pius XII, *Mystici Corporis*, it identified the mystical body of Christ with Roman Catholicism and so applied the term 'church' exclusively to the Roman Catholic Church. In the final days of the first session of the

Schmidthüs, 'Decree on the Instruments of Social Communication', in *Commentary on the Documents of Vatican II*, i, 89–104.

12. See Hünermann, '*Lumen Gentium*', *Herders Theologischer Kommentar*, ii, 269–563; Gérard Philips, 'History of the Constitution', in *Commentary on the Documents of Vatican II*, i, 105–37; id., *L'Église et son mystère au IIe Concile de Vaticane: histoire, texte et commentaire de la Constitution 'Lumen Gentium'*, 2 vols. (Paris: Desclée, 1967).

Council, this draft was sharply criticized by the bishops (1–6 December 1962).

Even before that, in October 1962, Cardinal Leo Jozef Suenens had asked Gérard Philips to 'revise, complete, and improve' this 'schema' on the Church.[13] As a result of the December debate, the 'schema' was removed, and over several months (February–May 1963) a new draft was prepared on the basis of a text authored by Philips (with the assistance of Karl Rahner and others).[14] For some weeks in the spring of 1963, Congar worked on the revision, which resulted in a new 'schema' being mailed to the bishops in the middle of the year. In that revised text, which, with some amendments, eventually became the final text of *Lumen Gentium* (promulgated on 21 November 1964), Congar worked on numbers 9, 13, 16, and 17 in Chapter 2 ('The People of God') and contributed to Chapter 1 ('The Mystery of the Church').[15] Number 16 of Chapter 2, with its positive regard for Jews, Muslims, and others, prepared the way for *Nostra Aetate*, Vatican II's Declaration on the Relation of the Church to Non-Christian Religions (28 October 1965) and also for *Ad Gentes*, the Decree on the Church's Missionary Activity (7 December 1965).

The Title and the Kingdom of God

(1) Before we come to the key articles in Chapter 2 of *Lumen Gentium* ('Light of the Nations') about 'the religious others' (nos. 16–17), we should pause to retrieve two items from Chapter 1. First, in richly biblical and patristic language, that chapter emphasized the sacramental reality of the Church, from which 'shines' the 'light' of Christ and which is 'the sign and instrument of intimate communion with God and of unity among the whole human race' (no. 1).[16] The opening words were obviously intended to evoke the strikingly universalist

---

13. Giuseppe Ruggieri, 'Beyond an Ecclesiology of Polemics: The Debate on the Church', in *The History of Vatican II*, ii, 281–357, at 282–4.
14. Jan Grootaers, 'The Drama Continues between the Acts: The "Second Preparation" and its Opponents', *History of Vatican II*, 359–514, at 391–412.
15. William Henn, 'Yves Congar and *Lumen gentium*', *Gregorianum* 86 (2005), 563–92.
16. Aloys Grillmeier points out how Pope John XXIII had already used the expression, *Lumen gentium* (light of the nations), to indicate a programme of reform; see Grillmeier, 'The Mystery of the Church', in *Commentary on the Documents of Vatican II*, i, 138–52, at 139.

texts of Second and Third Isaiah (40–55 and 56–66, respectively) about foreign peoples to whom divine salvation is extended and who join themselves to Israel. It is in these terms that a poem pictures the glorious restoration of Jerusalem: 'Arise, shine, for your light has come, and the glory of the Lord has risen upon you... Nations shall come to your light, and kings to the brightness of your dawn' (Isa. 60: 1, 3).

God has called his 'Servant' (primarily, either the whole covenant people, Israel, or a faithful remnant of Israel, or an individual, or some blend of these possibilities) to bring 'light to the nations' who fumble in the darkness of ignorance (Isa. 40: 6–7). The Israelites who have survived the Babylonian captivity, in general, or an individual, in particular, will have the mission of being 'a light to the nations' (Isa. 49: 6). In the New Testament, Luke picks up this language—for instance, in the prayer of old Simeon: 'My eyes have seen your salvation, which you have prepared for all nations, the light to enlighten the Gentiles and give glory to Israel your people' (Luke 2: 30–2). With its opening words, 'the Light of the Nations', the Dogmatic Constitution on the Church signals its universal outlook. The short, opening paragraph presses on to underline this mindset by introducing five equivalent expressions for 'the nations': 'all human beings', 'every creature', 'the whole human race', 'the whole world', and 'all human beings'. Chapter 7 will disclose the same universal mindset; it looks forward to the whole human race, along with the universe itself, being finally renewed in and through the risen Christ (*LG* 48).

(2) Second, when interpreting the way of salvation for 'the others', making a distinction (but not a separation) between the Church and the Kingdom of God is vital.[17] In official Roman Catholic teaching, Pope John Paul II drew this distinction clearly in his 1990 encyclical *Redemptoris Missio* (the Mission of the Redeemer). The Church is intimately and uniquely related to the kingdom and 'ordered towards' the kingdom, without being identical with it: 'the church is not an end unto herself, since she is ordered towards the kingdom of God of which she is the seed, sign and instrument'. The Pope summed up the

---

17. See Jacques Dupuis, *Christianity and the Religions: From Confrontation to Dialogue*, trans. Phillip Berryman (Maryknoll, NY: Orbis Books, 2002), 20–31, 195–217; Dupuis, *Toward a Christian Theology of Religious Pluralism* (Maryknoll, NY: Orbis Books, 1997), 330–57.

relationship by saying that 'the Church serves the kingdom'. While Christ 'endowed' the Church 'with the fullness of the benefits and means of salvation', 'Christ and his Spirit' also act 'outside the Church's visible boundaries' (*Redemptoris Missio*, 18, 20; ND 899c and 899d). In particular, John Paul II acknowledged how 'the Spirit's presence and activity affect not only individuals but also society and history, peoples, cultures and religions', sowing among them 'the seeds of the Word' and 'preparing them for full maturity in Christ' (*Redemptoris Missio*, 28; ND 1172).

Speaking of the Church as 'the people of God', *Lumen Gentium* recognized its 'purpose' to be that of embodying 'the Kingdom of God which God himself has begun on earth' and 'will complete at the end of time' (no. 9). The constitution had already described the coming of the kingdom in the ministry and person of Christ. With his death, resurrection, and outpouring of the Holy Spirit, the Church received 'the mission of proclaiming and establishing among all nations the Kingdom of Christ and of God, and she constitutes, on earth, the seed and beginning of this kingdom' (no. 5). In these two articles (nos. 5 and 9), Vatican II came close to distinguishing (but not separating) the Church from the kingdom of God, and to recognizing how the kingdom forms the more encompassing reality and how the Church serves the kingdom and not vice versa.

But, rather than pondering the issue of church/kingdom, this chapter of *Lumen Gentium* brought to the table the question: what is the identity of the Roman Catholic Church as 'the holy Church' founded by Christ (*LG* 5)? Famously the Council replied by saying that the holy Church 'subsists in (= continues to exist [fully] in)' the Roman Catholic Church (*LG* 8) and is not simply identical with the Roman Catholic Church, as Tromp and others claimed.[18] To be sure, the meaning of 'subsists in' remains controversial, with the Congregation for the Doctrine of the Faith offering over the years varying translations, as Frank Sullivan has pointed out.[19] But the conclusion that the

---

18. Alexandra von Teuffenbach, using the council diaries of Tromp, has argued for a narrow version of 'subsistit in' (simply 'is') in *Die Bedeutung des subsistit in (LG 8). Zum Selbstverständnis der katholischen Kirche* (Munich: Herbert Utz, 2002).

19. For a magisterial guide to the meaning of 'subsists' in this context and some of the controversy surrounding its meaning, see F. A. Sullivan, 'The Meaning of *Subsistit in* as explained by the Congregation for the Doctrine of the Faith', *Theological Studies* 67 (2006), 116–24; Sullivan, 'A Response to Karl Becker, SJ, on the Meaning of *Subsistit*

Church Founded by Christ is not *tout court* identical with the Roman Catholic Church does not simply depend on the translation of 'subsistit in'; it emerges clearly from several passages in Vatican II documents.

Recognizing how 'many elements of sanctification and grace' are found outside the 'visible' Roman Catholic Church (no. 8), *Lumen Gentium* would go on to specify some of these elements: 'believing the Sacred Scripture' to be 'the norm of faith and life'; belief in the Trinity; and the reception of baptism and 'other sacraments in their own Churches and ecclesial communities' (no. 15). Here the Council acknowledged as 'Churches' various bodies of Christians not (or not yet) in union with the Roman Catholic Church. Even more emphatically in its Decree on Ecumenism (*Unitatis Redintegratio* of 21 November 1964), Vatican II recognized how the principle 'the Eucharist makes the Church' operates also for the Eastern Churches not in communion with the Bishop of Rome: 'through the celebration of the Eucharist of the Lord in each of these Churches, the Church of God is built up and grows' (no. 15). In other words, while the Church of God continues to exist fully in the Roman Catholic Church, it also continues to exist in other churches or ecclesial communities, above all in the Eastern Churches, which enjoy almost all the elements of Christian sanctification and truth.

Here Vatican II officially recognized that, beyond the visible Roman Catholic Church, the Church of God also lives and grows among those whom the Council of Florence and the Council of Trent had labelled 'heretics' and 'schismatics'. Such teaching formed a background to Vatican II also recognizing that the kingdom of God extends beyond the Church, even if the Council did not anticipate the explicit language of Pope John Paul II on this issue. Among 'the religious others', who are not (or not yet) baptized Christians, Christ and his Holy Spirit are active and the kingdom grows towards its final consummation. Just as Roman Catholics should acknowledge that 'many elements of sanctification and grace' exist and are at work among their 'separated' Christian brothers and sisters, so too they should acknowledge the elements of truth and grace operating among the followers of other religions, who belong to the wider reality of God's kingdom.

in', *Theological Studies* 67 (2006), 395–409; Sullivan, 'Further Thoughts on the Meaning of *Subsistit in*', *Theological Studies* 71 (2010), 133–47.

Article 16

The key responses of *Lumen Gentium* to questions about understanding 'the religious others' in the light of Christian faith come in two articles (nos. 16 and 17).[20] An earlier article (no. 13) frames the scope of what will be said there. Holding in faith that, through Christ's redeeming work, 'all human beings are called to the new People of God', the Council now reflects on how, 'in different ways', they 'belong (pertinent)' or 'are ordered (ordinantur)' to 'catholic unity'. This is true, no matter whether 'they are Catholic faithful, or others who believe in Christ, or lastly all human beings without exception (omnes universaliter homines), called by God's grace to salvation' (*LG* 16). We saw in Chapter 2 how Thomas Aquinas prompted this language of all members of the human race being 'ordered' variously to 'catholic unity' under the universal headship of Christ.

In considering how the final group, 'those who have not yet received the Gospel', are 'ordered to the People of God for different reasons', our document distinguishes (a) Jews, (b) Muslims, (c) other believers in God, and (d) those who, through no fault of their own, have not yet come to an explicit knowledge of God (*LG* 16). The agenda of this book includes (b) and (c), but we will also examine what our document says about those who belong under (d).

For the first time since the Arab prophet Muhammad (d.632) founded Islam, an ecumenical council of the Catholic Church offered some explicit teaching on Muslims,[21] and it was teaching that highlighted common ground: the divine 'plan of salvation also embraces those who acknowledge the Creator, in the first place amongst whom are the Muslims. They profess to hold the faith of Abraham, and

---

20. On these two articles, see Hünermann, '*Lumen Gentium*', 397–405.
21. In no. 107 of his first encyclical, *Ecclesiam Suam* (dated 6 August 1964), Pope Paul VI had anticipated by a few months the positive teaching on Islam found in *Lumen Gentium*. He wrote of Muslims, 'whom we do well to admire on account of those things that are true and commendable (vera et probanda) in their worship' (*AAS* 56 (1964), 609–59, at 654). This encyclical encouraged the theme of dialogue taken up by *NA* and, especially, *GS*; for the encyclical's general impact on Vatican II, see Vilanova, 'The Intersession', 448–57. Meeting soon after the failure of the fifth and final (major) crusade, the Second Council of Lyons (1274) described 'the Saracens' as 'blasphemous', 'faithless', and 'the impious enemies of the Christian name'. See Norman P. Tanner (ed.), *Decrees of Ecumenical Councils*, vol. 1 (London: Sheed and Ward, 1990), 309.

together with us they adore the one, merciful God, who will judge human beings on the last day' (*LG* 16). While describing Muslims as those 'who profess to hold the faith of Abraham' rather than simply state that Muslims hold the faith of Abraham, the Council agreed that they 'acknowledge the Creator', 'adore with us the one, merciful God', and also share with Christians an expectation of a general judgement 'on the last day'. A year later in the Declaration on the Relation of the Church to Non-Christian Religions, Vatican II would fill out its positive picture of Islam.

Lumen Gentium raised and left open the question: if Muslims 'acknowledge the Creator' and, together with Christians, 'adore the one, merciful God', who will come in judgement at the last day, how can they do this without God having been revealed to them and their responding in faith? How can this happen, moreover, unless in some sense God has made Islam a way of salvation for them? It is hard to escape the conclusion that the constitution recognizes some revealing and saving efficacy in Islam. In some way the Muslim religion enjoys a specific role in mediating the knowledge of God and grace of God. Similar questions will emerge again when we come to *Nostra Aetate*.

After the Muslims, the same article in *Lumen* Gentium then turns to (c), other believers in God: 'nor is this God distant from others who in shadows and images seek the unknown God, since to all he gives life and breath and all things (cf. Acts 17: 23–8) and [since] the Saviour wills all human beings to be saved (cf. 1 Tim. 2: 4)'. Because God is both the Creator who gives life to all human beings and the Saviour who wishes all to be saved, the Council holds that the divine presence also embraces all God-seekers, even if it is 'in shadows and images' that they seek 'the unknown God'. Hence 'those who, through no fault [of their own], do not know Christ's Gospel and his Church and who, nevertheless, seek God with a sincere heart and, under the influence of grace, try in their actions to fulfill his will made known through the dictate of their conscience—these too may obtain eternal salvation'.[22]

We come here to a biblical passage that we already examined in detail in Chapter 1. Paul's speech in Athens, as presented by Acts 17, enjoyed a privileged role in shaping the thinking of Vatican II about 'the religious others'. As we have seen in Chapters 1 and 2, Christian

---

22. Rahner understood this passage to parallel somewhat his notion of 'anonymous Christians' (Chapter 2 above, n. 52).

teachers from Augustine, through Gregory VII and Aquinas, and down to modern times also reckoned with the classic passage in 1 Timothy 2: 4 and God's desire to save all people. When the paragraph in *Lumen Gentium* considers (c) other believers in God, it rightly prioritizes the divine initiative. It is God who comes close to all (as Creator) by giving them life and (as Saviour) by willing them to be saved. It is only through 'the influence of grace' that these 'others' can try to follow their conscience and do God's will. But when they 'seek the unknown God' and 'seek God with a sincere heart', can they do this only because God draws them? When they seek God, is this only because God has first 'found' them? While not clearly stated, an affirmative answer seems presupposed when no. 16 speaks earlier of 'all human beings without exception' being 'called by God's grace to salvation'.

Apropos of these other believers in God (c), the Council does not pick up traditional earlier terminology about their condition implying implicit faith in Christ and a baptism of desire which conveys (once again implicitly) membership in the Church (Chapter 2 above). Furthermore, while speaking of their 'salvation', the Council remains silent here about the other, inseparable dimension of the divine self-communication: revelation. In the light of the Scriptures and, in particular, of John's Gospel, one should maintain: no salvation without revelation.[23] This particular passage of *Lumen Gentium* has nothing to say, at least explicitly, about divine revelation and its correlative in human faith. Nevertheless, we should ask: while the voice of conscience dictates what the 'God-seekers' should do, how has the will of God been 'made known' to them at the heart of their conscience? Does the 'making known' imply some measure of revelation? Although they can be described as seeking 'the unknown God' and doing so 'in shadows and images', this language suggests that something has been disclosed to them. Shadows are not equivalent

---

23. Vatican II's Dogmatic Constitution on Divine Revelation (*Dei Verbum*) witnesses repeatedly to the way God's activity in being revealed to human beings remains inextricably intertwined with the divine activity in saving or redeeming them. As this document puts it, the history (or 'economy') of revelation is the history of salvation, and vice versa. Over and over again *Dei Verbum* moves between revelation and salvation as inseparable and almost equivalent realities (nos. 3, 4, 6, 7, 14, 15, 17, 21).

to total darkness, and images imply some resemblance to truth and reality.[24]

Finally, our passage refrains from specifying any particular religious situation of the 'God-seekers'. In Chapter 2 we recalled how, a year before Vatican II opened, Karl Rahner insisted that the social nature and radical solidarity of all human beings mean that, in practice, a saving relationship with God is possible only within and through the religion that is 'at their disposal'. A year after *Lumen Gentium* was published, in *Nostra Aetate* the Council, albeit cautiously, would begin to be more specific about this.

Article 16 in the constitution then moves at once to (d), 'those who, without any fault [of their own], have not yet reached an explicit/ express acknowledgment (expressam agnitionem) of God, and who, not without grace, strive to lead an upright life'. The 'divine providence' will not deny them 'the helps (auxilia) necessary for salvation'. As with the 'God-seekers', the grace of God makes it possible for such non-believers to follow their conscience and lead an upright life. Here the Council retrieves for the only time the terminology of 'implicit/explicit' as applied to faith (in God and Christ) and desire for baptism, which developed from Thomas Aquinas through to Pius XII (Chapter 2 above). Commenting after the Council closed, Karl Rahner believed his notion of 'anonymous Christians' to be vindicated by this picture of those who strive to lead an upright life but who, without any fault of their own, have not yet reached an explicit knowledge of God (Chapter 2). *Gaudium et Spes* will have more to say about agnostics and atheists, whether upright or otherwise (nos. 19–21).

After speaking of the morally upright atheists (d), the same article 16 adds three points: 'whatever good or truth is found among them (apud illos) is considered by the Church to be a preparation for the Gospel, and given by him [Christ] who enlightens all human beings so that they may at length have life'. An eminent expert at the Council, Aloys Grillmeier, understood that the Council spoke here of the 'atheists'.[25] But I wonder whether the 'apud illos' was intended to apply these

---

24. A year later, in *Ad Gentes*, the Council would add to this passage in *Lumen Gentium* by teaching something on revelation to all 'the others'.
25. Aloys Grillmeier, 'The People of God', trans. Kevin Smyth, in Herbert Vorgrimler (ed.), *Commentary on the Documents of Vatican II*, i (London: Burns & Oates, 1967), 153–85, at 184.

three remarks *also* to the 'God-seekers', considered under (c). In any case, of the three significant themes that emerge here, *Nostra Aetate* 2 would refer the first ('good and truth') and the third (enlightenment by the Word) to Hindus, Buddhists, and followers of other religions and not limit them to upright atheists. *Ad Gentes* 3 would likewise refer the second ('preparation for the Gospel') to 'God-seekers' in general. Even if the three themes may have been originally applied to upright atheists alone, a year later the Council deployed them more broadly.

First of all, *Lumen Gentium* followed the example of Pope Paul VI who wrote in *Ecclesiam Suam* of what was 'true and good' in the Muslim worship of God. Here the 'paired' blessings acknowledged by the Pope were clearly inspired by John's language about the Word being full of 'grace and truth' (Chapter 1 above). *Lumen Gentium* 8 picked up this 'double-sided' terminology when attending to Christ who, through the visible community of the Church, 'communicates truth and grace to all [human beings]'. Then at the end of article 17, our text uses Trinitarian language to envisage this universal mission: 'the Church prays and labours so that into the People of God, the Body of the Lord, and the Temple of the Holy Spirit may pass the fullness of the entire world'. We return later to the theme of the Church 'praying' for the entire world and mediating 'truth and grace to all'.

When reflecting on the religious condition of 'others' in terms of 'whatever good and truth is found' among them (*LG* 16), the Council suggested two distinguishable but inseparable dimensions of the divine self-communication that has blessed them: salvation ('good') and revelation ('truth'). Johannine language of revelation and salvation (in that order) followed at once when our passage introduced 'enlightening' and 'life'. The following year the final documents of the Council were to include similar 'double' terminology, and do so in a way that implied the order of revelation first and salvation second. In non-Christian religions one finds elements 'of what is true and holy' (*NA* 2). Six weeks later the Council followed the same order, while showing itself to be more critical of other religions. Missionary activity 'purges of evil associations every element of truth and grace which is found among peoples' (*AG* 9).

The second theme concerns the 'preparation for the Gospel'. As we recalled at the end of Chapter 1, Eusebius of Caesarea provided this terminology. In a footnote, *Lumen Gentium* refers to his work which bears that name (*LG* 16, n. 20). *Ad Gentes* was to introduce the same expression, but the accompanying footnote cited appropriate passages from Irenaeus and Clement of Alexandria, without mentioning Eusebius as such. What should we make of this 'preparation for the Gospel' to be recognized as present in upright atheists and others?

Here it would be inaccurate to represent the Council as alleging that the elements 'of what is true and holy' or of what is 'good and true', which constitute the 'preparation for the Gospel' among 'religious others', are only elements of goodness, holiness, and truth that human beings achieve for themselves in their search for God and in their practice of an upright life. Such 'merely natural' achievements, while in some sense preparing non-Christians for the gift(s) of grace, would not count towards their supernatural destiny. The 'preparation for the Gospel' would leave them on the side of nature and religion. They would be God-seekers who reach some true beliefs but who are not given the supernatural gift of faith.

This interpretation, however, lapses back into a natural/supernatural scheme of things, a presupposition that obscures what the Council says about those who have not yet received the gospel. It ignores the phrases that characterize *Lumen Gentium* 16: 'under the influence of grace', 'not without grace', 'the helps necessary for salvation'. The Council talks about God's free and loving self-gift that, already in the life of grace, raises human beings above what is due to their human nature and disposes them for the life of glory. There is a straight line back to Blessed Pius IX and his encyclical of 1863. He underscored 'the power of divine light and grace', which leads to eternal life upright non-Christians, who, through no fault of their own, have not embraced Christian faith. There is also a line that takes us forward to the language which *Ad Gentes* 9 borrows from John's Gospel: the elements of '*grace* and truth' to be 'found among peoples' (italics mine). One should take *Lumen Gentium* at its word: it is Christ who lovingly and supernaturally gives 'whatever good or truth' is found among those who have not or have not yet embraced the gospel. To echo the final words of Georges Bernanos's *The Diary of a Country Priest*, 'all is grace'.

Another faulty interpretation of 'preparation for the Gospel' would propose that the gifts of grace and truth may be supernatural but enjoy value only insofar as this preparation succeeds in bringing people to accept the gospel and baptism. But Vatican II never adds this qualification. As regards *Lumen Gentium* and *Ad Gentes*, a deeply spiritual and supernatural 'preparation for the Gospel' could be found in the lives of very many people, who, through no fault of their own, never seek baptism and join the Church. At least as the Council uses the terminology of Eusebius of Caesarea, a preparation for the gospel could involve many serious elements of grace and truth, without the recipients necessarily moving on to embrace the gospel. A 'preparation' may be genuinely present but never completed and brought to a full conclusion.

Then there is a third theme that invites comment: the words about Christ 'who enlightens all human beings so that they may at length have life'. This Johannine language of revelation and salvation (in that order) presents Christ as the light and the life of all human beings without exception. This language will be taken up by *Nostra Aetate* when it echoes John 1: 9 and refers to 'the Truth that illuminates all human beings' (no. 2), and then cites John 14: 6 to name Christ as 'the way, the truth, and *the life*' (italics mine). Here and elsewhere, *Lumen Gentium* expresses a faith in the universal presence and power of the risen Christ as the Light *and the Life* of the whole world.

Article 17

What the bishops at Vatican II endorsed in *Lumen Gentium* 17 about proclaiming the gospel and receiving into the community of the Church those who embrace faith opens a window on how they viewed the previous religious condition of 'the others'. Those who accept the gospel undergo a revelatory and redemptive process in receiving light and life.

Article 16 has already proposed, or at least implied, three schemes for interpreting the change in those who accept faith. (1) Where they do not yet expressly acknowledge God, they can move from an implicit to an explicit knowledge of God. (2) They can move from 'shadows and images' to light, and (3) from being prepared for the gospel to sharing its fullness. In all three pictures there is no question of starting from zero. Implicit knowledge, while not yet full and conscious acceptance, is still some form of knowledge; shadows and images rise above merely formless darkness; a preparation already sets people en route towards a goal.

According to article 17, when baptizing people and incorporating them in Christ, the Church 'snatches them from the slavery of error'. But at once our document mitigates this bleak and unqualified picture of the religious situation of those who have not (or have not yet) accepted the gospel.[26] It suggests that their pre-Christian condition has left them somehow wounded, at a lower level, and imperfect. Through the Church's missionary work, 'whatever good is found sown in the heart and mind of human beings or in the particular rites and cultures of peoples, so far from being lost, is *healed, elevated, and consummated* (sanetur, elevetur et consummetur) for the glory of God' (italics mine).[27]

This language evokes the traditional adage that 'grace does not take nature away but perfects [it] (gratia non tollit naturam sed perficit)'. It also echoes classical language about 'healing' and 'elevating' grace ('gratia sanans et elevans'). It encompasses both individuals ('the heart and mind of human beings') and societies ('the particular rites and cultures of peoples'). It mentions 'rites and cultures', but cautiously refrains from referring to religions.[28] The terminology of 'sown (*seminatum*) in the heart and mind of human beings' deftly recalls what St Justin Martyr, Clement of Alexandria, and other early Christian authors wrote about 'the seeds of the Word' being sown everywhere and not least in the knowledge of God displayed by classical Greek philosophers and others (Chapter 1 above). While the passage highlights the salvific impact of accepting Christianity, the reference to the

26. Miika Ruokanen missed this passage when he stated that 'the old terminology for pagan religions *and their errors* seems to be totally omitted from the documents of the Council': *The Catholic Doctrine of Non-Christian Religions According to the Second Vatican Council* (Leiden: E. J. Brill, 1992), 55; emphasis mine. He also missed what *AG* 9 said about 'purging of *evil associations* those elements of truth and grace found among peoples' (italics mine).

27. See *LG* 13: '[The Church] fosters and adopts, in so far as they are good, the abilities, resources, and customs of peoples. In adopting [them], she purifies, strengthens and elevates [them].' This passage highlights the activity of the Church, while that of *LG* 17, by using a 'divine passive', suggests more the primary initiative and causality of God. The 'good sown in the heart and mind of human beings or in the particular rites and cultures of peoples' is 'healed, elevated, and consummated' by God.

28. Twenty-six years later in *Redemptoris Missio* 28, John Paul II acknowledged how 'the Spirit's presence and activity affect not only individuals but also society and history, peoples, cultures, *and religions*', sowing among them 'the seeds of the Word and preparing them for full maturity in Christ' (italics mine).

good 'sown' in 'the mind of human beings' implies the divine self-revelation communicated and known even before people accept the gospel. In other words, those 'religious others' who become Christians bring with them some elements of salvation *and* revelation. All is not lost or discarded. The process of healing, elevating, and consummating (or finishing) obviously involves some measure of continuity, albeit a transformed continuity.

Taking articles 16 and 17 together, we can see that they deploy a variety of terms to indicate how God's self-communication includes a *revelatory* dimension ('the gospel', 'truth', 'enlightening', 'the good sown in the mind of human beings', and a 'knowing' of God that can lead to 'faith') and a *salvific* dimension ('salvation', 'the influence of grace', and 'the good sown in the hearts of human beings'). To remark on this double-sided terminology may seem to border on the banal. However, this persistent usage in *Lumen Gentium* and subsequent Vatican II documents carries two lessons. First, we may not raise the question of salvation without raising that of revelation, and vice versa. When interpreting the situation before God of individuals and groups, we need to recall the two inseparable dimensions of the divine self-communication. Second, the Council's terminology witnesses to the way the mediation of Christ entails his being universal Revealer as well as universal Saviour, both light and life for all people. Our document calls Christ 'the source of salvation for the whole world' (*LG* 17), but it has already named him as the one 'who enlightens all human beings so that they may at length have life' (*LG* 16).

This presence of Christ need not be 'felt' or explicitly known. Neither *Lumen Gentium* nor any of the later Vatican II documents ever allege that people must be aware of Christ's revealing and saving activity if it is to have its appropriate effect. Christ and his Spirit exercise their impact 'in an infinite series of unique acts of love, each new and different from all the others'.[29] But Christ and the Spirit, in operating for the good not only of Christian but also of 'religious others', do not necessarily and always make their presence consciously felt. In any case, as we know, 'we experience many things without knowing *what* we experience or *how* we experience them'.[30] To this

29. Ingolf U. Dalferth, *Becoming Present: An Inquiry into the Christian Sense of the Presence of God* (Leuven: Peeters, 2006), 147.
30. Ibid., 115; italics mine.

we might add that we may never, for instance, be in a position to know the identity of some agents who prove particularly helpful to us. The 'what', the 'how', and the 'who' of our religious, as well as our other, experiences can at times remain shrouded in mystery.

Finally, article 17 cites the mandate to baptize in the name of the Father, and of the Son, and of the Holy Spirit (Matt. 28: 19), but otherwise has only one thing to say about the Spirit: the Church 'is driven by the Holy Spirit to cooperate, so that the plan of God, who has constituted Christ as the principle of salvation for the whole world, should be fully realized'. *Ad Gentes, Gaudium et Spes*, and John Paul II, as we will see, recognize how the Spirit operates universally and not simply within the Church.

Some Provisional Conclusions

Before moving to *Nostra Aetate*, let me summarize what I have gleaned from *Sacrosanctum Concilium* and *Lumen Gentium* about the situation of 'the religious others'. I can set out schematically the teaching that is relevant to our topic.

∞ Christ is the Saviour of all people (*SC* 83; *LG* 1, 16, 17).

∞ Christ is the Revealer for all people (*LG* 1, 16).

∞ Christ is the head of the entire human race (*SC* 83, *LG* 16 and closing sentence of 17).

∞ Christ's divine presence and grace embrace everyone and move everyone towards unity (*SC* 83; *LG* 16).

∞ Vatican II attends to every human being (*SC* 1–2, 5, 83; *LG* 1, 8, 16, 17).

∞ The kingdom of God extends beyond the Church (*LG* 5, 9).

∞ All people are 'ordered', albeit differently, to the Church (LG 11, 13, 16).

∞ The Church prays for the entire world (*SC* 53; *LG* 17).

∞ The Church recognizes elements of 'grace and truth' (what is 'good and true') in the 'religious others' (*LG* 16).

∞ These elements can be 'healed, elevated, and consummated' when these 'others' come to faith and baptism.

∽ The Holy Spirit prompts the mission of the Church in the world (*LG* 17).

∽ Vatican II is the first council to speak expressly of Muslims and value positively their faith, worship, and hope in God our Creator (*LG* 16).

∽ Islam is in some sense a way of revelation and salvation for Muslims (*LG* 16).

FOUR

Nostra Aetate on Other Religions

From the unreal lead me to the real; from darkness lead me to light;
from death lead me to immortality.

Upanishads

Without beauty the good becomes a burden and the truth a useless
and empty struggle. It is in beauty that truth and goodness find their
supreme revelation.

Divo Barsotti, *'The Spirituality of Beauty'*

The Second Vatican Council's Declaration on the Relation of the
Church to Non-Christian Religions, *Nostra Aetate* ('In our age'),
promulgated during the fourth and final session of the Council on 28
October 1965, was quickly recognized not only for its significant
contribution to Catholic–Jewish dialogue but also for its fresh
approach to relations between Roman Catholics and followers of
other religions.[1] Building on some items in *Sacrosanctum Concilium*
and, even more directly on the teaching of *Lumen Gentium* (in particular, art. 16), this declaration has proved a genuine milestone in interreligious dialogue. While *Lumen Gentium* 16 had already broken new
ground in the history of the twenty-one ecumenical councils of
Catholic Christianity by its positive remarks about Judaism and
Islam, *Nostra Aetate* went further by reflecting on other religions and,
in particular, Hinduism and Buddhism, and by considering the human

---

1. If Vatican II had met thirty years later, it would have changed the title of the
   declaration to speak of 'Other Religions', 'Other Living Faiths', or, even better,
   'People of Other Living Faiths'.

condition and 'the riddles of the human condition' to which different religions provide an answer. On these and further questions, the first three articles of the declaration contribute much material for this book. For the first time in the history of Roman Catholicism an ecumenical council honoured as the work of the living God the truth and holiness to be found in certain other religions.

Somewhat like *Lumen Gentium* but for different reasons (mainly debates over what should be said about the relationship between Christians and Jews), the final text of *Nostra Aetate* had a troubled history as it moved towards the document finally approved in late 1965. Its first version (actually its second draft) came before the Council in November 1963 as Chapter 4 ('On the Relationship of Catholics to Non-Christians and especially to Jews') in a 'schema' for the Decree on Ecumenism. A new draft of this chapter was then moved to being an appendix in the same decree and became 'A Further Declaration on Jews and Non-Christians'. It was then proposed as an appendix to *Lumen Gentium*, with the title 'On the Relation of the Church to Non-Christian Religions'. Finally, it kept the same title but became a self-standing document. A debate in November 1964 opened the way for a final, emended form voted on and approved during the Council's last session.[2]

2. See Giovanni Miccoli, 'Two Sensitive Issues: Religious Freedom and the Jews', in Giuseppe Alberigo and Joseph A. Komonchak (eds), *History of Vatican II*, iv (Maryknoll, NY: Orbis, 2003), 135–93; Riccardo Burigana and Giovanni Turbanti, 'The Intersession: Preparing the Conclusion of the Council', in *History of Vatican II*, 546–59; Mauro Velati, 'Completing the Conciliar Agenda', in *History of Vatican II*, v (2006), 185–273, at 211–31; John M. Oesterreicher, 'Declaration of the Relationship of the Church to Non-Christian Religions', in Herbert Vorgrimler (ed.), *Commentary on the Documents of Vatican II*, iii, trans. William Glen-Doepel et al. (London: Burns & Oates, 1969), 1–136. Since Oesterreicher was concerned with the section of the declaration that addressed Judaism (*NA* 4–5), an excursus on Hinduism, another on Buddhism, and another on Islam were added; we come to those additions below. See also Michael Fitzgerald, '*Nostra Aetate*, A Key to Interreligious Dialogue', *Gregorianum* 87 (2006), 700–13; Daniel A. Madigan, '*Nostra Aetate* and the Questions It Chose to Leave Open', *Gregorianum* 87 (2006), 781–96; G. O'Collins, 'Implementing *Nostra Aetate*', *Gregorianum* 87 (2006), 714–26; Jacques Scheuer, 'The Dialogue with the Traditions of India and the Far East', *Gregorianum* 87 (2006), 797–809; Roman A. Siebenrock, 'Theologischer Kommentar zur Erklärung über die Haltung der Kirche zu den nichtchristlichen Religionen *Nostra Aetate*', in Peter Hünermann and Bernd Jochen Hilberath (eds), *Herders Theologischer Kommentar zum Zweiten Vatikanischen Konzil*, iii (Freiburg: Herder, 2005), 591–693; and Gregor Ahn, 'Religion', *TRE*, xxviii, 513–59.

The Unity of Human Beings

The declaration opened by observing how 'in our age' the 'human race is day by day becoming more closely united' and 'the obligations between different peoples are increasing'. But in 1965, when they pondered the crimes, tragedies, and traumas of the twentieth century and were painfully aware that the Cold War threatened human beings with nuclear death, many observers would have cast doubt on such a positive judgement. Was the human race in fact drawing closer together and were different peoples becoming more open and friendly towards each other? Did the United Nations, other world organizations, the explosion in international trade, the Olympic Games and burgeoning world sport, global tourism, and other developments signal such a growth towards a world in which people of different nations and cultures could face one another and say 'my neighbour'? Such a global village characterized by true friendship seemed more distant than ever. Nevertheless, years before the fall of the Berlin Wall (1989), the vast expansion in jet travel, the emergence of the Internet, stronger international cooperation in dealing with such matters as financial crises and the spread of infectious diseases, and other events and developments that marked milestones in the progressive bonding of the human race, Vatican II looked at the whole world and calmly concluded that we human beings were in fact drawing closer together in mutual obligations and even friendship. Half a century later and despite murderous tragedies of massive proportions that have occurred across the globe, the Council's judgement can still be endorsed.

The opening words of *Nostra Aetate* loom large as the first time that any of the twenty-one general councils recognized by Roman Catholics had ever made such a pronouncement on the state of global humanity. Popes had done so, notably Pope John XXIII in *Pacem in Terris* (1963), but never before had that kind of pronouncement come from any ecumenical council. Less than two months later the Pastoral Constitution on the Church in the Modern World (e.g. GS 4–11) would massively develop the vision of the whole human race with which the Declaration on the Relation of the Church to Non-Christian Religions began.

In both cases such judgements went far beyond merely theoretical pronouncements and flagged serious commitments. *Nostra Aetate* spoke at once of the Church's 'duty to foster unity and charity' between individuals and nations as belonging to its mission to serve the entire human race. This prompted the Council into showing (a) what human beings have in common and (b) what 'leads to mutual fellowship'. The declaration dedicated at once a paragraph to producing a summary answer to (a). Seemingly in all that followed about the 'various religions' of the world (*NA* 2–5), the Council engaged itself with (b): that is to say, religion as a major cause of fellowship among human beings. *Gaudium et Spes* would soon invest time in unpacking another, related major cause, the different cultures of global humanity (*GS* 53–62). *Nostra Aetate* touched only very briefly on the theme of cultures. It urged Catholics to 'recognize, protect, and promote those spiritual and moral goods, as well as those *socio-cultural values*, found among them [the followers of other religions]' (*NA* 2; italics mine).

Nostra Aetate named three basic reasons for acknowledging what all nations have in common, to the point of making them 'one community': their origin in God, the divine providence that extends to all people, and their common, heavenly destiny. First, the Council referred in a footnote to Acts 17: 26 in support of the statement that 'all nations have one origin, since God made the entire race of human beings to inhabit the whole face of the earth' (*NA* 1).[3] This way of citing Acts 17: 26 (but without literally quoting the verse) simply avoided the problem of deciding between the two possible Greek readings: '*ex henos* (from one human being, from one ancestor)' or '*ex henos haimatos* (from one blood, from one stock, from one blood-stock)'.

For the second statement (God's 'providence, witness of goodness, and plans of salvation extend to all human beings'), our document refers in a footnote to Wisdom 8: 1, Acts 14: 17, Romans 2: 6–7,[4] and, of course, 1 Timothy 2: 4, the classic verse about the universal scope of God's wish to save all people and help them 'come to the knowledge

---

3. In the NRSV translation Acts 17: 26a reads: 'from one ancestor he [God] made all nations to inhabit the whole earth'.
4. These two verses read: 'For he [God] will repay according to each one's works: to those who by patiently doing good seek for glory and honour and immortality, he will give eternal life'. Paul here speaks of future judgement that will be made on the basis of one's good (or bad) works (see 2 Cor. 11: 15).

of the truth'. The first text, which personifies the divine activity through the figure of Lady Wisdom, expresses satisfactorily the universal scope of divine providence: 'She [Lady Wisdom] reaches mightily from one end of the earth to the other, and she orders all things well.' The second text draws on what Barnabas and Paul said in Lystra to correct those who worshipped Zeus and Hermes and imagined the two apostles to be gods who had come down in human form: 'he [God] has not left himself without a witness in doing good—giving you rains from heaven and fruitful seasons, and filling you with food and your hearts with joy'. The true God shows a providential benevolence towards all human beings and supplies what is necessary and good for their life. The testimony of nature displays the divine concern for all people everywhere. The texts from Wisdom, Acts, and 1 Timothy support the claim that the divine providence, the witness of God's goodness, and plans for salvation, respectively, extend to all people. In this context the two verses from Romans introduce a somewhat different theme, one that touched not only on the present (good and evil human behaviour) but also on what is to come: the impartiality of God that will be revealed in his future, righteous judgement. All, whether Jews or Gentiles, will be judged according to the same standard, the good or evil works they have done (Rom. 2: 5–11).

Third, to support the third statement ('they have one [and the same] final end'), *Nostra Aetate* refers to (but without quoting) two verses in the Book of Revelation (21: 23–4): 'the elect are to be united in the Holy City which the brightness of God will illuminate [and] where the nations will walk in his light' (*NA* 1).

On the basis of the unity between all human beings finding its deepest foundation in what God has done, is doing, and will do, the declaration turns next to the common self-questioning that also—but this time, on the human side—bonds everyone. Its eloquent exposé of the deep questions that haunt human beings has no precedent in the teaching of earlier ecumenical councils. The theme of ever-recurring human questions will be taken up in *Gaudium et Spes* (*GS* 4, 10, 18, 21) and then correlated, as we shall see in Chapter 6, with the answer(s) that come from the crucified and risen Christ (*GS* 22).

It is worth observing here that *Nostra Aetate* could have followed another option by attending to the human drive to know truth and, in particular, religious truth. After all, Vatican II's Declaration on

Religious Liberty (*Dignitatis Humanae*), promulgated less than two months later, took as part of its starting point the innate human drive and obligation 'to seek the truth, above all that truth which concerns religion' (*DH* 2). The dynamic openness to truth has a respected place in the history of Christian thought. But *Nostra Aetate* preferred to begin from human self-questioning—an approach that reached back to Job, the Psalms, Plato's dialogues, St Augustine of Hippo (above all, in his *Confessions*), many later theologians and philosophers, the systematic theology of Paul Tillich (1886–1965),[5] and a common tradition that insists on clarifying questions before moving to any possible answers.

The Primordial Human Questions

Making a broad statement about the present and the past, *Nostra Aetate* observes that 'human beings expect from the various religions a response to the obscure enigmas of *the human condition*, which, today as in the past, intimately disturb the hearts of human beings' (*NA* 1; italics mine). After echoing the title of a 1933 novel by André Malraux (1901–76), *La Condition Humaine*, the declaration then lists pervasive and radical questions that unavoidably touch human hearts and minds:

What is the human being? What is the meaning and purpose of our life? What is good [behaviour] and what is sin? What is the origin of sufferings and what is their purpose? What is the way to obtain true happiness? What is death, judgement, and final accounting (*retributio*) after death? What, finally, is that ultimate and ineffable mystery which enfolds our existence, from which we take our origin and towards which we move? (ibid.)

These seven questions enjoy a long heritage, both in the Scriptures, literature of all kinds, and human thought.

Some, like Paul Gauguin (1848–1903), would shorten the list. Shortly before his death in Tahiti, this post-impressionist painter wrote out three questions on a large triptych he had completed: 'Where do we come from? What are we? Where are we going?' Robert Coles has reported how, with surprising feeling and subtlety,

5. P. Tillich, *Systematic Theology*, 3 vols (Chicago: University of Chicago Press, 1951–63).

children ponder similar questions about the human predicament, asking about our origin, our nature, and our destiny.[6] Famously Immanuel Kant raised only three questions at the end of his *Critique of Pure Reason*: 'All interest of my reason (the speculative as well as the practical) is united in the following three questions: What can I know? What should I do? What may I hope for?'[7] As for Vatican II itself, in *Gaudium et Spes* one passage reduced its list of seven questions to three: 'human beings will always want to know, if only in a vague way, what is the meaning of their life, their activity, and their death' (*GS* 41). But let us take up the fuller list, the seven questions raised by *Nostra Aetate*.

The Psalms show us ancient believers wrestling with the first question: 'what are human beings that you are mindful of them, mortals that you care for them?' (Ps. 8: 4) In the twentieth century, Wolfhart Pannenberg (b.1928) set himself to bring together in a tour de force the religious implications of human biology, cultural anthropology, psychology, sociology, and history to construct a religious account of human beings as created in the image of God and yet marred by sin that breaks and distorts their true identity. Part of the natural world, human persons are social beings, whose subjective identity is shaped by society, with its institutions, political order, and, in general, culture, which are all expressed and developed in particular ways by language. Pannenberg understood history to embrace all these realities and the concrete conditions of human life.[8] One could list numerous other biblical and post-biblical voices raising the question: who or what is the human being? Much of the work of Pannenberg's great contemporaries, Karl Rahner (1904–84) and Jürgen Moltmann (b.1926), was dedicated to raising and answering that question.

Second, what can be the meaning and purpose of life? So often, self-aggrandizing and powerful people seem to win out, while those who aim at lovingly helping others go to the wall. Was the doomed Macbeth right? Is life simply 'a tale told by an idiot, full of sound and fury, signifying nothing' (*Macbeth*, Act 5, Scene 5)?[9] The quest for

---

6. R. Coles, *The Spiritual Life of Children* (Boston: Houghton Mifflin, 1990).
7. I. Kant, *Critique of Pure Reason*, trans. Paul Guyer and Allen W. Wood (Cambridge: Cambridge University Press, 1998), A805/B833, 677.
8. W. Pannenberg, *Anthropology in Theological Perspective*, trans. Matthew J. O'Connell (Philadelphia: Westminster Press, 1985).
9. The full quotation runs: 'And all our yesterdays have lighted fools/The way to dusty death. Out, out brief candle!/Life's but a walking shadow, a poor player/That struts

meaning turns up everywhere. Let me offer two out of endless examples, one serious and the other more popular. Viktor Frankl (1905–97) embodied this question in his own life, surviving the Holocaust through his hunger for meaning. His *Man's Search for Meaning* (original ed. 1946) proved the key text for the school of Logotherapy (therapy through meaning) that he founded. He understood the struggle to find meaning to be the principal driving force in human beings.[10] Those who write and direct popular films recognize that, at least every now and then, they should throw in the question of meaning. Some years ago I was watching a well-acted and popular TV soap opera. After taking us through some minor storms in the domestic teacup, the central personality, an attractive wife and mother in her late thirties, looked off into the distance and asked: 'What's it all about?' Her woman friend seemed equally puzzled about the meaning of life and replied: 'You tell me.'

Christians and others resonate with St Paul's wrestling with good and evil and our seeming incapacity to resist the pull of evil (Rom. 7: 13–25)—the third question on the list from *Nostra Aetate*. In his *Divine Comedy* Dante Alighieri set himself to answer the question: what is good behaviour and what is sin? He took the reader through hell and the sins for which people have been condemned. He then constructed a long climb up the mountain of purgatory around seven terraces on which sinners were being cleansed from the seven deadly sins, which began with the worst (pride) and ended with the least serious (lust). It is only after this long pictorial and poetic treatment of sin that Dante moved to heaven and expounded directly the working of redemption. The movement of the *Comedy* is instructive. Reflecting on and discerning between good and evil behaviour is a basic challenge that people need to face and, sooner or later, do face.[11]

With the fourth question, 'what is the origin of sufferings and what is their purpose?', we reach a question that signals the way by which human beings can frequently open up, or rather are opened up, to

---

and frets his hour upon the stage,/And then is heard no more; it is a tale/Told by an idiot, full of sound and fury,/Signifying nothing.'

10. V. Frankl, *Man's Search for Meaning: An Introduction to Logotherapy*, trans. I. Lasch (London: Hodder & Stoughton, 1964).

11. See further G. O'Collins, *Jesus Our Redeemer: A Christian Approach to Salvation* (Oxford: Oxford University Press, 2007), 43–62.

religious experience and practice. As emeritus Linacre Professor of Zoology at the University of Oxford, Sir Alister Hardy (1896–1985) founded the Religious Experience and Research Centre. This centre put together a vast database of personal reports of spiritual experiences. The stories collected by Hardy and his collaborators from a wide range of 'ordinary' people showed how painful and even tragic events often trigger a vivid sense of the divine presence and relate to religious practice. Yet, unquestionably, the terrible suffering of innocent persons has also driven many away from God and the practice of religion. Here the Book of Job offers no answer but a different sequence. The unmerited sufferings of the innocent Job provide the agenda for thirty-seven chapters, but no conclusions are reached as to why he has suffered. Then it is God who finally addresses Job, not to explain anything but to illustrate the limits of human knowledge and power which leave suffering very mysterious (Job 38: 1–42: 6).[12]

The fifth question, 'what is the way to obtain true happiness', expresses the question that obviously summons up the moral code proposed by different religions. 'True' aims to exclude any shallow or short-lived pleasure that can masquerade as genuine happiness. All religions present a way of life that will make its committed followers genuinely and lastingly happy. With an eye on Aristotelian ethics, some may prefer to rephrase the question and ask: 'what is the way to genuine human flourishing?' Whether we speak of happiness or of flourishing, different religions offer their specific (often overlapping) protocols.

Sixth, we arrive at the enigma of death ('what is death, judgement, and final accounting after death?'), a theme that will be considered in *Gaudium et Spes* (no. 18). Years ago Ernest Becker (1924–74) cried out against the ultimate loss of death, for which he could see no remedy. He found 'the real dilemma of existence' in 'the mortal animal who at the same time is conscious of his mortality' and added:

A person spends years coming into his own, developing his talent, his unique gifts, perfecting his discriminations about the world, broadening and sharpening his appetite, learning to bear the disappointments of life, becoming mature, seasoned—finally a unique creature in nature, standing with some dignity and nobility and transcending the animal condition, no longer driven,

---

12. See David B. Burrell, *Deconstructing Theodicy: Why Job Has Nothing to Say to the Problem of Suffering* (Grand Rapids, MI: Brazos Press, 2008).

no longer a complete reflex, not stamped out of any mold. And then the real tragedy, as André Malraux wrote in *The Human Condition*: it takes sixty years of incredible suffering and effort to make such an individual, and then he is good only for dying . . . He has to go the way of the grasshopper, even though it takes longer.[13]

In differing ways, religious faiths respond to this challenge, whether they profess hope in a glorious resurrection of the body after death, propose reincarnation of the soul as the solution to Becker's question, or understand death as being peacefully absorbed back into the cosmos from which we came.

Seventh and finally, there is the question of the 'mystery [curiously written in lower rather than upper case] which enfolds our existence, from which we take our origin and towards which we proceed/move'. Here the God-question is phrased in terms of the mysterious Being who is our beginning, our total environment, and our end. Life is seen as a journey *from* God and *to* God, in a way that could evoke John's words about Jesus' 'coming from God and going to God' (John 13: 3). Or one might understand the question to be loosely based on what Paul said in Athens about everyone being God's 'offspring', about experiencing God as the One in whom 'we live and move and have our being', and about moving towards final resurrection and divine judgement (Acts 17: 28, 31).

Whatever precise sources we could suggest for this seventh question, here the list reaches its climax. 'The' question that any religion promises to answer is surely that of God. Interestingly, *Nostra Aetate* 'places' God before us (as 'our origin'), around us (as 'enfolding our existence'), and ahead of us (as the one 'towards whom we move'). It does not situate God immanently 'within' us, or transcendentally 'above' us, or coming to us (as a kind of 'Ad-vent God' who comes to us from the future).

The seventh question brings at once two comments on how human beings understand variously 'the mystery which enfolds our existence'. First, 'among different nations there is found a certain perception of that hidden power (virtutis) that is present in the course of things and the events of human life'. Yet, secondly, 'sometimes there is rather found a recognition of a Supreme Deity or even of a Father'. Both the

13. E. Becker, *The Denial of Death* (New York: Free Press, 1973), 268–9.

former 'perception' and the latter 'recognition' imbue life 'with an intimate religious meaning' (*AG* 2).

This list of seven questions includes some that are double questions (e.g. 'what is the origin of sufferings and what is their purpose?'), one that is triple ('what is death, judgement, and final reckoning after death?'), and one, the final God-question, that is quite complex. As providing a context for introducing the variety of world religions, the questions serve well by raising issues of meaning and truth (the first, second, fourth, sixth, and seventh questions), as well as ethical issues about good behaviour and what will lead to 'true happiness' (the third and fifth questions). The 'truth' to be known and the 'good' to be practised feature clearly and strongly. But what of the 'beautiful' to be loved? Surely religions are *also* in the business of responding to the question: where do we find something or rather Someone utterly and lastingly beautiful who will steal away our hearts forever? Without denying the place of beauty in religious faith, the list of questions proposed by *Nostra Aetate* quietly bypasses the 'beautiful dimension' of religions.[14]

The question of beauty (and, in particular, divine beauty) made only a few appearances at the Second Vatican Council (e.g. *SC* 122; *GS* 57, 76). On 8 December 1965, when he closed the Council and the bishops were about to leave for home, Pope Paul VI alerted them to seven messages he was sending to seven classes of people (from governments to the young). The third message went out to artists, and included a paragraph on beauty:

This world in which we live has need of beauty, so as not to collapse into despair. Beauty, like truth, is that which puts joy in the hearts of human beings; it is that precious fruit which resists the wear and tear of time, which unites generations and makes them share with others in admiration. And [all of] that [happens] through your hands.[15]

Here, of course, Paul VI did not present beauty precisely in terms of the God-question. Rather he appreciated how art counteracts despair,

14. At various points in other documents, including a reference to beauty would have enriched what was said. For example, instead of merely saying that God reveals 'love and truth' (*AG* 11), the statement would have been happily enhanced by saying that God reveals 'love, truth, and beauty'.
15. *AAS* 58 (1966), 8–18, at 12–13.

triggers deep joy, and brings together successive generations through their delight in beautiful works of art.

Augustine would encourage us to prioritize beauty when approaching questions of religious faith. As he said to God, 'late have I loved you, Beauty so ancient and so new. Late have I loved you!' He fastened upon the five senses to describe how the divine beauty took hold of him. He heard, saw, smelled, tasted, and touched God. Or rather God took the initiative and spoke to him, shone upon him, shed fragrance about him, touched him, and let him taste the divine goodness:

You called and cried aloud [to me], and you broke open my deafness. You flashed around me and shone upon me, and you put my blindness to flight. You shed your fragrance about me. I drew breath and I pant after you. I tasted you, and now I hunger and thirst for you. You touched me, and I burn for your peace. (*Confessions*, 10. 27; trans. mine)

All of this is nothing less than a powerful and poetic way of expressing Augustine's total experience of the beautiful God to whom he could respond only with radical love. Augustine's words leave us with a question when we investigate the religions of the world: does *this* religious faith let the divine beauty break in and change our lives?

If I missed a question about the divine beauty in the list offered by *Nostra Aetate*, what I appreciated was the way in which the seven questions not only spring from human existence as we constantly experience it but also join the question of self with the question of God. We cannot raise profound questions about human existence without raising questions about God, and vice versa. Augustine's prayer classically linked the search for oneself with the search for God: 'Lord, that I might know myself! That I might know thee!' As Augustine realized through all the troubled and elusive drama of his life, our radical restlessness and self-questioning are only a thin veil concealing our search for God.

Hinduism and Buddhism

After its introductory article that climaxed with the *unity* of the human race, *Nostra Aetate* turns to the manifold answers offered by the religions of the world, which 'in various ways attempt to engage with the restlessness of the human heart by proposing' three things: 'doctrines', 'precepts for life', and 'sacred rites' (*NA* 2). This triple scheme, which encompasses belief systems, codes of conduct, and modes of worship, may be conventional, but it remains enduringly serviceable for analysing what particular religions set before their followers.

In the event, the declaration attended only to Hinduism, Buddhism, and Islam.[16] It had nothing to say, for instance, about Confucianism, Shintoism, Sikhism, and Taoism, and, even more broadly, nothing to say about traditional religions to be found in Africa, Asia, Oceania, and the Americas. Both at the time of the Council and later, commentators have regretted the failure to address, even in passing, ethnic or tribal religions.

When it tackled specific religions, *Nostra Aetate* spoke about the religions themselves rather than about the followers of these or those religions. It concerned itself primarily with the systems they followed. Even then the declaration never attempted to describe fully the different religions.[17] It said nothing, for example, about various schools in Hinduism, or about any 'negative' Buddhist understanding of salvation, or about differences between Sunni and Shi'a Muslims. While acknowledging such limitations, this declaration did something no ecumenical council had ever done before in the history of Catholic Christianity: it reflected explicitly and positively on some aspects of Hinduism and Buddhism, two religious ways of life that existed centuries before the coming of Christ himself. It was not 'doing a theology of religion' but set itself only to indicate some of their key spiritual values which could serve as a basis for dialogue. As Siebenrock remarks, the declaration never aimed at a complete treatment; yet lengthy descriptions were not needed to achieve the purpose of the document—to lay the ground for dialogue and collaboration.[18]

Nostra Aetate begins with what it calls 'the religions connected with the progress of culture', which 'endeavour to reply' to the seven questions 'with subtler concepts and a more exact language'. Our document might have added a word about the classical religious texts of these religions, which deploy those 'subtler concepts' and 'more

---

16. See Heinz Bechert, 'Buddhismus', *TRE*, vii, 317–35; Heinrich von Stietencron, 'Hinduismus', *TRE*, xv, 346–55; Anton Schall et al., 'Islam', *TRE*, xvi, 336–58.

17. For all its limits, the declaration respected the irreducible particularity of these religions and what made them distinctive—a principle stressed by more and more specialists in recent years.

18. Siebenrock, '*Nostra Aetate*', 655.

exact language'. Instead, *Nostra Aetate* bypasses the status of the sacred scriptures of other religions, and moves at once to acknowledge features of Hindu teaching enshrined in those texts: 'in Hinduism, human beings examine the divine mystery and express [it] through the unspent fecundity of myths and acute efforts of philosophy' (*NA* 2). Here the well-founded reference to the exuberant 'myths' and brilliant 'philosophy' of India could distract us from a key issue: if Hindus have dedicated themselves to 'examining' and 'expressing the divine mys- tery', how did they personally know this mystery (revelation in the primary sense) or know about it (revelation in the secondary sense) in the first instance? Is it through some kind of revelation that the mystery of God has been disclosed to them? The declaration, while not expli- citly putting that question, encourages readers to raise it.

Apropos of the style of life practised by Hindus, our document adds: 'they seek liberation from the trials of our condition through forms of ascetical life, or through deep meditation, or through recourse to God with love and confidence'. What is involved in 'forms' of asceticism and 'profound meditation' is relatively clear and needs little comment. But what does the Council intend by loving and trusting 'recourse to God'? Does it refer here to Hindu practices of worship and religious festivals, which are persistently characterized by 'love', 'confidence', and, one should add, 'joy'? Once again the text leaves us with an intriguing question.[19]

Moving on to Buddhism, *Nostra Aetate* refers to the notable differ- ences between its 'various forms', presumably the more rational Theravada (developed from Hinayana) and the more religious Maha- yana traditions or 'vehicles'. In general, Buddhism 'acknowledges the radical insufficiency of this changing world', and teaches 'a path by which human beings, with a devout and confident spirit, can acquire a state of perfect liberation, or can—relying either on their own efforts or on higher assistance—reach supreme enlightenment' (NA 2). Besides naming the awareness of 'the radical insufficiency of this changing world' (something not peculiar to Buddhism but found in the religious experience of humanity), the document might have attended more precisely to the Buddhist view that it is desire which causes pervasive suffering and that 'a state of perfect liberation' is

19. On the treatment of Hinduism in *Nostra Aetate*, see Cyril B. Papali, 'Excursus on Hinduism', in *Commentary on the Documents of Vatican II*, iii, 137–44.

nothing else than total freedom from suffering or nirvana. The mention of 'enlightenment' obviously recalls the founder of Buddhism, even if he is not explicitly named: Siddhartha Gautama (d. around 480 BC), who through asceticism and meditation reached enlightenment.

While setting out some common characteristics of Buddhism, the decree distinguishes 'paths' of salvation pursued by one's 'own efforts' or pursued 'by higher assistance'. Theravada traditions typically propose a state of absolute freedom to be achieved through one's own exertions, whereas Mahayana traditions highlight supreme enlightenment that comes through higher assistance. The document acknowledges (but without taking a stand on the debates and conflicts) the unity *and* diversity in the religious traditions of Buddhism but leaves much unsaid. *Nostra Aetate* also largely puts aside the issue: is Buddhism a philosophy or is it a religion but a religion without a god? The declaration focuses on the religious character of Buddhism, and understands it as a religion of salvation.[20]

Before leaving Vatican II's brief treatment of Hinduism and Buddhism, we should recall how many Catholics and other Christians, sometimes long before the Council opened in 1962, explored ways in which they could incorporate into their spiritual lives, theological thinking, and ways of worship some Hindu and Buddhist ideas, themes, and practices. We should remember with gratitude Anthony de Mello, Bede Griffiths, Patricia Kinsey (Sister Vandana), Henri Le Saux (Swami Abhishiktananda), Raimon Panikkar, and others in India; and the work in Japan of Heinrich Dumoulin, William Johnston, and Hugo Lasalle (Makibi Enomiya); and many others in those countries and elsewhere who led the way in the cause of inculturating Christianity. At Vatican II, Asian and other bishops knew what living dialogue and collaboration with Hindus and Buddhists had been contributing. But it would have been unreasonable to have expected them to expand the Declaration on Relation of the Church to Non-Christian Religions by adding guidelines for such dialogue. The text already had enough fresh and significant teaching to offer. In any case, as we will see shortly, it endorsed such dialogue and collaboration.

---

20. On the treatment of Buddhism in *Nostra Aetate*, see Heinrich Dumoulin, 'Excursus on Buddhism', in *Commentary on the Documents of Vatican II*, iii, 145–50.

What is True and Holy in World Religions

Before moving on from article 2 and article 3 to Muslims, *Nostra Aetate* pauses to sum up Catholic belief and practice vis-à-vis the religions of the world. Quoting John 14: 6 and referring to 2 Corinthians 5: 18–19, our document makes it crisply and compellingly clear where we find the unsurpassable highpoint of divine revelation and salvation: Christ 'is the way, the truth and the life', the One in whom God has 'reconciled all things to himself'. That means that in Christ human beings 'find the fullness of religious life'. 'Fullness' proves a well-chosen and highly significant word. While the fullness of revelation and salvation is to be found in the Christian Church, those who live beyond that community are not left in a state of total emptiness.

Hence the declaration observes that 'the Catholic Church rejects nothing of those things which are true and holy in these [other] religions'. Rather, 'it is with sincere respect that she considers those ways of acting and living, those precepts and doctrines, which, although they differ in many [respects] from what she herself holds and proposes, nevertheless, often reflect a ray of that Truth, which illuminates all human beings' (*NA* 2). By recognizing what is 'true and holy' in other religions, *Nostra Aetate* follows the lead of *Lumen Gentium* in using a Johannine, double-sided terminology that distinguishes (but does not separate) the two dimensions of the divine self-communication: revelation and salvation. What or rather who has given rise to 'those things which are true and holy' in the other religions? The Council responds by pointing to the person of Christ.

Without condemning various 'ways of acting and living', as well as various 'precepts and doctrines' to be found in other religions, but simply saying that they 'differ' in many respects from what the Catholic Church teaches, the declaration then acknowledges something extraordinarily positive: the beliefs and practices of other religions 'often reflect a ray of that Truth, which illuminates all human beings' (John 1: 9). Since what is 'true' among the others reflects 'the Truth' that is the Word of God, presumably what is 'holy' among them also comes from the Word who is the life of humankind (John 1: 4). If Christ is 'the truth' for everyone, he is also 'the life' for them. This paragraph does not expressly state that Christ is both universal

Revealer and universal Saviour, but what it says amounts to that. How can he 'illuminate' all human beings, without conveying to them, through a personal, divine disclosure, something of God's self-revelation and hence also the offer of salvation?

The Council did not, however, enjoy the authority and 'resources' to attempt to identify precisely what shape the divine revelation has taken in other religious traditions. It is one thing to maintain the origin and common destiny of all people in God, along with the universal revealing and saving impact of the Word of God, but it would be quite another to risk spelling out precisely what is 'true and holy' in world religions and how that has come through the revealing activity of God. As we will see in the next chapter, *Ad Gentes* respected the mysterious ways in which the divine self-disclosure can call forth human faith.

On the basis of what article 1 has observed about the growing unity of the human race and of what article 2 has said about the followers of other religions, the declaration 'exhorts' Catholics, while acting 'with prudence and charity' and 'witnessing to Christian faith and life', to take up 'dialogue and collaboration with followers of other religions'.[21] Such dialogue and collaboration should involve Catholics in 'recognizing, protecting, and promoting those spiritual and moral goods, as well as those socio-cultural values' found among the followers of other religions (*NA* 2). Obviously 'recognizing, protecting, and promoting' such 'spiritual and moral goods' and 'socio-cultural values' embodies a loving concern for the religious others. But by 'recognizing, protecting, and promoting' these goods and values, do Catholics receive some of those 'spiritual and moral goods' for themselves, as well as being blessed by the 'socio-cultural values' of the others? No reply is given in our text, but we could look for an answer in the mutual fruits of the dialogue and collaboration that emerged around the world in the aftermath of Vatican II.[22]

---

21. Pope Paul VI's 1964 encyclical, *Ecclesiam Suam*, had firmly encouraged such dialogue: *AAS* 56 (1964), 609–59, at 639–40.

22. On some results and difficulties, see Daniel A. Madigan, 'Muslim-Christian Dialogue in Difficult Times', in James L. Heft (ed.), *Catholicism and Interreligious Dialogue* (New York: Oxford University Press, 2012), 57–87; Francis X. Clooney, 'Learning Our Way: Some Reflections on Catholic-Hindu Encounter', in Heft, *Catholicism and Interreligious Dialogue*, 89–125; James L. Fredericks, 'Off the Map: The Catholic Church in Its Dialogue with Buddhism', in Heft, *Catholicism and Interreligious Dialogue*, 127–68; Peter C. Phan, 'Catholicism and Confucianism: An Intercultural and Interreligious Dialogue', in Heft, *Catholicism and Interreligious Dialogue*, 169–207.

Muslims

Nostra Aetate devoted an entire article (no. 3) to the Muslims,[23] first acknowledging major features in their doctrine of God: 'they worship God, who is unique, living and subsistent, merciful and almighty, the Creator of heaven and earth, who has spoken (*allocutum*) to human beings'. This involves them in 'submitting themselves wholeheartedly to the hidden decrees' of God, 'just as Abraham submitted himself to God'. The declaration added at once that 'Islamic faith (fides Islamica) willingly refers itself' to Abraham—primarily, one presumes, to the *faith* of Abraham (and Sarah). The document remains silent, however, about the controversial issue of their historical descent from Abraham's son (Ismael), claimed by Muslims.

While reluctant to state straight out that Muslims share the faith of Abraham and Sarah, *Nostra Aetate* clearly recognized how Muslims want to share that faith by 'willingly' referring their faith to that of Abraham. Despite this reluctance, the article had already indicated how Islamic faith responded to God's revelation. It was because God had 'spoken [in some kind of personal self-revelation] to human beings' and, specifically, to Muslims that they came to faith in God as 'unique, living and subsistent, merciful and almighty, the Creator of heaven and earth'. Hence they could truly 'worship God', now revealed to them.[24] The divine self-revelation had made possible not only their worship of the true God but also their submission to God's decrees. To be sure, *Nostra Aetate* characterized the 'decrees' of God as 'hidden'. But, obviously, they cannot have remained totally and completely hidden. Otherwise how could Muslims have known what they should submit themselves to? God must have partially revealed the divine will to prompt such submission ('Islam' meaning 'submission [to God]').

23. See George C. Anawati, 'Excursus on Islam', in *Commentary on Vatican II*, iii, 151–4; Sachiko Murata and William C. Chittick, *The Vision of Islam* (St Paul, MN: Paragon House, 1994).
24. To say that God had 'spoken (*allocutum*) to human beings' obviously evokes a traditional way of expressing divine revelation as 'locutio Dei', or God breaking silence and speaking to and addressing human beings. The verb 'alloquor' corresponds to the noun 'locutio'.

From the doctrine of God, the decree moves its focus to Jesus: 'they [the Muslims] do not acknowledge Jesus as God but venerate [him] as a prophet'. They 'honour his virgin mother Mary', and 'at times even devotedly invoke' her. Since the Christian doctrine of God is Trinitarian, it would be more accurate to speak of acknowledging or not acknowledging Jesus as 'the Son of God'. The language about 'honouring the virgin Mary' forms a slightly oblique way of stating that, along with Christians, Muslims believe that Jesus was virginally conceived through the power of God.

Muslims sum up their doctrine in the profession of faith, 'there is no God but Allah and Muhammad is his prophet'. But *Nostra Aetate* does not mention either the person of Muhammad or his prophetic character, or—for that matter—the Koran, *the* holy book of Islam containing the revelations said to have come from the archangel Gabriel to Muhammad. Yet the decree has indicated much common ground: (a) monotheistic faith in God revealed as the Creator of the universe, (to which *Nostra Aetate* adds that Christians and Muslims alike 'expect' the day when all human beings will be raised from the dead and divine 'judgement' will be passed on them); and (b) the virginal conception of Jesus and his activity as prophet. Here it is worth emphasizing that Christians, while believing in Jesus as more than a prophet, *also* understand his redemptive role in terms of his threefold office (*munus triplex*) as 'priest, *prophet*, and king'. The Second Vatican Council was to make Christ's office as 'priest, prophet, and king' a major theme, by applying it to all the baptized, as well as to ordained priests and bishops.[25]

Finally, the declaration shows its esteem for 'the moral life' of Muslims, and the way they 'worship God in prayer, alms-giving, and fasting'. This is to mention three of the 'Five Pillars' of Islam, but leaves out two: (a) the profession of faith that includes the prophetic mission of Muhammad; and (b) the pilgrimage to Mecca, where Muhammad was born and received the first series of revelations. But *Nostra Aetate* never promised to provide a complete picture of Islam; it set itself to highlight some major features in the faith, practice, and worship of

25. See G. O'Collins, '*Ressourcement* and Vatican II', in Gabriel Flynn and Paul Murray (eds), *Ressourcement: A Movement of Renewal in Twentieth-Century Catholic Theology* (Oxford: Oxford University Press, 2012), 372–91, at 387–8.

Muslims which establish common ground for dialogue and collaboration.

The article on Muslims concludes by referring to the 'many' disagreements and the acts of open hostility between Christians and Muslims which have occurred over the centuries. The Council wants both sides to 'forget the past' and 'make a sincere effort at mutual understanding'. Then, for the sake of all people, they will be able together to 'protect and promote social justice, moral goods, peace and freedom'. This conclusion, by recommending fresh efforts at dialogue and collaboration, matches what *Nostra Aetate* had encouraged when ending the previous article on world religions (which paid specific attention to Hinduism and Buddhism). Like others, I have found the invitation to 'forget the past' not particularly helpful. Sincere attempts at mutual forgiveness could lay a healthier and happier foundation for dialogue and collaboration between Christians and Muslims.

The Divine Image, Human Dignity, and Divine Fatherhood

Before leaving *Nostra Aetate*, we do well not to neglect the final (brief) article (5), which, after the long article on Judaism (4), expresses Vatican II's frame of mind about all humanity. Three themes should seize our attention when we explore possibilities for relating to 'the religious others'.

First, the declaration recalled a theme from the Book of Genesis that fills out what has already been said about human beings having a common origin in God. Right from the very first human beings, they are all 'created in the image and likeness of God' (Gen. 1: 26, 27). A few weeks later, in the context of spelling out what Christ the New Adam has done, the Constitution on the Church in the Modern World was also to appeal to this conviction (22). Seeing all people as not only created by God but also created in the divine image will prove an effective mindset; it dramatically puts back on display how we should interpret and understand 'the religious others', whoever they may be.

Second, *Nostra Aetate* draws a practical conclusion from the doctrine of all people being created in the divine image: there is no basis for any 'discrimination' that offends or curtails 'human dignity and the rights that flow from it'. 'Human dignity' would become the title of the Declaration on Religious Liberty (promulgated a few weeks later on 7 December 1965). *Gaudium et Spes* (also promulgated on the same day) would insist on 'the extraordinary dignity of the human person' and the basic rights that flow from that dignity (*GS* 26). Since 'all are created in the image of God', 'every way of discriminating against the fundamental rights of a person on the grounds of sex, race, colour, social condition, language, or religion should be overcome and removed' (*GS* 29). Thus the final article of *Nostra Aetate* found a fuller form in the last document to be promulgated by Vatican II.

Third, early on *Nostra Aetate* had briefly mentioned God the Father. 'The mystery that enfolds our existence' (*NA* 1) is sometimes recognized as 'a Supreme Deity' and 'even a Father' (*NA* 2). In its closing article, the decree begins by echoing the opening words of the Lord's Prayer: 'we cannot truly invoke God the Father of all, if we refuse to behave in a brotherly fashion towards certain human beings', even though 'they have been created in the image of God' (*NA* 5). Hence 'the relation of human beings to God the Father and the relation of human beings to their fellow human beings are so closely connected that Scripture says: "whoever does not love does not know God"' (1 John 4: 8). The article and whole decree end by urging readers to be at 'peace with all human beings', so that, in the words of Matthew 5: 45, 'they may truly be children of the Father who is in heaven' (ibid.). The universal fatherhood of God is to be matched by a universal brotherhood/sisterhood of the human race, fashioned by those who know themselves to be fellow children of one and the same God.

Nostra Aetate thus treats faith in God the Father in terms of the moral obligations that faith entails (but not, for instance, apropos of the Father being the ultimate, efficient cause of human salvation). It has nothing to say about the Holy Spirit.

The Achievements and Limits of *Nostra Aetate*

We might sum up some of the major achievements and limits of the Declaration of the Relation of the Church to Non-Christian Religions as follows:

∞ It is within a vision of one world that *NA* reflects on other religions (*NA* 1).

∞ All human beings share a common origin, providence, and destiny (*NA* 1).

∞ All human beings are made in the divine image (*NA* 5; see GS 22, 29).

∞ Human dignity and rights come from being made in the divine image (*NA* 5; see GS 26, 29).

∞ All human beings share the same deep questions (*NA* 1; see GS 4, 10, 18, 21, 22).

∞ The questions that *NA* lists concern truth and goodness but not beauty (*NA* 1).

∞ *NA* does not reflect on ethnic, tribal religions (*NA* 2).

∞ In *NA,* for the first time an ecumenical council considers Hinduism and Buddhism (*NA 2).*

∞ *NA* does not attempt to summarize all key aspects of Hinduism, Buddhism, and Islam, but only some major features (*NA* 2, 3).

∞ *NA* does not consider the sacred scriptures of other religions (*NA* 2).

∞ *NA* follows *LG* in considering 'doublets', or what is 'true and holy' in other religions (*NA* 2).

∞ *NA* encourages dialogue and collaboration with other religions (*NA* 2) and, specifically, with Muslims (*NA* 3).

∞ *NA* introduces Christ (*NA* 3) and God the Father (*NA* 2, 5), but does not mention the Holy Spirit.

Finally, two issues of terminology call for attention. First, in its introductory article *Nostra Aetate* spoke of 'the mystery which enfolds our existence, from which we take our origin and towards which we move' (*NA* 1). Then in a section on Hindus and Hinduism, the declaration observed how they examine and express 'the divine mystery' (*NA* 2). Lastly, in the story of the Old Testament patriarchs, Moses, and the prophets, our document recognized 'the saving mystery of God' (*NA* 4). This preference for the singular ('mystery' rather than 'mysteries') reflects a pervasive tendency of Vatican II documents to highlight *the* mystery of God (or God who is *the* Mystery) revealed in the whole history of salvation and inviting human beings to share, through faith in the self-revealing God, in a new and final communion of love.

This linguistic preference is based on the Pauline letters and their message of 'the revelation of the mystery' or the great truth of salvation for all, now made known through Christ (Rom. 16: 25–6; see Eph. 1: 9; 3: 4, 9). The Dogmatic Constitution on Divine Revelation, *Dei Verbum* ('the Word of God'), five times invokes the 'mystery' in the singular (nos. 2, 15, 17, 24, and 26) and never 'mysteries' in the plural. The same tendency shows up in other texts from Vatican II: the sixteen documents use 'mystery' in the singular 106 times and 'mysteries' in the plural only 22 times. This preference suggests a single design of universal salvation, a mystery that is inseparably one, even if we can and should distinguish within it various stages and dimensions.

Second, what of revelation, the inseparable, other dimension of the divine self-communication? *Nostra Aetate*, in its article on the Jewish people, gratefully recalled 'the Revelation' that the Church had inherited from the Old Testament (*NA* 4). Otherwise, the declaration uses neither the noun 'revelation' nor the verb 'reveal'. This reticence prompted Miikka Ruokanen to maintain: 'any idea of applying the concept of revelation to any instance *outside Christianity* is totally missing in the Council documents'.[26] As the next chapter shall show, in the December 1965 Decree on the Church's Missionary Activity, the Council did explicitly acknowledge 'revelation' in the divine activity outside Christianity; moreover, as we have just seen, *Nostra Aetate* acknowledged how 'revelation' was already there in the history of the Old Testament, prior to the birth of Christianity.

Karl Rahner proved less sweeping than Ruokanen when he remarked on the Council being 'extraordinarily reserved when it comes to the question of how a salvific faith in a real revelation of God in the strict sense can come about outside the realm of the Old and New Testaments'.[27] Rahner rightly set the question of revelation alongside that of (salvific) faith. God's self-revelation calls forth human faith, while such human faith, wherever it exists, is always a response to the divine revelation. Yet I puzzle over the significance of 'real' in 'real

---

26. M. Ruokanen, *The Catholic Doctrine of Non-Christian Religions According to the Second Vatican Council* (Leiden: E. J. Brill, 1992), 66; italics mine.
27. K. Rahner, *Foundations of Christian Faith: An Introduction to the Idea of Christianity*, trans. William V. Dych (New York: Seabury Press, 1978), 313.

revelation', and over the qualification of 'in the strict sense'. Is God's revelation sometimes (often?) less than 'real'? When and how would such a revelation occur in less than 'the strict sense'? Perhaps Rahner has in mind a distinction between revelation as it occurs in the 'special' history of revelation and salvation (that the inspired Scriptures recorded and interpreted) and revelation as it occurs in the 'general' history of revelation and salvation that coincides with the history of humanity.[28]

Apropos of divine revelation, a danger exists of being bewitched by a hunt for the words 'revelation' and 'reveal'. Years ago Rudolf Bultmann highlighted the strong emphasis on revelation found in the Fourth Gospel.[29] Even if that Gospel never formally gives Christ the title of 'Revealer' and never uses the terminology of 'revelation (*apokalupsis*)' and 'reveal (*apokalupsō*)', it applies to him a rich and variegated revelatory language: 'glory' (and 'glorify'), 'light', 'signs', 'truth', 'witness' (as both noun and verb), the 'I am' sayings, 'disclose (*phaneroō*)', and so forth. The Johannine vocabulary concerned with Christ's identity and activity is heavily revelatory, without using 'revealer', 'reveal', and 'revelation'.[30]

When commenting on what was said in *Nostra Aetate* about Hindus examining 'the divine mystery', I raised the question: how did they come to know about that mystery in the first place? Was it by divine revelation? A few lines later the declaration spoke of what is 'true and holy' in Hinduism and other religions, and understood the beliefs and practices of those religions to 'reflect often a ray of that Truth, which enlightens all human beings'. How could Christ as the Truth enlighten all human beings without conveying to them something of the divine self-revelation? The Council presumably meant what it said (or, at least, clearly implied) about the light of God's revelation reaching everyone, including the followers of other religions.

The article which our decree dedicates to Muslims implies that they came to faith because God had spoken to them and revealed at least something of himself and his 'hidden decrees' (*NA* 3). They can truly 'worship' the one God and Creator of all, since God is somehow

---

28. Ibid., 138–75; see G. O'Collins, *Rethinking Fundamental Theology: Toward a New Fundamental Theology* (Oxford: Oxford University Press, 2011), 50–95, 292–321.
29. For details, see O'Collins, *Rethinking Fundamental Theology*, 68, n. 11.
30. Ibid., 68–70.

revealed to them. What *Nostra Aetate* highlights in the faith and practice of Islam does not seem compatible with holding that Muslims have not and do not receive in any sense God's self-revelation.

Nostra Aetate, with only five articles, may be the shortest of all sixteen documents promulgated by Vatican II. But half a century of post-conciliar history has seen it grow both in theological significance and in pastoral importance for interfaith dialogue and collaboration. We turn next to *Ad Gentes*. That Decree on the Missionary Activity of the Church had valuable items to add about the situation of 'the religious others' and not least about the divine revelation that has reached them.

FIVE

Ad Gentes on Other Religions

He became the source of eternal salvation for all who obey him.

Letter to the Hebrews 5: 9

No Council has ever so consciously emphasized and so insistently expounded the Church's pastoral work of salvation and its world-wide missionary function as Vatican II.

Heinrich Suso Brechter

A t the Second Vatican Council sharply different views of Christian missionary activity led to many difficulties in the drafting, discussion, and revision of the Decree on the Church's Missionary Activity (*Ad Gentes*).[1] At the end, however, 2,394 'fathers' voted 'yes' and only five voted 'no'—a striking tribute to the work of the Council's Missionary Commission and their experts who included, in particular, Yves Congar.

Congar played a major role in developing the text and, especially, in composing Chapter 1 ('Doctrinal Principles'), his own work from

---

1. See Heinrich S. Brechter, 'Decree on the Church's Missionary Activity', in Herbert Vorgrimler (ed.), *Commentary on the Documents of Vatican II*, trans. W. J. O'Hara, iv (London: Burns & Oates, 1969), 87–181, at 87–111; Yves Congar, 'Principes doctrinaux (nos 2 a 9)', in Johannes Schütte (ed.), *L'activité missionaire de l'Eglise* (Paris: Cerf, 1967), 185–221; Norman Tanner, 'The Church in the World (*Ecclesia ad Extra*)', in Giuseppe Alberigo and Joseph A. Komonchak (eds), in *History of Vatican II*, iv (Maryknoll, NJ: Orbis, 2003), 269–386, at 331–45; Riccardo Burigana and Giovanni Turbanti, 'The Intersession: Preparing the Conclusion of the Council', *History of Vatican II*, 453–615, at 573–84; Peter Hünermann, 'The Final Weeks of the Council', in *History of Vatican II*, v (2006), 363–483, at 427–51; Peter Hünermann, 'Theologischer Kommentar zum Dekret über die Missionstätigkeit der Kirche: *Ad Gentes*', in Peter Hünermann and Bernd Jochen Hilberath (eds), *Herders Theologischer Kommentar zum Zweiten Vatikanischen Konzil*, iv (Freiburg im Breisgau: Herder, 2005), 219–336.

'A to Z', as he put it.[2] This is the longest of the six chapters that make up *Ad Gentes*, as well as including more sources (either cited or referred to) in the footnotes than all the other chapters put together. 'The patristic references are particularly numerous and excellently chosen', Heinrich Suso Brechter wrote, 'whereas the following chapters quote almost exclusively from conciliar texts and papal allocutions'.[3] In a *tour de force,* Congar introduced quotations from or references to twenty-three Fathers of the Church, some of them, such as Irenaeus and Augustine, more than once. He retrieved remarkable texts that illuminate principles which guide the Church's missionary activity, itself based on the 'missionary activity' of the Trinity for the salvation of human beings.

The first doctrinal principle which founds the missionary activity of the Church according to Chapter 1 is its 'origin' in the plan of God the Father, whose 'love' and 'goodness' give rise to the mission of the Son and the mission of the Holy Spirit. Through those missions, God who 'in his great and merciful kindness has freely created us, graciously calls us to share in his life and glory' (*AG* 2).[4] This Trinitarian vision of the origin of missionary activity leads naturally to three matching images of the goal of that activity, when the whole human race 'form one people of God [the Father], come together into the one body of Christ, and are built up into the temple of the Holy Spirit'. Then 'all who share human nature, regenerated in Christ through the Holy Spirit', will be able to 'gaze together on the glory of God [the Father]' (AG 7). Thus, when reflecting on the religious state of the entire human race, both

---

2. Y. Congar, *My Journal of the Council*, trans. Mary John Ronayne and Mary Cecily Boulding (Collegeville, MN: Liturgical Press, 2012), 871.

3. Brechter, 'Decree on Church's Missionary Activity', 113.

4. On grounding the Church's mission in the mystery of the Trinity, see Brechter, 'Decree on the Church's Missionary Activity', 113–16; James B. Anderson, *A Vatican II Pneumatology of the Paschal Mystery: The Historical-doctrinal Genesis of 'Ad Gentes' 1, 2–5* (Rome: Gregorian University Press, 1988); Lesslie Newbigin, *The Relevance of Trinitarian Doctrine to Today's Mission* (London: Edinburgh Press, 1963). Although it would be published only in 2002, Anderson had access to Congar's diary (and some other personal papers) when telling the story of how Congar joined and worked on the editorial sub-commission appointed in late 1964 to draft a new 'schema' about the Church's missionary activity; in this he was ably assisted by another expert, Joseph Ratzinger (Anderson, *A Vatican II Pneumatology*, 94–137). After the debate in the Council on this new draft (7–13 October 1965), Congar and Ratzinger were once again at work considering, inserting, or rejecting proposed amendments, as they were yet again involved together after a further discussion of the amended text in the Council (10–11 November) (ibid., 151–95).

Christians and non-Christians alike, *Ad Gentes* wishes to consider everyone through the eyes of the Father, Son, and Holy Spirit.

Before examining in detail one example that takes further Vatican II's teaching on the divine self-revelation to all people, let me gather together five items, which illuminate the religious situation of 'the others' and which earlier Vatican texts had already developed or at least touched on.

Five Themes Already Developed

(1) *Ad Gentes* (and, in particular, Chapter 1) puts on display various New Testament texts already cited or at least referenced in documents previously promulgated by Vatican II. These biblical verses reflect the Council's mindset as it considers the religious situation of 'the others'. Naturally the decree cites (*AG* 7) the classical text about God wanting 'all human beings to be saved and come to the knowledge of the truth' (1 Tim. 2: 4), and echoes it in its closing article (*AG* 42). The same verse had already featured in the opening chapter of Vatican II's first promulgated text, *Sacrosanctum Concilium* (Chapter 3 above). The decree also appeals (*AG* 2) to the Johannine language about Christ's work in 'gathering the children of God who had been scattered' (John 11: 52), a verse that previously turned up in *Sacrosanctum Concilium* 2 and *Lumen Gentium* 13. In Chapter 1, we saw how *Lumen Gentium* 16 echoed what Acts 17 presents Paul as saying in Athens. With reference to the whole human race, *Ad Gentes* cites Acts 17: 27 to support the statement that 'God is not far from anyone' (*AG* 3).

As we showed in Chapter 1, the terminology of 'reconciliation' that Paul introduced played a role, albeit a minor role, when Vatican II reflected on the religious situation of the human race. *Nostra Aetate* confessed that in Christ 'God reconciled all things to himself' (*NA* 2). A footnote in the Decree on the Church's Missionary Activity picked up this language when it cited Cyril of Alexandria about 'all people being reconciled to the Father' (*AG* 7, n. 45). Earlier the decree spoke of God aiming through Christ 'to reconcile the world to himself', and added a footnote to 2 Corinthians 5: 19, the classic statement of that divine purpose which stopped at nothing less than universal reconciliation (*AG* 3, n. 10). There is one, further text that should be recalled.

In his Gospel and Acts, the central message of Luke is that human beings are saved only through the crucified and resurrected One. Jesus is the sole agent of final salvation, and this salvation is available for all human beings. Luke's two-part work on Christian origins climaxes with the claim: 'there is the salvation through no one else [than Jesus]; for there is no other name under heaven given among human beings by which we must be saved' (Acts 4: 12).[5] This claim from a speech by Peter fits into a whole pattern of speeches in Acts[6] and introduces some of its most recurrent themes: the *universal* significance of his message (for 'all human beings' 'under heaven') and the *name* of Jesus. In Acts, the apostles and others baptize 'in the name of Jesus', preach and teach in his name, and work miracles in his name. The 'name' is to be identified with Jesus himself; it re-presents Jesus really and effectively. When people put their faith in his 'name', they put their faith in Jesus himself and find salvation in him.[7] As regards salvation (*sōtēria*), Luke uses the word ten times in his Gospel and Acts. It is never found in Mark and Matthew and merely once in John (4: 22). It is only here in Acts 4: 12 that Luke attaches the definite article to 'salvation' (*hē sōtēria*). In short, the language of this verse suggests that it offers us Luke's primary message in miniature.[8]

Thus *Ad Gentes* introduces a verse of vast importance for Luke and Acts when citing Acts 4: 12 in support of the missionary activity of the Church and of the need for baptism (*AG* 7). This momentous verse

5. Joseph A. Fitzmyer, *The Acts of the Apostles* (New York: Doubleday, 1998), 297, 301–2; see also Marcel Dumais, 'Le salut universel par le Christ selon les Acts des Apôtres', *Studien zum Neuen Testament und seiner Umwelt* 18 (1993), 113–31.
6. While the substantial historical reliability of many of the narratives in Acts can be solidly defended (Fitzmyer, *Acts of the Apostles*, 124–8), the speeches and missionary discourses (which make up nearly one third of the whole book) appear to be Lukan compositions, albeit passages in which Luke draws on some historical sources and may give the general sense of what was actually said (ibid., 103–13). The speeches and discourses cannot be taken to be verbatim reports; they show repeatedly Luke's style and formulations.
7. To indicate that 'calling upon the *name* of the Lord' brings salvation, Acts 2: 21 has quoted Joel 2: 32. This prophetic text originally referred to calling on the name of the YHWH, to whom prayers and sacrifices were offered (e.g. Gen. 4: 26; 13: 4). Now Acts and other books of the New Testament (e.g. Rom. 10: 9–13) apply 'calling on the name of the Lord' to invoking and venerating Jesus in early Christian worship. Acts 4: 12 implies such cultic veneration of Jesus: salvation comes from calling on the name of the Lord Jesus. See Larry W. Hurtado, *Lord Jesus Christ: Devotion to Jesus in Earliest Christianity* (Grand Rapids, MI: Eerdmans, 2003), 179–85.
8. This conclusion emerges from the *whole* context of Luke's Gospel and Acts. In the *immediate* context of Acts 4: 12, Peter is talking only to fellow Jews ('we' in that sense) and not to those who adhere to other faiths.

appears only once elsewhere in the other documents of the Second Vatican Council (*GS*, 10). How does *Ad Gentes* envisage the situation of those who have not (or have not yet) come to Christian faith?

(2) Chapter 3 above remarked on the way the Constitution on the Church echoed the language of Justin Martyr and other early Christian writers when speaking of 'the good sown (*seminatum*) in the heart and mind of human beings or in the particular rites and cultures of peoples' (*LG* 17). Congar, who had played his part in drafting that article of *Lumen Gentium*, repeated those words in the decree on missionary activity when describing the passage to Christian faith, and indicated in a footnote their source in *Lumen Gentium* 17: 'whatever good is found sown (seminatum) in the heart and mind of human beings or in the particular rites [presumably religious rites] and cultures, so far from being lost, is healed, elevated, and consummated' (*AG* 9 and n.52).[9] Once again, while expressing the saving impact on those who move to faith in Christ (through the 'healing, elevating, and consummating'), the passage recognized 'the good' already 'sown in the mind and heart of human beings' and in 'their rites and cultures'; presumably we deal here with a 'divine passive' and the sowing that had been done by God, and hence with the prior presence in them of a measure of divine self-communication. Even before accepting the gospel, these religious 'others' already enjoy some elements of revelation and salvation. The process of 'healing', 'elevating', and 'consummating' embodies a degree of continuity between what God has already blessed them with and what they become.

Ad Gentes proceeds to talk of 'the seeds of the Word' that are 'hidden' in 'the national and *religious traditions*' of various peoples and that need to be 'gladly and reverently uncovered'. The decree then characterizes these 'seeds of the Word' as 'the riches which the bountiful God has distributed to the nations'. The disciples of Christ should 'try to illuminate these riches with the light of the Gospel, to set them free, and to bring them back to the dominion of God the Saviour' (*AG* 11; italics mine). Thus the move to Christian faith involves both a revealing or enlightening process (riches being illuminated 'with the

---

9. Earlier *Ad Gentes* used two verbs, 'illuminate' and 'heal' to describe what is needed for the religious 'undertakings (incepta)' that develop under the providential 'pedagogy' of God, with 'illuminate' applying presumably to ideas and 'heal' to practices (*AG* 3).

light of the Gospel') and a saving liberation (riches being set free). But this happens to people who have already been richly blessed by the grace of God and enjoy some measure of the presence of the Word. Talk of the 'seeds of the Word' that have been sown by God in 'the religious traditions' of various peoples and 'riches distributed' by 'the bountiful God' prioritize the divine initiative (and presence), rather than any human search. To be sure, the language about these riches being 'illuminated' and 'set free' obviously suggests that, before the gospel is accepted, the religious situation is not yet as complete and perfect as it could be. Nevertheless, the decree envisages what God has already done in the 'religious traditions' of different nations by 'sowing' in them the seeds of the Word and by 'distributing' to them 'the riches' of divine grace.[10]

A later article takes up again 'the seeds of the Word' by stating that 'the Holy Spirit calls all human beings to Christ through the seeds of the Word and the preaching of the Gospel' (*AG* 15). This is to picture the process of moving to Christian faith happening through the word of preaching being addressed to people who, through 'the seeds of the Word', already enjoy, albeit mysteriously, the hidden presence of Christ.

Finally, with an eye on Buddhist, Hindu, and Muslim prayer-life and asceticism, *Ad Gentes* encourages Roman Catholic religious who work in missionary situations to 'consider attentively how traditions of asceticism and contemplation, the *seeds* of which have been sometimes planted by God in ancient cultures, could be taken up into Christian religious life' (*AG* 18). This last appeal by *Ad Gentes* to the theological theme of 'seeds of the Word' clarifies quite explicitly what has hitherto taken the form of a 'divine passive': it is God the Holy Spirit who sows or plants these seeds. The passage also specifies one form of the 'good'

---

10. 'The riches distributed to the nations' deftly echo the promise to God's royal son in Ps. 2: 8: 'I will make the nations your heritage, and the ends of the earth your possession' (NRSV). Where *AG* 11 speaks of 'religious traditions' activated by 'seeds of the Word' and *AG* 18 points to 'traditions of asceticism and contemplation' as an example of such religious traditions, *AG* 22 shows itself more cautious by talking of 'the socio-cultural' regions of the world, with their 'customs and traditions, wisdom and teaching, professions and disciplines' and their 'philosophy and wisdom, customs, concept of life, and social order', without specifying anything of all that as 'religious'. However, this article remarks that Christians should carefully examine how 'faith can seek understanding by keeping in mind (ratione habita) the philosophy and wisdom of the peoples'.

that has been sown and 'the riches' that have been distributed by God: the ascetic and contemplative traditions that could be incorporated into the lives of Christian religious institutes. This clarification and specification complete the development *Ad Gentes* gave to what *Lumen Gentium* had retrieved from Justin and other early Church writers about the theme of 'the seeds of the Word'.

(3) *Ad Gentes*, when characterizing the religious situation of those who have not or who have not yet accepted faith in Christ, picks up the 'double terminology' we already saw in *Lumen Gentium* and *Nostra Aetate* but in this case follows the Johannine terminology precisely (see John 1: 14, 17). While 'the word of preaching and the celebration of the sacraments' 'make Christ, the author of salvation, present', what-ever elements of 'truth and grace', which are 'already found among nations', 'are, as it were, a secret presence of God'. This may sound like setting 'the presence of God' over against the presence of Christ. But the article at once makes it clear that Christ, 'the author of salvation' is also 'the author' of these elements of 'truth and grace', already found among the nations before they hear the word of Christian preaching (*AG* 9). The 'secret presence of God' is equivalently the secret pres-ence of Christ. As the giver of the gifts of truth and grace, Christ comes with the gifts.

'Truth and grace' characterize what 'the seeds of the Word' bring. It is a matter of the (a) revealing and (b) saving presence and activity of Christ, with 'truth' pointing to (a) and 'grace' to (b).

(4) At the close of Chapter 1, we recalled how a theme from Eusebius of Caesarea about 'the preparation for the Gospel' was retrieved by *Lumen Gentium* 16. *Ad Gentes* followed suit and acknowledged that 'human undertakings (incepta), also religious ones', through 'the providence of God' who is 'not far from any one of us' (Acts 17: 27), can prove a 'pedagogy' that leads to 'the true God' and 'a preparation for the Gospel' (*AG* 3). Unlike *Lumen Gentium* (16, n. 20), the decree does not refer in a footnote to Eusebius but cites Irenaeus and Clement of Alexandria (*AG* 3, n. 2).

The theme of 'the preparation for the Gospel' surfaces only three times in the sixteen documents of Vatican II: in the passages just indicated from *Lumen Gentium* and *Ad Gentes*, and within a somewhat different context in *Gaudium et Spes* (*GS* 40) where it concerns what the Church 'receives from the modern world' (*GS* 44). Where *Lumen*

Gentium 16 considers 'preparation for the Gospel' to be all that is 'good or true' (found before accepting faith in Christ) 'given by him who enlightens all human beings in order that they may finally have life' (John 1: 4, 9), *Ad Gentes* 3 speaks of this preparation taking place through 'human undertakings', including religious ones, that are providentially guided by God. John's Gospel inspires the first way (found in *LG*) of describing the 'preparation for the Gospel', and the Acts of the Apostles (esp. Ch. 17) the second way (found in *AG*). Neither way envisages the search for God involving merely human efforts. For the first way, the light and life coming from the Word of God are essential; for the second way, God is the intimately present Pedagogue whose providential guidance prepares people to receive the gospel.

When appropriating the language of Eusebius of Caesarea, Vatican II leaves the readers with the question: since God or, equivalently, the Word of God is constantly present in the preparation for the gospel, should we recognize this divine activity to be not only revealing and saving but also at work on people everywhere? Should we agree that, right there at the stage of preparation, the revelation and salvation of God are already having their impact on those who have not or have not yet explicitly embraced Christian faith?

(5) A fifth item to be retrieved from the missionary decree is the call to dialogue and collaboration which, in our previous chapter, we saw *Nostra Aetate* embracing. In lyric language, *Ad Gentes* describes the 'sincere and patient dialogue' with the religious others to be expected of Christians engaged in missionary activity. Thus the disciples of Jesus, 'profoundly imbued by' his Spirit, will be able to 'learn what riches the bountiful God has distributed to the nations', so that they might 'try to illuminate these riches with the light of the Gospel, to set them free, and bring them back to the dominion of God the Saviour' (*AG* 11).

This 'fraternal dialogue' should lead Christians to 'collaborate with all others', both Christians and non-Christians, 'in the right ordering of economic and social affairs'. Another lyric article spells out the collaboration called for in the areas of education, health care, and the work for 'better living conditions' and 'peace' (*AG* 12). Such collaboration should also look beyond 'Christians and non-Christians' to include 'members of international associations' (*AG* 41).

Naturally those being trained for the ordained ministry in missionary areas should study 'the social, economic and cultural conditions of their own people'. This will better prepare them 'for fraternal dialogue with non-Christians' (*AG* 16).[11] 'Dialogue with non-Christian religions and cultures' also requires taking advantage of the resources of institutes that specialize in missiology and in such disciplines as ethnology, linguistics, and the history of religions (*AG* 34; see 41).

In the early twenty-first century, interreligious dialogue and working together with others, including non-Christians, may appear obvious obligations to be embraced by Catholic and other Christian believers. But such interfaith consciousness took centuries to emerge. No previous ecumenical councils of Catholic Christianity ever imagined, let alone encouraged, the dialogue and collaboration with 'religious others' inculcated by *Nostra Aetate*, *Ad Gentes*, and *Gaudium et Spes*. These officially promulgated texts have shaped the story of Roman Catholicism in a way from which there is no turning back.

Revelation and Faith for All

To explain 'the preparation for the Gospel' (*AG* 3), the Decree on the Church's Missionary Activity quotes, in the corresponding footnote 2, two passages from Irenaeus: 'the Word existing with God, through whom all things were made, . . . was always present to the human race'. Hence, 'from the beginning the Son, being present in his creation, reveals (*revelat*) the Father to all whom the Father desires, at the time and in the manner desired by the Father' (*Adversus Haereses*, 3. 18. 1; 4. 6. 7). Thus *Ad Gentes* aligns itself with Irenaeus in acknowledging the Word of God as the agent in creating all things (see John 1: 1–3, 10; 1 Cor. 8: 6; Heb. 1: 2). Consequently the Word has 'always' been present to the entire human race, and not merely to certain groups or nations.

11. Vatican II's Declaration on Christian Education (*Gravissimum Educationis*), promulgated on 28 October 1965, emphasized the duty of all faculties and departments of theological studies, and not merely those in mission countries, to promote 'dialogue' not only 'with separated brethren' (= other Christians) but also 'with non-Christians' (*GE* 11).

Granted the Christological origin and character of creation, right 'from the beginning' of human history, the Son has been revealing the Father to human beings. In all its sixteen documents, it is only here that Vatican II quite explicitly applies the verb 'reveal' to the knowledge of God mediated through the created world. Clearly this revelation of God through creation and 'ordinary' human history allows for endless variety, as 'the Son reveals the Father to all whom the Father desires and at the time and in the manner desired by the Father'. In contemporary terms popularized by Karl Rahner (Chapter 2 above), Irenaeus spoke of the 'general' history of revelation (and salvation), in which from the origins of the human story the Son of God has been revealing the Father.

The two quotations from Irenaeus highlight the universal divine activity by which the Word/Son of God prepares people for the coming of the gospel. Using the term 'reveal' for the divine activity implies the counterpart of human faith. It is with true faith that human beings respond to the initiative of the Son of God who, being present in and through creation, reveals God to them. The decree expressly acknowledges a faith-response to the personal divine revelation made by the non-evangelized: 'in ways known to himself' God can lead 'those who, through no fault of their own, are ignorant of the Gospel to that faith without which it is impossible to please him (Heb. 11: 6)' (AG 7).

Unlike the First Vatican Council, which appealed to Hebrews 11: 6 with regard to Christian believers persevering in their faith (DzH 3012; ND 122), Vatican II appreciated the significance of this verse for humanity in general, even if it is only in *Ad Gentes* 7 that the text makes an appearance in any of the Council's documents.

Recognizing explicitly that the divine activity of revelation and the human response of faith also take place among those who follow other religions or none at all occurs briefly in *Ad Gentes*. But the decree stands apart in being the first text from the twenty-one ecumenical councils of Catholic Christianity to acknowledge expressly (a) that God's self-revelation reaches all people, and (b) that human beings, no matter who they are and where they are, can and should respond with faith.

In *Dominus Iesus*,[12] issued in September 2000, the Congregation for the Doctrine of the Faith taught that 'theological faith (fides theologalis)' was not found 'in other religions', since faith entails 'accepting

12. *AAS* 82 (2000), 742–65.

revealed truth'.[13] Other religions enjoy only 'belief (credulitas)', which is 'religious experience still in search of absolute truth and not yet reaching an assent to God who reveals himself'.[14] This teaching, however, seems to forget that God is already present in any religious search (Anselm, *Proslogion* 1). It also appears to be incompatible with *Ad Gentes* 7, which took seriously Hebrews 11: 6 ('without faith it is impossible to please God') and acknowledged that God can lead to faith those who do not know the gospel and who obviously in the vast majority of cases follow other religions. Briefly but clearly, Vatican II's Decree on the Church's Missionary Activity, unlike *Dominus Iesus*, allowed that the divine self-revelation and responding human faith can take place among those who follow 'other religions'.

Ad Gentes respected the mystery of how such revelation may achieve its goal by calling forth faith (in 'ways known' to God), but through citing Hebrews it lets us fill out some of what can be said about the faith of 'others' who belong to the 'general' history of revelation and salvation. *Ad Gentes* set the stage for us to unpack the key verse in the Letter to the Hebrews. But before doing that, let me summarize what we have drawn from the decree.

- ✎ Besides repeating classic texts on God's saving plans for all 'others' (1 Tim. 2: 4; John 11: 52; 2 Cor. 5: 19), the decree (*GS* 7) introduces a key verse about salvation coming only through Jesus (Acts 4: 12).

- ✎ Far beyond *LG* 17, the decree develops the theme of 'the seeds of the Word' sown by God and 'hidden' everywhere, in particular, in 'religious traditions' (*AG* 9, 11, 15, 18).

- ✎ The 'secretly present' Christ is 'the author' of elements of 'truth and grace' found 'among the nations' (*AG* 9).

---

13. This is to take 'faith' primarily in the sense of believing that what God has revealed is true, as taught by Vatican I in *Dei Filius*, its 1870 constitution on Catholic faith (DzH 3008; ND 118). Yet *Dominus Iesus*, as we will see at once, by also speaking of 'an assent to God who reveals himself', approaches the primary sense given to faith by the Vatican II in *Dei Verbum*, its 1965 constitution on revelation: namely, faith as the personal response of the whole human being (and not merely the assent of one's intellect) in obedience to the self-revealing God (*DV* 5).

14. Here 'credulitas' has been regularly translated as 'belief', but clearly both in Latin and in English, 'credulity' has negative connotations, suggesting someone who is gullible and naïve. As we will see in Chapter 8, years earlier (in 1979) in *Redemptor Hominis* Pope John Paul II had chosen a different term, 'firm conviction (firma persuasio)', when referring to strongly committed adherents of other religions.

∽ The divine pedagogy prepares the way for the gospel (*AG* 3).

∽ The Holy Spirit calls human beings to Christ through 'the seeds of the Word' (*ad intra*) and 'the preaching of the Gospel' (*ad extra*) (*AG* 15).

∽ In the case of those who accept the gospel, the good already 'sown in their hearts and minds' is 'healed, elevated, and consummated' (*AG* 9).

∽ The decree calls for dialogue and collaboration with the religious 'others' (*AG* 11, 12, 16, 34, 41).

∽ Most importantly, the decree states that the Son, 'present in creation', reveals the Father universally (*AG* 3, n. 2) and human beings can respond with saving faith (*AG* 7).

The Structures of Faith

Ad Gentes appeals to Hebrews and its unqualified statement that 'without faith it is impossible to please God'. This statement leaves behind any talk about merely human (religious) *beliefs* elaborated through an unaided search for God. Without responding in *faith* to the divine revelation, no one can 'please' God and receive salvation. Putting this positively, we can say that the offer of light and life to everyone makes possible, respectively, faith and salvation.

The verse that concerns us fits into a long section on faith: Hebrews 11: 1–12: 27. The passage opens by declaring: 'Now faith is the assurance [or reality or evidence/proof] of things hoped for, the proof of things not seen. By this [faith] the elders [our ancestors] received approval. By faith we understand that the universe was fashioned by the word of God, so that from what cannot be seen that which is seen has come into being' (Heb. 11: 1–3). This prepares the way for the verse which is central to our issue: 'without faith it is impossible to please God; for whoever would approach him must believe that he exists and that he rewards those who seek him' (Heb. 11: 6).[15] But, before examining this key verse, what do the opening three verses say about faith and its 'content'?

15. On these and other relevant verses on faith, see Christopher R. Koester, *Hebrews* (New York: Doubleday, 2001), 468–553.

Those verses hint at the future. Divine promises (presumably of some eternal inheritance) have aroused the hope of human beings and their trust that God will keep these promises, which involve future 'things that are not [yet] seen' but are to come. Faith also entails a view of the past. We understand by faith the unseen origin of the world: it 'was fashioned by the word of God'. Just as people of faith rely on the word of God about the *genesis* of the universe, so they rely on the word of divine promise when considering the *goal* of the world and their own existence now and in the future. Both in their view of the past and their hope for the future, the existence of those who have faith remains entwined with the life of the invisible God.

Faith cannot prove the unseen 'things' of God; rather, faith itself is 'the proof' of these things. As Christopher Koester comments, 'the unseen realities of God give proof of their existence by their power to evoke faith'. It is the divine reality that creates faith, not faith that 'creates' the divine reality. The divine 'object' of faith and hope 'can be known by its effects on human beings'.[16] The invisible power of God evokes faith and hope, and directs human beings towards their, as yet invisible, goal. One cannot see God and the power of God, but one can know the divine power from its results. Both faith and the created universe witness to the invisible power of God, and the reality of the unseen world of God.

In Hebrews 11, the opening description of faith makes no mention of Christ. He will appear later, when the list of the heroes and heroines of faith culminates with the case of 'Jesus, the pioneer and perfecter of [his own] faith' (Heb. 12: 2), who was, one might say, 'faith personified'. The first verses of Hebrews 11 invoke 'the elders' or 'ancestors', people who have been honoured and approved by God for their perseverance in faith. Then follow examples of those who have lived on the basis of faith, with particular attention paid to Abraham, Sarah, and Moses. Some of those who exemplified faith (Abel, Enoch, and Noah) were understood to have existed prior to Abraham, Sarah, and the formation of the chosen people. One significant figure of faith is 'Rahab the prostitute', an outsider who appeared in the story of the conquest of the promised land. Abel and Noah are identified as 'righteous'—a useful reminder that their faith *and* righteousness

16. Ibid., 480.

responded, respectively, to the revelatory and salvific dimensions of the self-communication of God. They found in God the light of faith and the life of a righteous existence.

Even though it does not explicitly do so, the opening account of faith in Hebrews allows us to glimpse the human questions to which faith supplies answers. (1) Is there anything beyond the visible world? Are we bonded with things unseen or, rather, with the unseen God? (2) Where do we and our universe come from? Has 'that which is seen' come into being from 'that which cannot be seen': that is to say, from God and his creative word? We come into a world which is not of our making. Do we nourish faith in the invisible Creator from whom all things have come? Such faith is close to gratitude towards the unseen Giver, a gratitude for the past from which we have emerged and for the future to which we have been summoned. (3) Does it matter how we behave? Should we imitate our 'ancestors', approved by God for their persevering faith? Should we live as pilgrims afflicted by various sufferings,[17] but always hoping for 'a better country' (Heb. 11: 10) and yearning for a God-given life to come? In short, may we trust God as the One who 'rewards those who seek him'?

These questions are obviously not limited to Christians but belong to everyone, and form a shorter version of the list of questions provided by *Nostra Aetate* (Chapter 4 above). They yield a vision of the questions that the Holy Spirit can stir in the hearts of people everywhere and so open them to the hidden but powerful presence and activity of Christ. Hebrews 11: 6, in particular, lets us glimpse something of the shape that faith can take in human beings anywhere.

The Faith of the Religious Others

Five elements show up in Hebrews 11: 6 and are clarified by related statements occurring elsewhere in Hebrews.

---

17. Right from the example of Abel (Heb. 11: 4) through to the end of the list of named or unnamed heroes and heroines of faith (Heb. 11: 38), sufferings of various kinds are recalled as having afflicted those who persevere in faith. This feature of Hebrews 11 calls to mind findings about suffering and deep experiences of the mysterious God gathered by the Religious Experience Research Unit established in Oxford by Sir Alister Hardy and later directed by David Hay (see Chapter 4 above).

(1) First, subsequent exhortations fill out what 'pleasing God' entails: 'let us give thanks, by which we offer God worship in a pleasing way with reverence and awe' (12: 28). Such grateful worship of God issues in acts of kindness that build up community: 'do not neglect to do good and to share what you have; for such sacrifices are pleasing to God' (13: 16). A further verse pulls together such 'pleasing God' in terms of doing the divine will: 'May the God of peace . . . make you complete in everything good so that you may do his will, working among us that which is pleasing in his sight' (13: 20–1). We could sum up what this view of 'pleasing God' involves: it envisages a faith that gratefully offers to God a reverent worship and does the divine will through kindly deeds in the service of others. Obviously explicit faith in Christ should vigorously empower the life of faith. Yet a vertical relationship with God (through grateful worship) and a horizontal relationship with other human beings (through self-sacrificing kindness), while calling for the invisible support of 'grace' (emphasized by *Lumen Gentium* [Chapter 3 above]), do not as such depend on a conscious relationship with Christ. A faith that pleases God is a possibility open to all.

(2) Various other passages in Hebrews illustrate what 'drawing near to God' (11: 6) involves. It means approaching God in prayer and worshipping God. Thus the anonymous author of Hebrews writes of 'drawing near to the throne of grace' (4: 16). Christians will be conscious of doing this through Jesus, 'since he always lives to make intercession for them' (7: 25). But approaching God in prayer and worship does not demand an awareness that such 'drawing near' depends on the priestly intercession of the risen and actively present Christ. That intercession functions, whether or not worshippers are conscious of the presence of Christ when they approach God in prayer.

(3) Obviously those who approach God in prayer display faith that he *exists*. They answer the question 'is there anything beyond the visible world?' by bonding with the invisible God. Their faith inevitably involves accepting that the world has been made by God, whom they worship as the unseen Creator from whom all things come and towards whom all things are directed. God is both the origin and the goal of the world (Heb. 2: 10).

(4) Faith accepts God not only as the origin of the universe but also as the One who 'rewards those who seek him'. This means letting God be the future goal of one's existence. God is accepted as just and faithful to his promises, however they are construed. In some way those with faith live as pilgrims who hope for 'a better country'. Clearly those who embrace faith do not always enjoy the 'normal' (material) blessings in this life. It is precisely that challenge which prompts the author of Hebrews into appealing for endurance: 'do not abandon that confidence of yours; it brings a great reward' (10: 35). At least here, the author does not specify what shape this great reward will take, nor does he distinguish between 'rewards' for his Christian readers and for those others who 'seek' God. Christians and other 'God-seekers' alike are summoned by faith to put their future in the hands of the just and faithful God (see 10: 23).

(5) 'Seeking God' expresses a permanent attitude that a sincere 'drawing near to God' in worship and prayer presupposes. One approaches God in prayer, because one hopes to receive a favourable response, whatever form it may take. 'Drawing near to the throne of grace' calls for a confidence that one's prayers will be heard. The author of Hebrews leaves matters quite open—as regards the when, the where, and the how of the 'reward' for those who seek God in prayer. What emerges here recalls the open-ended confidence inculcated by Jesus' teaching: 'Ask and you will receive. Seek and you will find. Knock and the door will be opened to you' (Matt. 7: 7). Nothing is indicated about when, where, and how persevering prayer will be answered. Everything is concentrated in the assurance that it will be answered.

As I stated above, the five major themes contained in Hebrews 11: 6 let us glimpse something of the shape taken by the faith of the religious 'others'. But to appreciate the richness of this verse, one must read it not only within its immediate context but also, as we have done, within the context of the entire letter. That is rarely, if ever done by theologians who cite the verse. Admittedly, the Letter to the Hebrews addresses Christians and does so in the knowledge that they have been enduring persecutions and sufferings of various kinds. Yet, as is clear from the majestic opening verses (1: 1–4), salvation through faith is offered to all people and on the basis of the universal sovereignty of Christ as Son of God and unique high priest. A comment made by

Luke Timothy Johnson on 1 Timothy 2: 5 ('God is one') applies
equally well to Hebrews and the vision it offers about God and faith:
'If God is to be more than a tribal deity, then God must be one for all
humans; and if God is to be righteous (fair), then there must be some
principle by which all humans can respond to God: faith.'[18] Here we
might take up a text originally applied to Christians (Col. 3: 3) and
extend it to God's other peoples: 'through faith your life is hidden with
Christ in God's kingdom'.

Divine Initiative and Obedience for Salvation

(1) A casual reading of Hebrews 11: 6 and the use made of it by some
theologians might encourage the conclusion that faith is shown by
'outsiders' through their 'performance' in seeking and approaching
God. It could seem that it is a question of their successful initiative in
seeking God rather than God's prior initiative in seeking them. They
would differ then from Abraham, Sarah, and others listed in Hebrews
11, who by faith obeyed a call that came to them from God. In such
cases drawn from the particular story of Judaism, human faith
responded to a prior initiative from God. But what of the view of
'outsiders' taken or, at least implied, by Hebrews?

Does Hebrews endorse or at least allow for the notion that we
human beings may seek God in ways that can bring us to the goal of
our existence in God? Several hundred years after Hebrews was
written, such an idea lay behind the position taken by Symmachus
(d.402), a rhetorician who defended the ancient Roman religion and
petitioned the emperor to reinstate the goddess 'Victory' in the senate.
In his memorandum he justified his request by arguing for a plurality of
ways to God: 'we cannot arrive by one and the same path at so great a
secret'.[19] Clearly Symmachus presupposed that it is we human beings
who approach and come to God, rather than vice versa. Hebrews,
however, begins by highlighting the prior initiative of God who 'in
these last days has spoken to us by a Son' (1: 2). Other New Testament

---

18. L. T. Johnson, *The First and Second Letters to Timothy* (New York: Doubleday, 2001),
    197.
19. For the plea of Symmachus and St Ambrose's reply to him, see J. Stevenson (ed.),
    Creeds, Councils and Controversies (London: SPCK, 1981), 121–5, at 122.

authors agree with this conviction about the divine initiative being the pre-eminent factor (e.g. John 3: 16–17; Rom. 8: 3–4; Gal. 4: 4–7). Right from the start of its description of faith and examples of faith, Hebrews points to the prior activity of God in rousing faith. By calling faith 'the assurance of things hoped for', our text implies prior promises coming from God and evoking the response of human hope. By naming faith as 'the proof of things not seen', Hebrews suggests the unseen reality of God that gives proof of its existence by its power to call forth faith.

Right from New Testament times and the teaching of Hebrews, Paul, and John, Christians have insisted on the prior action of God in summoning forth human faith (in the divine self-revelation) and hope (in the divine promises of salvation). In the second century Irenaeus wrote: 'no one can know God unless God teaches [him or her]; that is to say, without God, God is not to be known (Deum scire nemo potest, nisi Deo docente; hoc est, sine Deo non cognosci Deum)' (*Adversus Haereses*, 4. 6. 4).

The roll call of heroes and heroines of faith in Hebrews 11 introduces only once 'obedience', a theme closely allied to that of faith. It does so when expounding the central example of Abraham: 'by faith Abraham *obeyed* when he was called to set out for a place that he was to receive as an inheritance; and he set out not knowing where he was going' (Heb. 11: 8). Elsewhere obedience is a key feature in the plot of Hebrews, not least when it portrays the prayer and obedience of Jesus himself. By obediently submitting to the divine will and facing death, he 'became the source (cause) of eternal salvation for all who obey him' (5: 7–9). Thus the faithful obedience of Jesus formed God's way of saving human beings.

But where does that leave all those innumerable 'outsiders' who do not know Jesus and hence cannot consciously obey him and experience in him the cause/source of their eternal salvation? This question can be met by observing the qualification that Hebrews 11 introduces into the drama of human salvation. We presume that the 'great cloud of witnesses' (Heb. 12: 1) cited in the previous chapter of Hebrews, either by name or in general, were eventually blessed with eternal salvation. Yet they all existed before Christ and could not have consciously obeyed him. If they had known, they would presumably have obeyed him. The same, one can argue, is true of all those innumerable 'outsiders' whose faith enables them to 'please' God.

Without knowing Jesus and hence without the possibility of consciously obeying him, they mysteriously experience in him (and his
Holy Spirit) the cause of their salvation. In their case faith does not
include conscious obedience towards Jesus, but that does not prevent
him from proving 'the pioneer of their salvation' (Heb. 2: 10).

SIX

The Contribution of
Gaudium et Spes

It is clear that day by day all nations are coming into closer unity, that people of different culture and religion are being bound together with closer considerations, and, finally, that there is a growing consciousness of each one's own responsibility.

Vatican II, Declaration on Religious Liberty, 15

In the relation of human beings to this world, there are certain transitions to the infinite, perspectives opened out, to which all are led, so that their mind may find the way to the universe.

Friedrich Schleiermacher, *On Religion: Speeches to its Cultured Despisers*

Any integral account of what the Second Vatican Council taught about the religious situation of 'the others' requires that we treat a final document promulgated on the same day as *Ad Gentes*, 7 December 1965. The last and longest text to come from the Council and the first conciliar document in the history of Catholic Christianity to be addressed to all human beings, the Pastoral Constitution on the Church in the Modern World (*Gaudium et Spes*) develops some of the themes that we have already retrieved, especially from *Nostra Aetate* and *Ad Gentes*, as well as adding its own new accents. We begin with its version of the unity of the human race.[1]

---

1. See Charles Moeller, 'Pastoral Constitution on the Church in the Modern World: History of the Constitution', in Herbert Vorgrimler (ed.), *Commentary on the Documents of Vatican II*, trans. W. J. O'Hara, v (London: Burns & Oates, 1969), 1–76; Hans-Joachim Sander, '*Gaudium et Spes*', in Peter Hünermann and Bernd Jochen Hilberath (eds), *Herders Theologischer Kommentar zum Zweiten Vatikanischen Konzil*, iv (Freiburg im Breisgau: Herder, 2005), 581–886; Giovanni Turbanti, *Un Concilio per il Mondo*

The Unity of All Human Beings

Like the Declaration on the Relation of the Church to Non-Christian Religions, *Gaudium et Spes* points to their common origin (as created in the image of God) and their common destiny (with God) when establishing the unity and equality that exists between all human beings, Christians and non-Christians alike (*GS* 22). But, where *Nostra Aetate* mentioned only once how everyone is created in the image and likeness of God (*NA* 5), this becomes a leitmotif in *Gaudium et Spes* (*GS* 12, 22, 24, 29, 34, 41, 52, and 68).[2] The constitution explores the possibilities of establishing on this basis the essential equality of all people and the social justice that follows from that equality: 'all human beings are created in God's image'; hence 'every form of social or cultural discrimination in fundamental personal rights, on the grounds of sex, race, colour, social condition, language, or religion, must be overcome and eradicated as contrary to God's design' (*GS* 29).

Nostra Aetate, as we saw, introduced a consequence that follows closely from being created in the divine image and likeness: namely, the *dignity* of all human beings 'and the rights that flow from it' (*NA* 5). *Ad Gentes* hoped that collaboration with others in providing education would help to 'raise human dignity and promote more human conditions' of life (*AG* 12). *Gaudium et Spes* presses on to speak of 'the sublime dignity of the human person', who 'stands above all things and

Moderno: La Redazione della Costituzione Pastorale 'Gaudium et Spes' del Vaticano II (Bologna: Il Mulino, 2000); Norman Tanner, 'The Church in the World (*Ecclesia ad Extra*)', in Giuseppe Alberigo and Joseph A. Komonchak (eds), *History of Vatican II*, iv (Maryknoll, NY: Orbis, 2003), 269–386, at 270–330; Riccardo Burigana and Giovanni Turbanti, 'The Intersession: Preparing the Conclusion of the Council', in *History of Vatican II*, iv, 453–615, at 518–31; Gilles Routhier, 'Finishing the Work Begun: The Trying Experience of the Fourth Period', in *History of Vatican II*, v (2006), 49–184, at 122–77; Peter Hünermann, 'The Final Weeks of the Council', in *History of Vatican II*, v, 363–483, at 386–427.

2. See Joseph Ratzinger, 'The Dignity of the Human Person', in *Commentary on the Documents of Vatican II*, v, 115–63, at 119–23; Otto Semmelroth, 'The Community of Mankind', in *Commentary on the Documents of Vatican II*, v, 164–81, at 166, 175–6. Vatican II was the first ecumenical council in the history of Catholic Christianity to introduce the theme of human beings created in the image and likeness of God—a theme retrieved from Irenaeus, Athanasius of Alexandria, Basil of Caesarea, Gregory of Nyssa, and other early Christian writers; see Gerald O'Collins and Mario Farrugia, *Catholicism: The Story of Catholic Christianity* (Oxford: Oxford University Press, 2003), 169–73.

whose rights and duties are universal and inviolable'.[3] The document lists various universal rights and ends with the right 'to act according to the right norm of conscience' and to safeguard 'just freedom also in matters of religion' (GS 26).

The dignity and rights of all human beings, whatever their religious convictions and observance, also form a leitmotif in the Constitution on the Church in the Modern World. One article emphasizes 'the dignity of human nature', 'the personal dignity and freedom of human beings', and 'the dignity of conscience'. Not surprisingly it also emphasizes the personal rights of human beings, and sees these rights being 'promoted all over the world' (GS 41).

Gaudium et Spes, as we have just observed, develops massively the brief remarks of *Nostra Aetate* about all human beings sharing the dignity and rights that flow from being created in the divine image and likeness. The constitution adds two further, related realities that underpin the unity of all human beings: the voice of *conscience* and the *natural law* which should guide the actions of everyone. As we showed in Chapter 3, *Lumen Gentium* presented positively the eternal prospects of those who, through no fault of their own, do not know the gospel of Christ and who, nevertheless, 'seek God with a sincere heart and, under the influence of grace, try in their actions to fulfil his will made known to them through the dictate of their conscience' (*LG* 16). This document paid brief respect to the guidance of one's conscience and spoke, albeit generally, about fulfilling the divine will. *Gaudium et Spes* has much more to say about both themes.

'Human beings have a law written in their heart by God', the constitution declares, and at once adds: 'Their very dignity consists in complying with this law, according to which they will be judged. Conscience is their most private core and sanctuary. There they are alone with God, whose voice echoes in their inmost being' (*GS* 16).[4] The Declaration on Religious Liberty (*Dignitatis Humanae*), promulgated on the same day as

---

3. In his encyclical *Pacem in Terris* (1963), Pope John XXIII had much to say about human dignity and rights.
4. Ratzinger commented on this article: 'conscience is presented as the meeting-point and common ground of Christians and non-Christians and consequently as the real hinge on which dialogue turns. Fidelity to conscience unites Christians and non-Christians and enables them to work together to solve the moral tasks of mankind, just as it compels them both to humble and open inquiry into truth' ('The Dignity of the Human Person', 136).

Gaudium et Spes, proposes the same equation of law–conscience–God: 'It is through their conscience that human beings perceive and acknowledge the decrees of the divine law, which they are bound to follow faithfully in all their activity, so that they may come to God, their final end' (*DH* 2). Given its central theme, *Dignitatis Humanae* stresses that 'the very dignity of the human person' involves 'the duty and therefore the right to seek for the truth in religious matters' (*DH* 2, 3). *Gaudium et Spes* applies the equation more broadly: for instance, in its attempt to curb the savagery of war as being incompatible with the natural law that binds all human beings. 'The Council intends to recall the permanent force of the natural right of peoples and its universal principles. The very conscience of the human race firmly and ever more emphatically proclaims these principles' (*GS* 79).[5]

Gaudium et Spes here speaks of 'the natural right of peoples' and 'its universal principles'. Elsewhere it speaks of 'the divine law' (*GS* 43, 50, 51, 87, 89), 'the natural law' (*GS* 74, 87, 89), 'the eternal law' (*GS* 78), or 'the law written in the human heart by God' (*GS* 16).[6] It is through the voice of conscience that all human beings, whatever their religious convictions, can hear and follow the universal law of God. Christians and those of other faiths all possess a conscience that enables and summons them to follow the requirements of the natural law. On the human side, conscience and, on the divine side, 'the eternal law' bind people together, and play their essential role in constituting the unity of all human beings—a solidarity (*GS* 32) that embraces the world and makes every person 'my neighbour' or 'my other self' (*GS* 27).[7]

A growing worldwide sensitivity to the universal rights and duties of human beings belongs to that 'evolution towards the unity' of all peoples which, like *Nostra Aetate* (see Chapter 4 above), *Gaudium et Spes* finds in contemporary society (*GS* 42). The Declaration on Religious Liberty put this conviction firmly on display: 'it is clear that day by day all nations are coming into closer unity, that people of different culture and religion are being bound together by closer

5. On *GS* 79, see René Coste, 'The Fostering of Peace and the Promotion of the Community of Nations', in *Commentary on the Documents of Vatican II*, v, 347–69, at 352–6.
6. This language about God 'writing in the human heart' and the divine voice 'echoing in the inmost being' of human beings (*GS* 16) makes sense only if we recognize that the divine self-revelation reaches every human heart and every human being.
7. See Semmelroth, 'The Community of Mankind', in *Commentary on the Documents of Vatican II*, v, 172–3.

considerations, and, finally, that there is a growing consciousness of each one's own responsibility' (*DH* 15).

Questions and Mystery

The way that *Gaudium et Spes* also follows and expands the 'questioning' approach of *Nostra Aetate* (Chapter 4 above) should seize and hold our attention. Right from its preface, the constitution recognizes how 'the human race is often disturbed by troubling questions about the contemporary evolution of the world, about its place and role in the universe, about the meaning of individual and collective endeavour, and, finally, about the purpose [or final end] of things and human beings' (*GS* 3). The very next article takes up again 'the constant questions human beings [raise] about the meaning of the present and future life, and about their mutual relationship' (*GS* 4).

The introduction to the constitution then dedicates a whole article to the deeper questioning that human beings cannot avoid. It lists 'the most fundamental' of such questions: 'What is the human being? What is the meaning of suffering, evil, and death, which continue to exist, despite so much progress? What is the purpose of [all] those achievements, purchased at so high a price? What can human beings contribute to society, and what can they expect from it? What will follow after this earthly life?' (*GS* 10).[8] Back in Chapter 4, we discussed a similar list of pervasive and perplexing questions, to which, according to the opening article of the Declaration on the Church's Relation to Non-Christian Religions, the various religions of the world offer their answers. Given that *Gaudium et Spes* addresses human 'society' in general and scrutinizes its 'progress' and 'achievements', it phrases the questions differently. Where *Nostra Aetate* asked succinctly, 'What is good, what is sin, and what is the way to true happiness?', the constitution asks: 'What is the purpose of all those achievements, purchased at so high a price? What can human beings contribute to society, and what can they expect from it?' The seven questions raised by *Nostra Aetate* climaxed with the God-question: 'What is that ultimate and ineffable mystery which enfolds our existence, from which we

8. On *GS* 10, see Moeller, 'Preface and Introductory Statement', in *Commentary on the Documents of Vatican II*, v, 77–114, at 111–14.

take our origin and towards which we move?' The six questions listed by *Gaudium et Spes* do not explicitly include one concerned with God, but they lead to the Council announcing its intention to clarify 'the *mystery* of the human person' (*GS* 10; italics mine). Here 'mystery' points to the deepest truths about the meaning of existence.

What would become the most famous article in *Gaudium et Spes* unfolds the 'mystery' of human beings and the 'mystery' of God (*GS* 22).[9] But before reaching that article, the constitution answers its first question ('What is the human being?') by presenting all human beings, whether Christians or others, as created in the image of God (*GS* 12) and five essentially related themes: the essential nature and experience of human beings (*GS* 14), the human intellect and the need for greater wisdom (*GS* 15), the dignity of conscience (*GS* 16), true human freedom (*GS* 17), and the human future in death and resurrection (*GS* 18).

Then, without specifying the questions at stake, the constitution reiterates that 'all human beings remain a question to themselves, one that is dimly perceived and left unanswered. For, in certain moments, especially in the major events of life, no one can altogether avoid such questioning'. The document adds, however, that God and 'only God replies to this questioning' and does so 'fully and with complete certainty' (*GS* 21).

This sets the stage for the next article which brings Chapter 1 to a climax: 'it is only in the mystery of the Word incarnate that the mystery of human beings becomes truly clear'. In revealing 'the mystery of the Father and his love', Christ 'fully discloses human beings to themselves and brings to light their noblest calling' (*GS* 22). In these few, dense words, the constitution sets out the solution to the self-questioning that leaves us a mystery to ourselves. Through his self-revelation, which also reveals the mystery of God, Christ illuminates once and for all the mystery of the nature and destiny of all human beings. Later in this chapter we will return to article 22, in which Vatican II made one of its most significant contributions to teaching about the religious situation of all human beings.

A later article (on what the Church offers to the world) acts as a postlude to the theme of that questioning which opens up the way to Christ's revelation of two 'mysteries', that of God and that of human

---

9. This was the article from Vatican II that was most quoted or referred to by Pope John Paul II in his official, papal statements; see Sander, '*Gaudium et Spes*', 859–61.

beings. When the Church discloses 'the mystery of God', it 'simultan-eously illuminates for human beings the meaning of their own exist-ence: namely, the inmost truth' about themselves. This postlude reduces the fundamental questions to three: the 'significance' of 'life', 'activity', 'and death'. The 'fullest answer to these questions' is to be found in 'God alone', or, more precisely, 'in the revelation of Christ his Son' (GS 41).

Thus *Gaudium et Spes*, when compared with *Nostra Aetate*, offers a fuller treatment of (a) the fundamental questions that, sooner or later, trouble all human beings and of (b) the answer given by the revelation brought by Jesus Christ. It also adds something further: through this revelation light is shed not only on the 'divine mystery' but also on the 'human mystery'.

Seeds, Preparation for the Gospel, Doublets, Verbs, and Dialogue

Let me turn now to some ideas which concern other living faiths and which earlier documents of the Council attended to, but to which *Gaudium et Spes* hardly adds any particular flavour.

(1) We have already discussed the major role that the theme of 'the seeds of the Word' plays in *Ad Gentes*. The preface to *Gaudium et Spes* recalls 'a certain divine seed planted in human beings' (GS 3). Later the constitution will call this 'the seed of eternity', and does so when reflecting on the mystery of death (GS 18). Finally, when speaking of humanity as a whole, the constitution recognizes how 'every part of the human family carries in itself and in its better traditions some part of the spiritual treasure (thesauri spiritualis) that God has entrusted to humanity' (GS 86). This global affirmation obviously respects the 'better traditions' of other religions, but does not take time out to discern 'the spiritual treasure' God might have entrusted to them. One can make the same comment when the constitution recognizes 'the spiritual ornaments and endowments (animi ornamenta dotesque) of each people or age' (GS 58), without going into detail. At all events, the passage implies that 'ornaments and endowments' come from God—a kind of elegant variation for 'the seeds of the Word' with which 'each people and age' are gifted by God.

(2) Like 'the seeds of the Word', the notion of 'preparation for the Gospel' hardly surfaces in *Gaudium et Spes*. When acknowledging various kinds of help the Church can receive from human society, the constitution understands such help to work towards 'the preparation for the Gospel' (*GS* 40).[10] Specifically, the 'positive values of modern culture' can 'yield some preparation towards accepting the message of the Gospel' (*GS* 57). *Gaudium et Spes* invokes an ancient commonplace coming from Eusebius of Caesarea but leaves its approbation at a very general level.

(3) When examining *Lumen Gentium*, *Nostra Aetate*, and *Ad Gentes*, we noted how they used a 'double' terminology when considering human beings at large—in particular, the state of those who have not yet embraced Christianity or perhaps never will do so. *Gaudium et Spes* follows suit. In a lyrical passage on wisdom, which evokes the wisdom books of the Bible and inserts in a footnote a reference to Sirach (often known as Ecclesiasticus) 17: 7–8, the constitution applauds the way in which wisdom can 'sweetly draw the human mind to look for and to love what is *true and good*' (*GS* 15; italics mine). The same pair ('true and good') turn up again when the document reflects on those with whom Christians engage in dialogue: 'courtesy should not leave us indifferent towards truth and goodness' (*GS* 28). With regard to the great variety of human 'institutions', the Council expresses its esteem for 'whatever that is true, good *and just* to be found in them'(*GS* 42). While justice belongs closely with goodness, presumably our text mentions it explicitly because it has here an eye also on human institutions dealing with fashioning and administering law.

Gaudium et Spes edges beyond earlier documents of the Council by finally adding 'beauty' to the scheme of 'truth and goodness'. In the course of developing some principles on the interaction of culture and faith, the constitution cast its eye over those who work in 'the fields of philosophy, history, mathematics, and natural science' and cultivate the arts. They can bring 'the human family to a higher understanding of what is true, good, and beautiful' (*GS* 57). When commenting on *Nostra Aetate* in Chapter 4, I noted how truth and goodness, but not beauty, feature in its list of primordial questions that lay the ground for

10. On *GS* 40, see Yves Congar, 'The Role of the Church in the Modern World', in *Commentary on the Documents of Vatican II*, v, 202–23, at 217.

religious answers. Now *Gaudium et Spes* makes up for this deficit. It might have done so earlier when remarking on the way human beings 'love what is true and good' (*GS* 15). Augustine vigorously reminds us that beauty, and, above all, the divine beauty elicits our love. But in the spirit of better late than never, we can welcome the addition of beauty. Genuine religious faith, wherever it is found, responds to God, who is infinitely true, good, *and* beautiful.[11]

(4) The triad of truth, goodness, and beauty recurs towards the end of *Gaudium et Spes*, and in the context of some significant *verbs*. The constitution underlines the duty of the Church to '*foster* and *elevate* all that is true, good, and beautiful to be found in the human community' (*GS* 76; italics mine).[12] My last chapter drew attention to the process of 'healing, elevating and consummating' whatever good is found in the hearts and minds of human beings, a process that *Ad Gentes* set at the heart of missionary activity (*AG* 9 and n. 52). A year earlier *Lumen Gentium* had described this process as 'healing, elevating, and consummating' (*LG* 17). The Dogmatic Constitution on the Church had already spoken of the Church 'fostering and adopting, in so far as they are good, the abilities, resources, and customs of people. In adopting [them], she purifies, strengthens, and elevates [them]' (*LG* 13). Beyond question, fostering and elevating 'all that is true, good, and beautiful' in the worldwide community of human beings presupposes recognizing what is 'true, good, and beautiful' in other faiths. Here *Gaudium et Spes* adds something momentous (the beauty already present) to add to the Council's teaching on the religious 'others', and on how the Church should act towards those who come from other faiths and seek baptism.

11. In its very first document, Vatican II observed that religious art is 'directed towards expressing in some way the infinite beauty of God' (*SC* 122). The theme of beauty then slid off the table, but found again its proper place in the final document of the Council.

12. Elsewhere *Gaudium et Spes* uses two verbs when presenting the Church's task to 'heal and elevate' the dignity of the human person (*GS* 40), and to 'purify and elevate' the morality of peoples (*GS* 58). It uses three verbs to speak of how Christ 'enlivens, purifies, and strengthens the generous desires of human kind' (*GS* 38), and four verbs in saying that the Church 'renders fertile, strengthens, completes, and restores in Christ (*fecundat, communit, complet atque restaurat*) the spiritual ornaments and endowments of each people or age' (*GS* 58).

(5) Finally, the pastoral constitution on the Church endorsed the call to dialogue and collaboration with those of other faiths, which we found developed in *Nostra Aetate* and *Ad Gentes*. Its preface announced an intention to enter into 'dialogue (colloquium)' with 'the whole human family' (*GS* 3). Later the constitution named 'love' and 'courtesy' among the essential conditions for practising dialogue with those who differ from us 'in social, political, *and also religious* matters' (*GS* 28; italics mine). The Council set itself to develop 'some general principles' towards fostering 'mutual exchange and help' in matters that affect alike the Church and the whole world (*GS* 40). Facing the enormous human needs created by lack of food, health care, education, and employment, as well as by the sufferings of refugees and the constant outbreak of war, the constitution warmly welcomed collaboration on these common causes 'between Christians and non-Christians' (*GS* 84).

In line with a mindset open to the whole world, the constitution concluded by expressing its eagerness for dialogue with everyone and, not least, with 'all who acknowledge God and maintain precious religious and human elements in their traditions' (*GS* 92). As it did in its very first document, *Sacrosanctum Concilium* (see Chapter 3 above), Vatican II reached out to the entire human race and, in a particular way, to the 'religious others', and recognized precious elements in their religious traditions. Presumably 'dialogue' with them, conducted with openness to 'the impulses of the Spirit' (*GS* 92), would make Catholics even more aware of those precious elements.

Signs and Voices of the Times

Its sensitivity to human life in all its dimensions leads *Gaudium et Spes* to attend to the 'signs of the times'. The constitution speaks, on the one hand, of these signs as 'out there' and requiring to be interpreted 'in the light of the Gospel' (*GS* 4). On the other hand, 'the events, needs, and desires' of our times can prove to be 'true signs of the presence or purpose of God' (*GS* 11). In other words, the signs of the times, whether at first glance positive ('desires') or negative ('needs'), may reveal something about *where* God is especially present and *what* God aims to bring about in our world. A later article draws together what we find in these two articles, by spelling out the responsibility of discerning the 'voices of our times', so that the reality of revelation might be more effectively communicated: 'with the help of the Holy Spirit, it is the task of the whole People of God, particularly of the pastors and theologians, to hear the various voices of our time, and to discern and interpret them in the light of the divine word, so that the revealed Truth may always be more deeply perceived, better under-stood and more suitably presented' (GS 44). To read the signs and hear the voices of yesterday is comparatively easy. To read the signs and understand the voices of today, and not least in the area of interfaith relations, can pose considerable difficulties. But it is a task that cannot be shirked. In particular, discerning the special presence and purpose of God in and through interreligious dialogue belongs to an integral Christian openness to God's revelatory and redemptive self-communication.

The Holy Spirit, Faith, and the Risen Christ

Studying *Gaudium et Spes* resembles mining a vast archive of rich material that continues to yield up treasures for Christian living, thinking, and worshipping. Three such treasures involve the Holy Spirit, the faith of 'religious others', and the impact of the risen Christ on the entire world.

(1) The presence of the Holy Spirit pervades the whole constitution—from the first article to the last (GS 1, 93). Many of these references to the Spirit concern the Church and her mission (e.g. GS 3, 21, 40, 43, 44). But some involve the whole of humanity: for instance, the belief that 'Christ, who died and was raised for all, will through his Spirit give light and strength to human beings so that they can respond to their supreme calling' (GS 10). Indeed, 'the people of God believes' that 'the Spirit of the Lord fills the whole world' (GS 11). Observing how an awareness of 'the supreme dignity' of human persons and their 'universal rights and duties' has been growing in the whole world, *Gaudium et Spes* states: 'the Spirit of God, who with wonderful provi-dence directs the march of time and renews the face of the earth, assists at this evolution'. This is to assign to the Holy Spirit a leading role in the development towards a social order, 'founded on truth, built on justice, and enlivened by love' (GS 26).

Some of this teaching links up with the central scope of this book. To maintain, for example, that the Spirit gives all human beings the 'light and strength' they need to fulfil their divinely given vocation raises pressing questions: what then is the presence of the Holy Spirit in the religions of the world if it is from the Spirit that the followers of these living faiths receive the light (= revelation) and strength (= salvation) they need for their destiny with God? Since all human beings receive through the Holy Spirit the 'light' needed for their eternal vocation, how can any Catholics loyal to Vatican II allege that the revelation of God through Christ and his Spirit is not available universally, albeit not necessarily with complete clarity? In a later article, the constitution acknowledges that 'human beings are being continually (*incessanter*) stirred up by the Spirit of God and can never remain utterly indifferent to the issue of religion' (*GS* 41). This vision of the Spirit being universally active (to raise questions of revelation and salvation) in all human hearts and minds was to be developed by Pope John Paul II, as we will see in Chapter 8.

(2) To speak of divine revelation inevitably brings up the human response of faith. *Gaudium et Spes* makes this link in reflecting on the importance and role of wisdom (*GS* 15).[13] When the document speaks of human beings 'drawn through visible things to those which cannot be seen', we could catch an echo of Hebrews 11: 3 and its account of faith: 'by faith we understand that the worlds were prepared by the word of God, so that what is seen was made from things that are not visible' (see Heb. 11: 27). But a footnote directs us to Sirach. Then the five appeals made to 'wisdom' in *Gaudium et Spes,* in what is only a brief article, ensure that we think of wisdom literature and its wonder at the design and beauty of the created world. Yet the article concludes: '*by the gift of the Holy Spirit and through faith*, human beings come to contemplate and savour the mystery of the divine plan' (italics mine). It is the Holy Spirit who, through the gift of faith, draws people 'through visible things' to the invisible God and to wonder at and delight in 'the mystery' or deep truth of the divine plan for humanity and the universe.

Relentlessly neglected in the literature concerned with 'the religious others', this final statement of article 15 strengthens the hand of

---

13. On *GS* 15, see Ratzinger, 'The Dignity of the Human Person', 130–4.

theologians who understand not only the presence of the Holy Spirit but also the gift of faith to be universally available. Those human beings, who know nothing of Christ and his Church, can be drawn by the Spirit to faith in God through the things they see and experience. Presumably an earlier statement in the same article about the initiative of wisdom—presumably in some sense divine wisdom—who 'sweetly draws the human mind to look for and to love what is true and good' fills out the nature of faith. Human beings are always drawn 'to look for and to love' God, who is infinitely true, good, and beautiful.

The last chapter showed how *Ad Gentes* recognized faith as found in the 'general' history of revelation and salvation. But that decree circumspectly said that such faith arose 'through ways known' to God. *Gaudium et Spes* 15, however, offers some clues about how the faith of the 'religious others' might arise.

(3) Finally, *Gaudium et Spes* moved decisively beyond *Lumen Gentium* in what it taught about the 'upright' non-believer.[14] The latter document had addressed the case of 'those who, through no fault [of their own], have not yet reached an explicit acknowledgement of God and who, not without grace, strive to lead an upright life'. 'Divine providence', the Council affirmed, will not deny them 'the helps necessary for salvation' (*LG* 16). *Gaudium et Spes* called all such non-believers 'people of good will', explained that 'grace is at work invisibly in their hearts', and added: 'since Christ died for all and since human beings have in fact one and the same final calling, namely a divine one, we ought to hold that the Holy Spirit offers to all the possibility of being united, in a way known to God, to the paschal mystery' (*GS* 22).[15]

Put in personal terms, this means that through the Holy Spirit all people, no matter whether they follow some faith or not, can be joined, albeit mysteriously, to the crucified and risen Jesus. After all, he is in person 'the paschal mystery'. Unlike *Gaudium et Spes* 15, the point at explicit issue here is salvation and not the revelation that can give rise to faith. In article 22, the constitution recalls the past ('Christ died for all'), affirms the present action of the Spirit (who 'offers to all

14. See ibid., 161–3.
15. On *GS* 22, see ibid., 161–3. By applying here 'the paschal mystery' to the salvation of humanity in general, *GS* echoed and extended what *SC* had said two years earlier about 'the paschal mystery' in the context of the Church's liturgical year (*SC* 106).

the possibility of being united' with 'the risen Christ'), and looks to the future ('the same final calling' for all). The document finds in the past (the death and resurrection of Christ) and in the future (the call of all human beings to share in the final vision of God) the basis for what happens now (the initiative of the Holy Spirit in bringing all people into union with the crucified and risen Christ).

Such sharing in the life of the crucified and risen Christ takes place 'in a way known to God'—that is to say, not in a way publicly known to other human beings. When people profess faith in Christ, receive baptism, and enter the Church, this is a public and not a private affair. *Gaudium et Spes* is talking here, however, about people in whose 'hearts' grace acts 'invisibly' or, to put this personally, in whose hearts the Holy Spirit acts and offers the chance of sharing in the life of the exalted Christ.

A later article adds to this picture of the intimate collaboration between Christ and the Spirit: 'constituted Lord by his resurrection and given all power in heaven and on earth, Christ is already at work through the power of his Spirit in the hearts of human beings, not only arousing a desire for the world to come but also enlivening, purifying, and strengthening the generous desires of human kind' (GS 38). Where the earlier article highlighted the activity of the Holy Spirit in joining people to the crucified and risen Christ, this article 'reverses' the roles and portrays Christ acting through the Spirit and doing so in the hearts of all human beings, whatever their religious adherence.

After setting out various contributions of *Gaudium et Spes*, let me summarize what it taught about the 'religious others' before pressing on to draw together the achievement of the Second Vatican Council:

- *Gaudium et Spes* is the first ecumenical council to teach that all human beings are created in the image of God (e.g. GS 12).
- All human beings enjoy the same basic dignity, from which flow universal rights and duties (e.g. GS 26).
- All human beings raise the same fundamental questions (GS 3, 4, 10, 21).
- The voice of God heard in the human conscience and the law written by God on human hearts (GS 16) imply some kind of divine self-revelation to all human beings.
- In Christ both the mystery (or deep truth) of human beings and the mystery of God are disclosed (GS 22).

∞ *Gaudium et Spes* has little to say about 'the seeds of the Word' and 'the preparation for the Gospel'.

∞ *Gaudium et Spes* adds 'the beautiful' to 'the true and the good' to be found in human beings and their cultures (*GS* 57, 76).

∞ *Gaudium et Spes*, from start to finish, endorses dialogue and collaboration with 'others' (*GS* 3, 28, 40, 84, 92).

∞ The 'signs of the times' and 'the voices of our age' can convey God's intentions about such issues as interreligious dialogue (*GS* 4, 11, 44).

∞ The Holy Spirit gives all human beings 'the light and strength' needed 'to respond to their supreme calling' (*GS* 10).

∞ Through the Holy Spirit, all human beings can receive the gift of faith (*GS* 15).

∞ Through the Holy Spirit, all human beings can be united with the crucified and risen Christ (*GS* 22).

∞ Through the Holy Spirit, the risen Christ is at work in the hearts of human beings everywhere (*GS* 38).

SEVEN

Putting It Together

Inter-religious dialogue is a part of the Church's evangelizing mission.[1] Understood as a method and means of mutual knowledge and enrichment, dialogue is not in opposition to the mission *ad gentes* [to the nations]; indeed, it has special links with that mission and is one of its expressions.

Blessed John Paul II, Redemptoris Missio

Five documents from Vatican II have held our attention during the last four chapters, in which we examined what the Council taught about the religious situation of those who follow other religions and, indeed, of those who do accept any particular faith. Before pulling together systematically the main lines of this teaching, we can pause to observe the tension in the Council between (a) a positive account of the 'religious others' (and the 'upright' atheists and agnostics), and (b) a massive reaffirmation of the Church's mission.

Mission Includes Dialogue, Justice, and Peace

Earlier chapters have repeatedly pointed to (a) the different ways in which the Second Vatican Council offered startlingly new (and courteous) teaching on the followers of other faiths, and did so in a number of documents of different purposes. In terms of their official or 'canonical'

---

1. On interreligious dialogue, see James L. Heft (ed.), *Catholicism and Interreligious Dialogue* (New York: Oxford University Press, 2012); Ataullah Siddiqui, *Christian-Muslim Dialogue in the Twentieth Century* (London: Macmillan, 1997), esp. 23–48.

authority, these five documents ranged from a dogmatic constitution, *Lumen Gentium*, a pastoral constitution, *Gaudium et Spes*, through a decree, *Ad Gentes*, to a declaration, *Nostra Aetate*. At the same time, however, (b) the Council repeatedly underlined the missionary nature of the Church, and in no way confined that theme to its decree on missionary activity. Heinrich Brechter rightly commented: 'no Council has ever so consciously emphasized and so insistently expounded the Church's pastoral work of salvation and its worldwide missionary function as Vatican II'.[2] The documents of Vatican II pervasively proposed not only (a) dialogue 'with the others' but also (b) mission 'to the others'.

Chapter 5 (above) noted how closely Joseph Ratzinger supported his fellow 'peritus' Yves Congar (and others) in developing the draft that, with some emendations, became the final text of *Ad Gentes*. Shortly after the Council ended, he also collaborated with Congar (and others) in producing a volume on that decree, and took as his topic the task of examining and evaluating what Vatican II said about the Church's missionary vocation in documents other than *Ad Gentes*.[3] Ratzinger trawled through *Lumen Gentium*, *Nostra Aetate*, the Decree on the Apostolate of Lay People (*Apostolicam Actuositatem*), *Dignitatis Humanae*, and the Decree on the Ministry and Life of Priests (*Presbyterorum Ordinis*). He established mission as an important, if not leading, theme in all these texts. But he did not include anything about *Sacrosanctum Concilium* or about *Gaudium et Spes*. Chapter 3 above illustrated the missionary outreach which the former document inculcated. There is a missionary aspect to liturgy; public worship (and private prayer) serves humanity. And then to pass over in silence *Gaudium et Spes* remains even more astonishing, and can perhaps be explained on the grounds that Ratzinger, like some other German theologians and some German bishops, had serious reservations about *Gaudium et Spes*.[4] One should be grateful for the way in which

---

2. H. S Brechter, 'Decree on the Church's Missionary Activity', in Herbert Vorgrimler (ed.), *Commentary on the Documents of Vatican II*, trans. W. J. O'Hara, iv (London: Burns & Oates, 1969), 87–181, at 87.

3. J. Ratzinger, 'La mission d'après les autres textes conciliaires', in Johannes Schütte (ed.), *L'activité missionaire de l'Église* (Paris: Cerf, 1967), 121–47.

4. Ratzinger expressed his dislike for *GS* even before the Council in its fourth session began to discuss 'schema XIII', as it was then named, on 21 September 1965. Gilles Routhier recalls how on 17 September 1965 'Ratzinger attacked the text radically and violently' ('Finishing the Work Begun: The Trying Experience of the Fourth Period', in Giuseppe Alberigo and Joseph A. Komonchak (eds), *History of Vatican II*, v

Ratzinger's chapter demonstrated a pervasive concern with mission that distinguishes the documents of Vatican II. But something should be added to fill up a serious lacuna that he left, and show how the theme of mission is present in the Pastoral Constitution on the Church in the Modern World. One may not simply ignore, let alone repudiate, its vision of a mission that also involves dialogue and collaboration with 'others' in the cause of justice, peace, and evangelization.

In addressing the people of today and explaining to them what the Church offers to contemporary society, *Gaudium et Spes* followed *Lumen Gentium* by characterizing the Church's mission as follows: 'in Christ she is, as it were, a sacrament or sign and instrument of intimate union with God and of the unity of the human race'. Hence the Church can 'show to the world that true, social, [and] external union flows from the union of hearts and minds: namely, from that faith and charity, by which her union has been indissolubly founded in the Holy Spirit.' By 'her nature and *mission*', the Church is 'universal' and not 'bound to any particular form of human culture or political, economic, or social system'. Thus she is in the position to 'serve the good of all' (*GS* 42; italics mine), and not least by bringing together human beings who are often ferociously divided from one another, above all through the cruel absurdity of war.

The constitution, when treating the Church and the political community, returns to its vision of the servant Church: she 'is not confused with a political community nor bound to any political system. She is the sign and the safeguard of the transcendence of the human person'. More specifically, 'being founded in the love of the Redeemer, she contributes to the flourishing of justice and charity between nations and within the borders of [any given] nation. By preaching the truth of the Gospel and illuminating all sectors of human activity, through her teaching and the witness shown by the faithful, the Church also respects and promotes the political freedom and responsibility of citizens.' This article ends by stating: it is by 'exercising her *mission* in the world' that the Church 'fosters and elevates all that is found to be true, good, and beautiful in the

[Maryknoll, NY: Orbis, 2006], 49–184, at 126). On Ratzinger's (and Rahner's) objections to the text, see also Peter Hünermann, 'The Final Weeks of the Council', in *History of Vatican II*, v, 363–483, at 387. On Ratzinger's 'reception' of *GS*, see also Hans-Joachim Sander, 'Die Rezeption [von *Gaudium et Spes*] bei Kardinal Ratzinger sowie der Glaubenskongregation und Papst Benedikt XVI', in Peter Hünermann and Bern Jochen Hilberath (eds), *Herders Theologisches Kommentar zum Zweiten Vatikanischen Konzil*, iv (Freiburg im Breisgau: Herder, 2005), 838–44.

human community', and 'strengthens peace among human beings to the glory of God' (*GS* 76; italics mine). Unquestionably, promoting justice, love, responsible freedom, and peace belongs essentially to the mission of the Church. Witnessing through words and, even more, through deeds to the truth of the gospel, the Church should change and has in fact changed for the better the face of human society.[5]

Gaudium et Spes moves to its conclusion by affirming that 'in reliance on her divine *mission* and by preaching the Gospel to all human beings and dispensing the treasures of grace, the Church contributes to strengthening peace all over the world' and 'laying a solid foundation' for fellowship among people (*GS* 89; italics mine). 'In virtue of her *mission* to enlighten the whole world with the Gospel message and to gather together in one Spirit all human beings of every nation, race, and culture', the Council pledges itself to a dialogue inspired by love and leading to truth, which will enable Catholics to work together with everyone and so build up the world in 'true peace' (*GS* 92; italics mine). Thus the closing passages of the constitution add their own, particular vividness to the sense of the Church being missioned to spread peace everywhere through global dialogue and fellowship.

As much or more than any other section in the Vatican II documents, the final articles of *Gaudium et Spes* place firmly together dialogue and mission or, better expressed, mission through dialogue.[6] The constitution not only embodies the theme of mission and dialogue in the service of justice, peace, and evangelization, but also conveys some major principles towards carrying out this task. Where *Sacrosanctum Concilium* (*passim*), *Lumen Gentium* (e.g. 7, 10–11), and *Ad Gentes* (e.g. 14, 15) illuminate the 'liturgical mission' of the Church, *Gaudium et Spes* does not add any teaching on baptism, the Eucharist, or the other sacraments but concentrates on translating into the public scene the social commitment which the sacraments entail. They remain essentially

---

5. The Decree on the Church's Missionary Activity points out how 'in the history of human beings, even in their secular [history], the Gospel has been a leaven of liberty and progress and constantly presents itself as a leaven of fraternity, unity, and peace' (*AG* 8). This obviously endorses the conviction that nourishing liberty, unity, and peace also belongs to the mission of preaching and spreading the good news.
6. Here the constitution developed extensively what was only sketched in the Declaration on the Relation of the Church to Non-Christian Religions (Chapter 4 above). By insisting that interreligious dialogue belongs to the Church's evangelizing mission, *NA*, *AG*, and *GS* vindicated the vision of Ramon Llull (Chapter 2 above).

incomplete, wherever and whenever the Church fails to press her public mission of promoting dialogue, justice, peace, and fellowship between all human beings. Her mission takes the Church beyond the realm of the 'sacred' sacraments into the realm of her 'secular' responsibilities.[7]

Three 'pontifical councils', which belong to the direct fruit of the Second Vatican Council, embody the conviction that the Church's mission also calls her to dialogue with others and work towards justice and peace in the world. First of all, the Pontifical Council for Promoting Christian Unity, which was founded in preparation for Vatican II by Blessed John XXIII in June 1960 as the Secretariat for the Promotion of the Unity of Christians, has been responsible for dialogue and relations with non-Catholic Christian churches and communities and with Judaism (through the Commission for Religious Relations with Jews). This secretariat, which was renamed in 1988 the Pontifical Council for Promoting Christian Unity, received its brief from the Vatican II through two documents: the Decree on Ecumenism, *Unitatis Redintegratio* (the renewal of unity), and the second half of *Nostra Aetate* (nos. 4–5). The Decree on Ecumenism depended on *Lumen Gentium*, which recognized how 'many elements of sanctification and truth are found outside the visible confines' of the Catholic Church (no. 8), and listed the many ways in which the Catholic Church is 'joined' with other Christians (no. 15).[8]

Second, the Secretariat for Non-Christians, founded in 1964 by Pope Paul VI and in 1988 renamed the Pontifical Council for Interreligious Dialogue, has strikingly institutionalized (in the good sense of that word) the dialogue and collaboration with the religious 'others' that *Nostra Aetate*, *Ad Gentes*, and, most of all, *Gaudium et Spes* called for. In May 1991 this council published 'Dialogue and Proclamation', a

---

7. In his 1987 encyclical *Sollicitudo Rei Socialis*, John Paul II (pope 1978–2005) underlined the social implications of the Eucharist as empowering work for development and peace in the service of the coming kingdom of God (no. 48; ND 1592). In his 1991 encyclical *Centesimus Annus* ('the Hundredth Year' since Leo XIII's encyclical *Rerum Novarum*), John Paul II stated: 'to teach and to spread her social doctrine belongs to the Church's evangelizing mission and is an essential part of the Christian message, since this doctrine points out the direct consequences of that message in the life of society and situates daily work and struggles for justice in the context of bearing witness to Christ the Saviour' (no. 5).

8. On the work of the Council for Promoting Christian Unity, see G. O'Collins, *Living Vatican II: The 21st Council for the 21st Century* (Mahwah, NJ: Paulist Press, 2006), 29–33.

document that illustrated how dialogue and mission do not merely face each other but belong essentially together.[9] By publishing the text jointly with the Vatican's Congregation for the Evangelization of Peoples, the Council for Interreligious Dialogue expressed the conviction founded solidly in *Gaudium et Spes*, as well as in *Nostra Aetate* and *Ad Gentes*, that both dialogue and mission characterize what, through the Holy Spirit, Christ summons his Church to grapple with.

Third, by founding in 1967 the Pontifical Commission 'Justitia et Pax', renamed in 1988 the Pontifical Council for Justice and Peace, Pope Paul VI placed firmly before the world a central theme of *Gaudium et Spes*: the Church has a public mission to promote justice and peace, and aims to carry out this mission not only with her own resources but also through dialogue and collaboration with 'others'. This council's commitment to furthering the observance of human rights and the progress of all peoples includes collaborating with various non-Catholic groups in achieving these ends. The Constitution on the Church in the Modern World remains the *magna carta* guiding the Council for Justice and Peace when it works for justice as a constitutive part of the good news which the Church is missioned to preach.

Gaudium et Spes also inspired directly the Third Synod of Bishops in Rome (1971), which took up the theme of 'justice in the world'. Faced with the present character of human society in which many 'are silent, indeed voiceless, victims of injustice', the synod declared: 'action on behalf of justice and participation in the transformation of the world fully appear to us a constitutive dimension of the preaching of the Gospel, or, in other words, of the Church's mission for the redemption of the human race and its liberation from every oppressive situation' (ND 2159).[10]

There is probably no need to drum up further arguments to show that Vatican II's vision of the Church's mission in no way excluded dialogue with 'others' and collaboration with them in the cause of justice and peace. The creation and ongoing work of three pontifical councils vividly vindicated and embodied the Second Vatican Council's integral view of what Christ missioned his Church to do.

---

9. For key extracts from this document, see ND 1059–63, 1176–9.
10. For further extracts from this document, see ND 2160–71.

The Church's Repentance and Self-Reformation

In its Decree on Ecumenism, *Unitatis Redintegratio* (the renewal of unity), promulgated on 21 November 1964, the Second Vatican Council acknowledges that 'every renewal of the Church essentially consists in an increased fidelity towards her vocation'. In fact, 'the Church is called by Christ' to 'a constant reformation which she invariably needs inasmuch as she is a human and earthly institution' (*UR* 6). The decree adds: 'there can be no ecumenism worthy of the name without interior conversion'. Such conversion involves deep love and 'the grace of humility and gentleness in serving' others with 'generosity' (*UR* 7). 'This conversion of heart and holiness of life, along with private and public prayers for the unity of Christians, should be considered the soul of the whole ecumenical movement' (*UR* 8). Finally, one should not ignore the indispensable role of serious 'study', undertaken with 'a spirit of good will', so that Catholics can know better 'the doctrine, history, spiritual and liturgical life, religious psychology, and culture' of other Christians. This can be facilitated by 'meetings of both sides'. Through such 'dialogue' it will 'also become more clearly known what the condition of the Catholic Church really is' (*UR* 9).

What the Decree on Ecumenism said about the Catholic Church and her relations with other Christians can be transferred directly to her relations with those who follow other faiths (and those who follow none). In a situation of 'renewal' in every area of Catholic life required by Vatican II, 'increased fidelity to her vocation' should make the whole Church sensitive to the need for a 'reformation'—or to put it more bluntly, the need for 'repentance'—in her attitude towards and relations with those of other living faiths. Yet it is with difficulty that one speaks here of a 'constant' reformation, since for centuries, apart from such shining exceptions as St Francis of Assisi, Ramon Llull, and Cardinal Nicholas of Cusa, official teachers (e.g. those at the Council of Florence) seemed to presume that, along with 'heretics and schismatics', 'Jews and pagans' were destined to eternal damnation. Chapter 2 (above) showed how, right down to the twentieth century, changes in attitude and official teaching came ever so slowly. The Catholic Church at large needed an 'interior conversion', so that it could recognize all human beings as our brothers and sisters and learn to love them as our 'other selves' and those whom we should serve with 'generosity'.

The five texts we examined from Vatican II document that 'reformation' and deep 'conversion' in attitudes towards the 'religious others'. This 'reformation' and 'conversion' involved *retrieving* the generous openness of such early Christian writers as Justin Martyr and Clement of Alexandria (Chapter 1 above) and the ancient practice of praying at the Eucharist for all human beings (*Sacrosanctum Concilium* in Chapter 3 above). What *Unitatis Redintegratio* maintained about relations with other Christians carries more or less the same weight when applied to relations with those of other living faiths. 'Conversion of heart and holiness of life, along with private and public prayers' for the religious others, 'should be considered the soul' of all interreligious dialogue and collaboration.

Where *Nostra Aetate*, through its call to dialogue with 'the others' and own example of such dialogue, implied the need to examine seriously what they believe and practise, *Ad Gentes* placed such study firmly on the agenda (Chapter 5 above). This study is simply indispensable if Catholics and other Christians are to know adequately 'the doctrine, history, spiritual and liturgical life, religious psychology, and culture' of those who follow other faiths. Once again what Vatican II taught about ecumenism in its 'strict' sense (of relations between 'separated' Christians) clarifies admirably the 'academic' task of followers of Christ who commit themselves to interreligious dialogue. They must, like Ramon Llull, know those of other living faiths if dialogue with them is to prove fruitful.

Lastly, the confident promise of the Decree on Ecumenism that dialogue will let us 'know more clearly what the condition of the Catholic Church really is' can be applied to all Christians who apply themselves to interreligious dialogue. Such a dialogue, when undertaken with love, humility, and a spirit of service, will obviously let Christians know more clearly the beliefs and practices of the 'others' with whom they wish to share the good news of Christ. But it should also illuminate who they themselves are and what they themselves believe. Sharing with 'the others' and learning to know them better will inevitably lead to a deeper self-knowledge and appreciation of Christian faith. In particular, what *Lumen Gentium*, *Nostra Aetate*, *Ad Gentes*, and *Gaudium et Spes* teach about Jesus Christ and the Holy

Spirit being actively present everywhere to enlighten and save all people expresses the experience of those dedicated to interreligious dialogue. Becoming familiar with those of other living faiths, Catholics and other Christians can experience the universal presence of Christ and his Spirit and be provided with the chance of hearing what Christ wants to say to them through 'the others'.

In its closing message the 1977 Synod of Bishops on Catechesis exhorted catechists not only to maintain towards other religions 'respect and understanding' but also to 'develop an attitude which listens to these religions and discovers the *semina Verbi* hidden in them' (no. 5).[11] That entails going beyond merely reading the classic texts of other religions and coming to know the spiritual experiences of the followers of these living faiths and the ways in which they interpret and express their experiences. Listening to what the 'religious others' have to say and watching them engaged in practising their faith will lead to 'discovering' Christ mysteriously present and active in the adherents of these faiths and to hearing something he may wish to say to us through these 'others'.

Nostra Aetate, as we saw in Chapter 4, promised that 'dialogue and collaboration with the followers of other religions' should include 'recognizing, protecting, and promoting those spiritual and moral goods' found among them (*NA* 2). Here the decree with its talk of 'recognizing spiritual goods' left matters unspecified, as it did with its talk about 'rejecting nothing of those things which are true and holy in these [other] religions' (ibid.). The 1977 synod made things more specific and personal by urging catechists to 'discover the seeds of the Word'. It is, after all, the Word of God hidden in other religions and their followers who is the supreme 'spiritual good' and Truth and Holiness in person.

The Human Condition

Nostra Aetate addressed itself not only to Catholics and other Christians, Hindus, Buddhists, Muslims, Jews, and followers of other religions

---

11. *Synod of Bishops, 1977: Fourth General Assembly, Rome, September 30–October 29, 1977; Message to the People of God and Interventions of the U.S. Bishops* (Washington, DC: United States Catholic Conference, 1978).

(*NA* 1–4) but also to human beings at large (*NA* 5). This declaration was followed six weeks later by *Gaudium et Spes*, a document addressed to all people of the contemporary world. How did the two texts understand and interpret the fundamental condition of those with whom they wished to be in conversation? Beyond question, the way in which they made sense of human existence would affect the way they understood the religious situation of those who follow other faiths.

Vatican II might have identified the human condition by speaking primarily of *homo dolens* (the human person who suffers). Human beings suffer through all that they have lost and continue to lose, as well as by what they fear about the present and the future. Loss, sometimes terrible loss, and fear, sometimes paralysing fear, characterize the lives of men and women around the globe. In a remarkable poem written during the Second World War, 'Ecce Homo', David Gascoyne (1916–2001) pictured the awful story of human pain and linked it to the passion of Christ: 'He is in agony till the world's end,/ And we must never sleep during that time!'[12] Everywhere suffering marked and marks human existence.

The many bishops and experts who collaborated in drafting *Gaudium et Spes* and the smaller number responsible for the text of *Nostra Aetate* might have privileged suffering in presenting the universal condition of human beings. After all, in his particular way Christ drew near to all men and women in their pain. His body on the cross expressed his presence with those who suffer anywhere and at any time. His death on Calvary between two criminals symbolized forever his solidarity with those who suffer and die, an identification with human pain defined also by the criteria for the last judgement (Matt. 25: 31–46). The final blessings of the kingdom will come to those who, even without recognizing Christ, have met his needs in the people who suffer by being hungry, thirsty, strangers, naked, sick, or imprisoned. To articulate the worldwide presence of Christ in all who suffer, we might say: *ubi dolor, ibi Christus* (where there is suffering, there is Christ). A *homo dolens* version of the human condition could display this radical need met by the redemption revealed and embodied

12. D. Gascoyne, *Collected Poems* (Oxford: Oxford University Press, 1965). He quotes here Blaise Pascal, *Pensée* 919 in A. J. Krailsheimer's trans. (Harmondsworth: Penguin, 1966), numbered 553 in some other editions.

in Christ. In dialogue with those of other faiths, the Council might have concentrated on this vision of humanity and, in an evangelizing mode that imitated St Paul and his message of the cross (1 Cor. 1: 23), have announced to them the crucified Christ.

Nostra Aetate and *Gaudium et Spes*, as we saw in Chapters 4 and 6, respectively, included but went beyond a vision of *homo dolens* to sketch a more complete range of questions. Sooner or later, human beings question themselves about a number of deep issues: where do we come from? Who are we? What does our suffering and struggling existence mean—in all its sinful failures, apparent successes, and future destiny? Is there a supreme Being in whose presence we play out our lives? Human beings put everything into question and do so within an infinite horizon of questioning. Every answer prompts a new question. Human beings are the question that they can never adequately settle and answer for themselves.

A *homo interrogans* anthropology (in the sense of a philosophical and/ or theological vision of humanity) aligns itself with a tradition that goes back to Paul and his radical questions (Rom. 7: 13–25). Without using the term, the Second Vatican Council in *Gaudium et Spes* took over a method of 'correlation' practised by Paul Tillich and others: 'human beings will always want to know, if only in a vague way, what is the meaning of their life, their activity, and their death'. The divine revelation correlates with our most serious questions: 'the fullest answer to these questions is provided by God alone, who created human beings in his own image and redeemed them from sin'. This answer has come 'through the revelation in his Son' (*GS* 41). This revelation fully matches the reality and need of human beings as those who are essentially questioners. *Nostra Aetate* had already remarked that 'human beings expect from the various religions a response to the obscure enigmas of the human condition', which, 'today, as in the past, disturb their hearts'. It singled out 'the religions connected with the progress of culture', which 'endeavour to reply' to the seven questions it listed (*NA* 1, 2). The decree pressed on to state briefly the answer that Christian faith gives to radical human self-questioning: the Church 'proclaims' Christ who is the way, the truth, and the life, in whom human beings find the fullness of religious life and 'in whom God has reconciled all things to himself'(*NA* 2). But it was left to *Gaudium et Spes* to present Christ much more fully as *the* answer to fundamental human questions (e.g. *GA* 22).

Under the Word of God

When reassessing and realigning its attitude to those of other living faiths, Vatican II allowed itself to be enlightened and guided by the inspired Scriptures. The Dogmatic Constitution on Divine Revelation, *Dei Verbum* (the Word of God), promulgated on 18 November 1965, acknowledged how the Catholic Church's official teachers are not above the Word of God but serve it (*DV* 10). The closing chapter of that constitution dreamed of a spiritually renewed Church, in which all its members would let their lives and work become much more deeply nourished and illuminated by the Scriptures, as well as by public worship and personal prayer (*DV* 21, 23–5). We can spot something of that biblical renewal already moving the Council towards a more truthful and loving way of reimagining other living faiths and their followers. One cannot talk of a tectonic shift, but some kind of shift unquestionably took place.

(1) From the time of Pope Gregory VII (Chapter 2 above) and earlier, certain New Testament texts, such as John 1: 9 (about 'the true Light that enlightens everyone') and 1 Timothy 2: 4 (about God who 'desires everyone to be saved and to come to the knowledge of the truth'), shaped Christian thinking, or at least better Christian thinking, about the 'religious others'. In particular, the language of John's opening chapter quickly assumed its place in discourse about all those human beings who were not or who were not yet Christians.

(2) Some biblical passages turned up, which had previously been applied in odd ways or at least cited without their full relevance being acknowledged. This happened to Hebrews 11: 6 ('without faith it is impossible to please God'). In 1415 the Council of Constance, before condemning various propositions from John Wyclif, declared: 'we learn from the writings and deeds of the holy fathers that the catholic faith "without which it is impossible to please God" has often been attacked by false followers of the same faith'.[13] But the anonymous author of Hebrews praised the faith of a long list of people from Abel to Jesus himself, all of whom lived and died before the Catholic

---

13. Norman P. Tanner (ed.), *Decrees of the Ecumenical Councils*, i (London: Sheed & Ward, 1990), 411.

Church and strictly 'catholic faith' came into existence (Heb.
11: 4–12: 2). The nature of the faith described by Hebrews, as we
saw in Chapter 5 above, enjoys universal application and may not be
limited to the Roman Catholic faith and its specific followers, whether
these followers are to be reckoned 'true' or 'false'. When introducing
its decree on original sin, the Council of Trent in 1546 also limited the
application of Hebrews 11: 6 to 'our Catholic faith' (DzH 1510; ND
507). It did better, however, in the 1547 decree on justification when it
cited the verse to support the more *general proposition that faith is 'the
foundation and root of all justification'* (DzH 1532; ND 1935; italics mine).
The First Vatican Council once again limited the scope of Hebrews
11: 6 to the case of Catholics persevering in 'the divine and Catholic
faith' or 'the true faith' (DzH 3011–12; ND 121–2). *Ad Gentes*,
however, as we showed in Chapter 5, recognized the universal import
of this text ('without faith it is impossible to please God'), a verse that
we can happily exegete by recalling other passages in Hebrews.

(3) Chapter 5 also attended to Acts 4: 12, a verse that sums up the
central message of Luke's two-part work on Christian origins: 'there is
salvation in no one else [than Christ], for there is no other name under
heaven given among human beings by which we must be saved'. In
1274 the Second Council of Lyons had pressed this verse into service
in the cause of encouraging devout and reverent behaviour when
the faithful met in church![14] The Council of Trent, however, drew
closer to Luke's intentions when it cited Acts 4: 12 in its decree on
original sin; it associated the text with the unique 'merits of the
one mediator our Lord Jesus Christ', merits applied 'to adults and
children alike through the sacrament of baptism' (DzH 1513; ND
510). *Ad Gentes* aligned itself even more closely with Luke by saying
nothing of original sin when introducing the verse in support of the
universal missionary activity of the Church and the need for baptism
(*AG* 7).

(4) Some further texts that promised, among other things, to shed
light on appropriate Christian attitudes towards those of other faiths
had not even rated footnote status before Vatican II. The Genesis
teaching about the creation of human beings in 'the image and likeness' of God (Gen. 1: 26–7) was *never* taken up by Trent or by any

14. Ibid., 328.

other ecumenical council prior to Vatican II. In his April 1963 encyclical *Pacem in Terris*, Blessed John XXIII (pope 1958–63) briefly alluded to humanity being created in God's 'own image and likeness' (no. 3), and its consequences (the 'conscience' [no. 5] and 'personal dignity' [no. 10] of human beings), before moving to a long discussion of the 'rights' and 'duties' of individual members of society (nos. 11–45). As we saw in Chapter 6, these three themes (conscience, dignity, and rights) were to feature in *Gaudium et Spes*, with creation in God's image being nothing less than a leitmotif that runs right through the constitution.[15] Renewed biblical studies and a modern retrieval of the thought of St Irenaeus, who repeatedly threw a searchlight on humanity being created 'in the image and likeness of God',[16] ushered in a deeper appreciation of what the Genesis text implied, on the one hand, for the universal rights and duties of human beings and, on the other hand, for the way Christians should value those of different living faiths. Since every man and every woman in the world carries the very image of God, this sets on them a seal of divine approval that calls for the deepest respect. Even if, to use Vatican II's language, their faith needs to be 'healed, strengthened, and elevated', they enjoy an unqualified dignity and worth that calls on Catholics and other Christians to reverence them as fellow pilgrims journeying together towards our common destiny with God.

(5) The fruits of biblical renewal registered themselves also in an unprecedented move towards distinguishing (but not separating) the kingdom of God from the Church. Deeper study of the Gospels—and, in particular, the Synoptic Gospels—had spread a new appreciation for the fact that the preaching of the kingdom constituted the heart of Jesus' ministry. New Testament scholarship had stressed how, in season and out of season, he proclaimed the divine kingdom *already*

---

15. Being created 'in the divine image', all people share a common origin, but this says little, at least explicitly, about the common human destiny. To be sure, *GS* recalls that all human beings 'have one and the same final calling' (*GS* 22), and brings together 'being destined to the same end' with 'being created in the divine likeness' (*GS* 24); *NA* cites the Book of Revelation's vision of the nations gathered in the new Jerusalem to come (*NA* 1). But the Council, at least in *GS*, has much more to say about creation in the divine image and what that *common origin* entails.

16. See Eric F. Osborn, *Irenaeus of Lyons* (New York: Cambridge University Press, 2001), 211–16.

present in our world but *not yet* consummated.[17] To be sure, he gathered disciples, selected a core group of twelve for a special leadership role in his community, and may have spoken of the coming Church (Matt. 16: 18; 18: 17).[18] But, for Jesus, the heart of the matter was the divine rule breaking into the world in his own person, words, and deeds. This sense that the kingdom of God had already begun in human history and would be completed at the end of time registered itself in the opening chapter of *Lumen Gentium* (*LG* 5 and 9) and provided, in official teaching, an early intimation of the kingdom forming a more encompassing reality than the Church, an intimation that would flower in a 1990 encyclical of John Paul II (Chapter 3 above). The conviction that, with the kingdom being the wider and greater reality, the Church serves the kingdom and not vice versa opens up space for a more Christian and generous appreciation of where other faiths and their followers belong in the one great divine design to save all human beings.

(6) A broader view brought by respect for the scope of the divine kingdom was matched by a presentation of Christ as head of the whole human race and then of the Church—a priority rooted in the New Testament which must shape any reflections on the religious others. Chapter 3 above recalled the image of Christ as musical director for all humanity adopted by the Constitution on the Sacred Liturgy (*SC* 83), a striking picture which obviously put in first place his cosmic headship but which, at least directly, retrieved the language of Clement of Alexandria and other early Christian writers rather than that of the Scriptures. *Lumen Gentium* 16 and 17 followed Thomas Aquinas in setting Christ's headship of the human race above his being head of the Church (Chapter 2 above). In making his case, Thomas (*Summa Theologiae*, 3a 8. 3) relied on two New Testament texts concerned with Christ being the saviour of all people (1 Tim. 4: 10; 1 John 2: 2). But, as we will argue in a moment, the order of creation, and not merely the order of redemption, underpins Christ's role as head of the human race.

17. On Jesus' proclamation of the kingdom, see G. O'Collins, *Christology: A Biblical, Historical and Systematic Study of Jesus* (2nd edn; Oxford: Oxford University Press, 2009), 54–62.
18. On Jesus as founder of the Church, see G. O'Collins, *Rethinking Fundamental Theology: Toward a New Fundamental Theology* (Oxford: Oxford University Press, 2011), 265–79.

A now classical article from Vatican II proposes the title of Christ as the 'last (novissimus) Adam' to portray his being the head of all human beings (*GS* 22). When expounding this role, the same article quotes Colossians 1: 15 and calls him 'the image of the invisible God'. It might have exploited what follows in that remarkable hymn about Christ having the primacy first in the order of creation (Col. 1: 15–17) and then in that of redemption (Col. 1: 18).[19] Yet the appeal to Christ being the 'second' or 'last' Adam does enough here to display his role as the head of humanity and thus head not merely of all the baptized but also of all the religious 'others'.

The Universal Presence of Christ and his Holy Spirit

A strong sense of the universal presence of Christ contributes to Vatican II's fresh understanding of the religious situation of those who follow other faiths (or none at all). Thus 'whatever good or truth is found among them' should be considered given by Christ, 'who enlightens all human beings so that they may at length have life' (*LG* 16). He is the 'source of salvation for the whole world' (*LG* 17). Since the giver comes with the gift, such language necessarily implies the active presence of the one who is both the Light of the world and the Life of the world. The elements of 'truth and grace', found 'among the nations' before they hear and, hopefully, receive the gospel, come from a 'secret presence' of God that is equivalently a secret presence of Christ (*AG* 9).

When articulating this mysterious, universal presence of Christ, Vatican II retrieved from the early Church the theme of 'the seeds of the Word'. After an initial use of this theme in the Dogmatic Constitution on the Church (*LG* 17), the Decree on the Church's Missionary Activity deployed it more fully (*AG* 9, 11, 15, 18). These 'seeds', or equivalently, the invisible Christ himself, are 'hidden' in 'the national and religious traditions' of various peoples (*AG* 11). The language of 'seeds being sown' obviously raises a question about the identity of the sower. The decree answers this question when characterizing the 'seeds' as 'the riches which the bountiful God has distributed to the

---

19. On this hymn, see Markus Barth and Helmut Blanke, *Colossians* (New York: Doubleday, 1994), 193–251.

nations' (ibid.). In his 1990 encyclical *Redemptoris Missio*, John Paul II spoke specifically of the Holy Spirit as sowing these seeds and doing so not only in individuals but also in 'peoples, cultures, and religions' (no. 28). A recognition of the universal presence and activity of Christ and his Holy Spirit was beginning to replace earlier, less personal expressions about 'the power of divine light and grace' available to all human beings and not merely to Christians (Pius IX in Chapter 2 above).

Where *Lumen Gentium* limited what it said about the Holy Spirit to the activity of the Church (twice in *LG* 17) and where *Nostra Aetate* had nothing to say about the Spirit, *Ad Gentes* named the Spirit as 'calling all human beings to Christ through the seeds of the Word and the preaching of the Gospel' (*AG* 15). This message about the Holy Spirit active on behalf of all humanity, as we pointed out in Chapter 6 above, reaches its climax in *Gaudium et Spes*. It is through the Spirit that Christ gives 'light and strength to human beings so that they can respond to their supreme calling' (*GS* 10). A few articles later, the constitution declares that it is 'by the gift of the Holy Spirit and through faith' that human beings in general 'can come to contemplate and savour the mystery of the divine plan' (*GS* 15). It is the Holy Spirit who 'offers to all the possibility of being united, in a way known to God, to the paschal mystery' (*GS* 22). Put in personal terms, this means that through the Spirit all people, no matter whether they follow some faith or no faith, can be joined, albeit mysteriously, to the crucified and risen Jesus. Or, to put matters equivalently, through the power of the Holy Spirit, the risen Christ 'is at work in the hearts' of all people (*GS* 38).

Revelation and Salvation for the Others

Clearly many Roman Catholics and other Christians find it unsettling or even disturbing to acknowledge that God's revelation and salvation are available for 'the others'. They would either prefer to leave matters shrouded in mystery, or else allege that those of other religions are left searching for God and may reach some true beliefs that, with the grace of God, help them to be finally saved. Such Christians, concerned as they are to limit the divine revelation to themselves and the Jews, are loathe to join Vatican II in reimagining the light and life offered to all through Jesus Christ and the Holy Spirit. Let me gather some of the relevant passages from the Council's documents, concentrating on the neuralgic issue of God's self-revelation, in some measure and some real sense, being universally, if not fully, available.

Apropos of Islam, *Lumen Gentium* confidently stated that, together with Christians, Muslims 'acknowledge the Creator' and 'adore the one, merciful God', who will come in judgement at the last day (*LG* 16). How can this be the case, unless God has been revealed to them and they have responded in faith? To be sure, the constitution does not raise this precise question and answer it in the affirmative. But such an affirmative answer seems called for by the common ground that *Lumen Gentium* recognizes between Christians and Muslims. In the very same article, the constitution speaks of sincere God-seekers who, 'under the influence of grace, try in their actions to fulfil his will made known through the dictate of their conscience'. Once again the question presses itself upon our attention: how has the will of God been 'made known' to them at the heart of their conscience, unless some kind of revelation has taken place? We return below to the rule of conscience made known by the Holy Spirit, when we reach *Gaudium et Spes*.

Here the impact of John's Gospel proves decisive: echoing its prologue, *Lumen Gentium* speaks of Christ 'who enlightens all human beings that they may at length have life' (*LG* 16). While, as we observed in Chapter 5, John does not use the verb 'reveal' or the noun 'revelation', his Gospel talks in various ways of the divine self-revelation, that 'light' which enlightens all human beings (and not simply Christians and Jews) so that they may receive life or salvation. Christ can be actively present to impart revelation and salvation without that being 'felt' or explicitly known. Neither *Lumen Gentium* nor any other Vatican II document alleges that people must be aware of Christ's revealing and saving activity for it to have its appropriate effect.

Apropos of Islam, *Nostra Aetate* shows reserve in not introducing, for example, the person of Muhammad or the Koran. But, like *Lumen Gentium*, it implies that Muslims come to faith because God has spoken to them and revealed something of himself and his 'hidden decrees' (*NA* 3). They can truly 'worship' the one God and Creator of all, since God has been in some way revealed to them. In short, what *Nostra Aetate* highlights in the faith and practice of Islam does not seem compatible with holding that Muslims have not received and do not in any sense receive God's self-revelation.

Nostra Aetate moves beyond *Lumen Gentium* in what it says and suggests about Hindus and their examining 'the divine mystery'. This brings up the question: how did Hindus come to know or know about that mystery in the first place, unless it was through some form of divine revelation? A few lines later the declaration, after referring to what is 'true and holy' in Hinduism and other religions, interprets the beliefs and practices of those religions to 'reflect often a ray of that Truth, which enlightens all human beings' (*NA* 2). Once again we can only ask: surely this means that all receive something of the divine self-revelation? The light of God's revelation, in some true sense, reaches everyone.

What we recalled above from *Ad Gentes* on 'the seeds of the Word' is compellingly clear about the mysterious but real presence and activity of Christ everywhere, including his hidden presence in 'the national and religious traditions' of various peoples (*AG* 11). Most importantly the decree explicitly states that the Son, being present in creation to the whole human race, 'reveals' the Father universally (*AG* 3, n. 2); human beings can and should respond to this revelation with saving faith (*AG* 7). Chapter 5 emphatically rules out views that wish to restrict revelation to biblical history and the Jewish and Christian tradition.

Finally, *Gaudium et Spes* plays a crucial role by introducing the activity of the Holy Spirit. It is the Spirit who gives all human beings 'the light and strength' they need 'to respond to their calling' (*GS* 10). Here 'light' points to revelation and 'strength' to salvation. A little later the constitution declares that the Holy Spirit, through the gift of 'faith', draws people 'through visible things' to the invisible God, so that they can wonder at 'the mystery' or deep truth of the divine plan for humanity and the universe (*GS* 15). Without mentioning explicitly the Spirit, the constitution speaks of 'the law written in the human heart by God' (*GS* 16)—an obvious echo of Paul: 'they [the Gentiles] give proof that what the law requires is written on their hearts, to which their own conscience bears witness' (Rom. 2: 15). Writing implies a writer, in this case a divine Writer, the Holy Spirit. The operation of the Spirit reveals to those of other faiths the rule of conscience by which they can be guided.[20] Then *Gaudium et Spes*

20. See G. O'Collins, *Salvation for All: God's Other Peoples* (Oxford: Oxford University Press, 2008), 131–8.

decisively teaches the universal role of the Spirit who offers to all the possibility of being joined with the crucified and risen Jesus (*GS* 22).

Putting all this teaching together, we can only conclude that the bishops at Vatican II taught that God's revelation and salvation are, in some sense, universally available. Some commentators try to shelter behind the position that this divine self-communication mysteriously reaches individuals but does not do so *through* the religious faith that they follow. This view can go so far as to allege that they will be saved *despite* the religion they accept and practice. But this interpretation is incompatible with what Vatican II proposes about the 'other' religion which it considers most of all: namely, Islam. Clearly what the Council says about the faith and practice of Muslims (*LG* 16; *NA* 3) supports the conclusion: it is precisely through their religion that they can acknowledge and worship the one God and Creator of all. It is only in *Nostra Aetate* that Vatican II refers explicitly to Hinduism (*NA* 2). But what is said about Hindus examining and expressing 'the divine mystery' leaves readers with the initial question: how do or did they know this 'divine mystery' except through God's self-revealing activity? A second question breaks through at once: surely their knowing, in one way or another, the divine mystery happens in and through following their religion? Both questions require a positive answer—at least for those who decline to torture the Council's texts and force them to mean something different.

What Karl Rahner wrote (Chapter 2 above) about the followers of other religions reconstructs convincingly what happens to human beings through their essentially social nature. It is within the religious system 'at their disposal' that they will come to know the self-revealing God and through faith enjoy a saving relationship with God. They have 'the right and indeed the duty' to live their relationship with God within the religious realities offered by their 'particular, historical situation'.[21]

Before leaving the theme of the Council's teaching on the divine revelation available to the 'religious others', we should note its happy parallel to what was taught on revelation within the Jewish–Christian tradition, which constitutes what Rahner and others have called 'the

21. K. Rahner, 'Christianity and the Non-Christian Religions', in *Theological Investigations*, trans. Karl-Heinz Kruger, v (London: Darton, Longman & Todd, 1966), 115–34, at 121, 122, 130.

special history of revelation'. *Dei Verbum* presented the divine self-revelation as primarily a personal event, in which God, through the incarnate and risen Christ and the Holy Spirit, invites people into a living relationship of dialogue and love (*DV* 1–4). Secondarily, revelation involves knowing new truths about God, which make up what has been traditionally called the 'deposit of faith' (*DV* 10). But primarily revelation entails knowing the divine Truth (in upper case) and only secondarily the revealed truths (in lower case). Likewise, with those of other living faiths, through the personal activity of the Holy Spirit (*GS* 10, 15, 16, and 22) they believe and practise things that 'often reflect a ray of that Truth [upper case] who enlightens all human beings' (*NA* 2). Obviously the adherents of these religions do not know and profess the full range of revealed truths that Christians do. In the case of Islam, Muslims share some of these revealed truths, accepting, for instance, the divine judgement to come. But, according to what we have gleaned from the Vatican II documents, official Catholic teaching acknowledges the living, personal relationship between these 'others' and God, mediated by the One who is the Truth of God in person. They are mysteriously enlightened by the Truth, even though they know few, if any, of the revealed truths.

The Church and the Other Faiths

We have pressed the case for recognizing that Vatican II, in several relevant documents, considers other living faiths to be ways of revelation and salvation. To be sure, the Council does not expressly speak of 'ways of revelation and salvation', but what it says of Islam and, to a lesser extent, Hinduism, Buddhism, and other religions, amounts to recognizing them to be such 'ways' to God. Yet this is not the same thing as (a) alleging that that they are equally effective at putting people in contact with God, or (b) acknowledging them to be complete and clear ways, equivalent to what God offers through Jesus Christ and the community called into being by the Holy Spirit. *Lumen Gentium* and *Ad Gentes*, when addressing the situation of those who move from another living faith to accept baptism and enter the Church, talk of the need for 'purifying, elevating, strengthening and consummating' the good already found in their hearts, minds, and lives (*LG* 13, 17; *AG* 3, 9). While their religions provide ways to know God and be saved, the community founded by Christ offers decisively fuller knowledge of God and richer means for salvation. How then should we conceive the relationship of the Church to 'the religious others' and her role in their path to salvation?

The language in *Lumen Gentium* about 'the others' being in various ways 'ordered' to the Church (*LG* 16) has suggested to some commentators a shift—one must say, a decisive shift—from maintaining 'outside the Church no salvation' (*extra ecclesiam nulla salus*) to 'without the Church no salvation' (*sine ecclesia nulla salus*). If the 'others' are 'ordered' to the Church, is this a reciprocal relationship, with something flowing, so to speak, in the opposite direction? The constitution itself spoke of Christ, through the community of the Church, 'communicating truth and grace to all human beings' (*LG* 8). Can we say anything more about the ways in which such communication happens?

Lumen Gentium uses Trinitarian language to describe the mission of the community of the baptized: 'the Church *prays* and labours so that into the People of God, the Body of the Lord, and the Temple of the Holy Spirit may pass the fullness of the entire world'(*LG* 17; italics mine). This statement strikingly names prayer as the first task of the Church vis-à-vis 'the others'. A year before promulgating *Lumen Gentium*, the Council had reinstated in the liturgy the 'prayer of the faithful', in which 'intercessions are to be made' for 'all human beings and for the salvation of the whole world' (*SC* 53). In other words, the members of the Church at worship should put no limits to its prayers for the human race. They may not be able to preach to all people, but they are called to pray for all people. Where *Lumen Gentium* spoke in general of praying for the entire world, *Sacrosanctum Concilium* set such prayers within the specific context of the Eucharist.

Some play down the role of such prayer, as if it were nothing very robust and 'merely a moral cause'. But any downplaying of prayers for the salvation of the world faces two challenges. First, it is love that motivates prayers for the whole human race, and love should not be belittled as if it were only a subjective disposition. Love constantly proves itself to be a power in our world that shapes lives[22] and can

---

22. See Vincent Brümmer, *The Model of Love: A Study in Philosophical Theology* (Cambridge: Cambridge University Press, 1993); Gerald O'Collins and Daniel Kendall, *The Bible for Theology: Ten Principles for the Theological Use of Scripture* (Mahwah, NJ: Paulist Press, 1997), 53–73 (on 'Redemption through Love').

even be understood as a cosmic force, albeit a mysterious cosmic force. Pierre Teilhard de Chardin called love 'the most universal, the most tremendous, and the most mysterious of the cosmic forces'.[23] He worked out a view of love as *the* most enormous and omnipresent force in a world which is dynamically converging towards Christ, the unifying point of everything.[24] The power of prayer is the power of love, and should not be written off as merely a minor, secondary cause.

Along with love, its Eucharistic setting forms a second, characteristic feature of the Church's prayer for 'the others' and its power to communicate 'truth and grace'. On the one side, the Church mediates truth and grace to its members principally, although not exclusively, through the proclamation of the word and the administration of the sacraments, the centre of which is the Eucharist. On the other hand, the Church 'intercedes' for the others. The liturgy distinguishes between calling down the Holy Spirit on the faithful and the intercessions made in the name of Christ for 'the others'. One should not blur the distinction between the Church's role for the salvation of her members and for the salvation of 'others'.

Nevertheless, we ignore at our peril how the prayers of the faithful for 'the others' join, or rather are taken up into, the high priestly intercession of Christ himself. These prayers are presented to the Father with and through the self-offering on behalf of all that as high priest Christ makes forever 'at God's right hand'.[25] When interceding for 'the others', the members of the Church are joined to the eternal intercession Christ makes for the entire world. The principle of Prosper of Aquitaine (*legem credendi lex statuat supplicandi*) deserves to be applied here. The 'law' of Christian prayer to and with Christ for 'the religious others' establishes the 'law of belief': namely, that Christ communicates, albeit mysteriously, his truth and grace to them. He does this supremely as the high priest, who at every Eucharist, invisibly yet really and effectively, is present and intercedes *for the whole human race*.

23. P. Teilhard de Chardin, *Human Energy*, trans. J. M. Cohen (London: Collins, 1969), 32.
24. Christopher F. Mooney, *Teilhard de Chardin and the Mystery of Christ* (London: Collins, 1966).
25. See Gerald O'Collins and Michael Keenan Jones, *Jesus Our Priest: A Christian Approach to the Priesthood of Christ* (Oxford: Oxford University Press, 2010), 261–2.

Before leaving the Church's role for those of other living faiths, we may not pass by what *Lumen Gentium* teaches about the Church as 'the visible sacrament of saving unity' (*LG* 9), 'the universal sacrament of salvation' (*LG* 48), or, more fully, as 'a sign and instrument of intimate union with God and of the unity of the whole human race' (*LG* 1), words repeated a year later by *Gaudium et Spes* (*GS* 42).[26] The world-wide community of the Church offers its most precious gift to the entire world: faith in Jesus Christ as our light and our life, now and forever. The Christian faithful have received this gift, but not as something that gives them a huge religious advantage and a head start in the matter of salvation, as if they might boast: 'the others walk lesser ways of salvation but we can take the highway'. The gift of Christian faith involves rather an awesome responsibility to announce and live up to this uniquely good message.

In considering other faiths, Vatican II might have noted the devout holiness that distinguishes the lives of many who belong to other religions, a holiness that contrasts with shortcomings and scandalous failures of very many Christians. In his first encyclical John Paul II drew attention to such a contrast. We turn now to him and the post-Vatican II situation.

---

26. John Friday, '*Universale Salutis Sacramentum*: Understanding the Church as the Universal Sacrament of Salvation in Relation to the Challenge of Interreligious Dialogue', *Pacifica* 25 (2012), 82–99.

EIGHT

John Paul II on Other Religions

Thanks to Vatican II, the Catholic Church is irrevocably committed
to meeting other believers.

Cardinal Francis Arinze, *Vatican II: Forty Personal Stories*

As followers of different religions we should join together in promoting
and defending common ideals in the spheres of religious liberty, human
brotherhood, education, culture, social welfare, and civic order. Dialogue and collaboration are possible in all these great projects.

Pope John Paul II, 'Address to the Leaders of Other Religions in Madras
(Chennai)', 5 February 1985

How has the teaching of the Second Vatican Council on other
religions been received and implemented around the world?
What impact has that teaching enjoyed on interreligious (or, as it is
often now called, 'interfaith') relations and dialogue?

One can point to the institutional reception led by the Pontifical
Council for Interreligious Dialogue, which regularly sends messages to
Buddhists, Hindus, and Muslims on the occasion of their major religious feasts, takes part in bilateral meetings with representatives of
other faiths, attends world conferences of religions, and in further
ways constantly meets and interacts with other believers. Particular
dioceses (or eparchies among Eastern Catholics), national episcopal
conferences, and international bodies, such as the Federation of Asian
Bishops' Conferences (FABC) and international unions of bishops'
conferences in Africa, continue to implement the teaching and policies
of Vatican II through various interfaith commissions and meetings.
Within individual dioceses, as at the national and international level,
the degree of vibrant reception of what the Council proposed about
those of other faiths has depended not only on the bishops themselves

but also on the quality of the specialists who collaborate with them by serving on commissions or helping in other ways.

Here one should not forget what many Catholics (and other Christians) continue to do for interfaith relations through their parishes, universities, colleges, seminaries, hospitals, schools, houses and monasteries of religious men and women, and journals and publishing houses. Some monks and nuns have, for instance, proved outstanding leaders in implementing the teaching and mandate of Vatican II in the cause of interreligious dialogue and service. The 2010 film *Of Gods and Men* vividly presented a commitment to such service that brought martyrdom to seven Cistercians in 1996. They had lived peacefully with and cared for the local Muslims until being kidnapped by fundamentalist terrorists and assassinated. Nor should we pass over the innumerable laymen and laywomen who, without being members of their parish councils or of any other groups or movements, have set themselves to meet, serve, and pray for those of other living faiths.

Through what it said and mandated about 'the religious others', Vatican II set in motion a huge, intercontinental project that involves, or should involve, Catholics (and other Christians) in relating actively and lovingly with more than half of the world's population. I leave to someone else to tell the full story of how the teaching and decisions of the Council about relations with other faiths have been interpreted, implemented, and at times frustrated. This chapter limits itself to presenting some major ways in which John Paul II (pope 1978–2005) creatively received the conciliar teaching on other religions.[1] He devoted, for instance, more attention to Christian–Muslim dialogue that any pope who preceded him. This chapter and the next chapter focus on what one pope and one theologian contributed towards receiving Vatican II's teaching on other faiths.

---

1. See Aleksander Majur, *L'insegnamento di Giovanni Paolo II sulle altre religioni* (Rome: Gregorian University Press, 2004); Christian W. Troll, 'John Paul II and Islam', in Gerald O'Collins and Michael A. Hayes (eds), *The Legacy of John Paul II* (London: Continuum, 2008), 203–18; Simonetta Calderini, 'Response to Professor Christian Troll', in O'Collins and Hayes, *The Legacy of John Paul II*, 219–27; Troll, 'Mohammed—Prophet for Christians also?', in O'Collins and Hayes, *The Legacy of John Paul II*, 252–68. Although this lies outside the scope of this present book, we should never forget how John Paul II did more than any previous pope (with the exception of Blessed John XXIII) to heal the wounds of Christian–Jewish relations; see Margaret Shepherd, 'John Paul II and Catholic-Jewish Dialogue', in O'Collins and Hayes, *The Legacy of John Paul II*, 228–51.

Two Encyclicals and a Memorable Speech

Right from his first encyclical, *Redemptor Hominis* (1979), John Paul II creatively developed what Vatican II had taught about other living faiths.[2] While paying homage to a theme that he would develop in later encyclicals, the universal activity of the Holy Spirit (no. 6),[3] he remained true to the title of the encyclical by concentrating on the redeeming function of Jesus Christ. In speaking of 'the mystery of the redemption', the Pope called it 'the mystery in which each and every one of the four thousand million human beings living on our planet have become sharers from the moment they are conceived beneath the heart of their mothers' (no. 13).

Here John Paul II built on two key texts from *Gaudium et Spes* (both of them found in GS 22) but introduced a significant development. The first text spoke of the actual impact of incarnation: 'the Son of God by his incarnation, in a certain way, united himself with every human being'.[4] The second highlighted a possibility offered to all by the Holy Spirit: 'since Christ died for all and since human beings have in fact one and the same final calling, namely a divine one, we ought to hold that the Holy Spirit offers to all the possibility of being united, in a way known to God, to the paschal mystery'. In *Redemptor Hominis* the Pope first wrote of Christ 'penetrating in a unique, unrepeatable way into the mystery of human beings and entering their heart' (no. 8; see GS 38). He then went beyond a possibility to present *actual* results coming from Christ's death and resurrection to all human beings and in fact coming to them from the very first moment of their human existence. From the time of their conception, they all, without exception, begin to share in 'the mystery of redemption' (no. 13): that is to

---

2. For the original (Latin) text of *Redemptor Hominis*, see *AAS* 71 (1979), 257–324; for this and the other two encyclicals by John Paul II that I will discuss, *Dominum et Vivificantem* and *Redemptoris Missio*, an English translation is found on the Vatican website, as well as in Michael J. Miller (ed.), *The Encyclicals of John Paul II* (Huntingon, IN: Our Sunday Visitor, 1996).

3. We will see how John Paul II moved official doctrine forward by his vision of the universal presence and activity of the Holy Spirit, an activity also exercised among members of other religions; see Jacques Dupuis, *Toward a Christian Theology of Religious Pluralism* (Maryknoll, NY: Orbis, 1997), 173–7, 360–2.

4. On this theme retrieved from the Fathers of the Church, see Chapter 1, n. 10. John Paul II quotes these words from *GS* in *Redemptor Hominis*, 8.

say, right from the beginning of their existence and before they make any free decisions, they share in the mysterious and dynamic reality of Christ, who became light and life for all people, Christians and others alike, by dying on the cross, rising from the dead, and sending the Holy Spirit from the Father.

What John Paul II said about Christ entering the inward 'mystery of human beings' and being united with them right from their conception could easily evoke what Karl Rahner wrote about 'the supernatural existential', or the way in which, as a result of Christ's redemptive work, God has positively preconditioned human beings even before they can exercise their freedom in accepting (or rejecting) divine grace. Through his reference to the statistics of world population at the end of the 1970s ('four thousand million') and the concrete imagery of human beings 'conceived beneath the hearts of their mothers', the Pope put more picturesquely what Karl Rahner expressed through his 'supernatural existential' (Chapter 2 above). Every human being, even before he or she makes any conscious decisions, is already sharing in the reality of the crucified and risen Christ. The Pope and Rahner converge in the same vision of all human life as Christ-oriented and Christ-supported.

Juan Alfaro (1914–93), a friend and close collaborator of Rahner, admitted to me that he was consulted by John Paul II when the Pope was preparing *Redemptor Hominis* for publication. Alfaro (who had a passion for John's Gospel) may well have encouraged not only the remarkable use of that Gospel in the encyclical but also the echo of (or, at least, convergence with) Rahner's supernatural existential in the two passages just mentioned (8, 13).

In *Redemptor Hominis*, John Paul II cited *Nostra Aetate* as being 'filled with deep esteem for the great spiritual values, indeed for the primacy of the spiritual, which in the life of human kind finds expression in religion and then in morality' (no. 11). He also referred to what *Ad Gentes* and *Lumen Gentium* expounded on the 'seeds of the Word': 'the Fathers of the Church rightly saw in the various religions, as it were, so many reflections of the one truth, "seeds of the Word", attesting that, although the routes taken may be different, there is but a single goal to which are directed the deepest aspirations of the human spirit as expressed in its quest for God' (ibid.). Mixing images in this dense statement (shining reflections, growing seeds, and routes taken), the Pope makes three points: (a) as *Ad Gentes* had already stated, in some sense Christ, the Word of God is present 'in the various religions'; (b) the routes taken by these religions differ but the goal (God) remains the same; (c) the religions express the human 'quest for God'. How (a) happens (through the work of the Holy Spirit) will be explained in a later encyclical, *Redemptoris Missio* of 1990. Apropos of (b), the centrality clearly given to Christ right through the encyclical shows that the Pope did not endorse the view that the different 'routes' are equally efficacious in bringing believers to their common goal in God. (c) John Paul II unquestionably assigned the priority to the divine initiative of Christ 'entering the human heart' and associating all people with his death and resurrection before they could ever take any route in their search for God. They seek God because God had first found them through Christ and the Holy Spirit.

Early in the encyclical, John Paul II made *two significant advances* when referring briefly to 'the representatives of the non-Christian religions'. He spoke of Catholics coming closer together with them 'through dialogue, contacts, *prayer in common*, investigation of the treasures of human spirituality, in which we know well the members of these religions also are not lacking'. He added the rhetorical question: 'does it not sometimes happen that the firm belief/conviction (*firma persuasio*) of the followers of the non-Christian religions—a belief that is also an effect of the Spirit of truth operating outside the visible confines of the mystical body—can make Christians ashamed at being often themselves so disposed to doubt concerning the truths revealed by God and proclaimed by the Church and so prone to relax moral principles and open the way to ethical permissiveness?' (6; italics mine). Recognizing how the Holy Spirit also operates 'outside' the visible Church picked up what *Gaudium et Spes* had already taught about the Spirit's activity throughout the world (Chapter 6 above). With an eye on an episode in which the Holy Spirit descended on those not yet baptized (Acts 10: 23–48), *Ad Gentes* had specifically observed that the Spirit 'at times anticipates apostolic activity' (*AG* 4).[5] However, John Paul II struck a new note by contrasting 'the firm

---

5. The public outpouring of the Spirit upon Cornelius and his party spectacularly exemplifies the Spirit acting on those who are not or are not yet baptized Christians (Acts 10: 23–48); for some theological implications of the story of Cornelius, see G. O'Collins, *Salvation for All: God's Other Peoples* (Oxford: Oxford University Press, 2008), 149–52.

belief' displayed 'sometimes' by followers of other faiths with what happens 'often' with Christians, who can doubt 'truths revealed by God' and lapse into 'ethical permissiveness'. Vatican II had acknowledged in other faiths elements of 'truth and grace' and even 'riches' distributed by 'the bountiful God' (*AG* 11). The Pope now added: the way some followers of other religions live up to the (lesser) blessings they have received through the Holy Spirit stands in judgement on the way that Christians often fail in belief and practice.

Like *Nostra Aetate*, *Ad Gentes*, and *Gaudium et Spes*, John Paul II supported coming together in dialogue with followers of other faiths. But he went a step further by proposing 'prayer in common' (see above).[6] In October 1986, he boldly broke new ground by doing just that and going off to Assisi with the Dalai Lama and other heads or representatives of the world's religions to pray for peace. Some Catholics, including some members of the Roman Curia, judged this event in Assisi harshly as if it somehow betrayed Christian faith in Jesus. The Pope replied to his critics in his Christmas address to the Roman Curia, delivered on 22 December 1986.[7] He echoed and extended a dictum that goes back many centuries ('every truth, no matter who says it, comes from the Holy Spirit').[8] John Paul II spoke not so much of truth but of prayer: 'every authentic prayer is called forth by the Holy Spirit'. For good measure, he added that the Spirit 'is mysteriously present in the heart of every person'. That same year he had already put the Holy Spirit firmly on the agenda of papal teaching.

John Paul II dedicated a long encyclical letter, *Dominum et Vivificantem* (Lord and Giver of life), published at Pentecost 1986, to the Holy Spirit active in the life of the Church and in the whole world.[9] According to God's plan of salvation, the 'action' of the Spirit 'has

---

6. See Jacques Dupuis on interreligious prayer, *Christianity and the Religions: From Confrontation to Dialogue*, trans. Phillip Berryman (Maryknoll, NY: Orbis, 2002), 236–52.

7. See *AAS* 19 (1987), 1082–90, at 1089.

8. In the form of 'omne verum, a quocumque dicatur, a Spiritu Sancto est', it turns up eighteen times in the works of St Thomas Aquinas. Like others, Thomas thought that the saying came from St Ambrose of Milan. In fact, in a slightly different form, 'quidquid enim verum a quocumque dicatur, a Sancto dicitur Spiritu (for whatever that is true, said by anyone, is said by the Holy Spirit)', it went back to an anonymous fourth-century author, now known as Ambrosiaster (*Corpus Scriptorum Ecclesiasticorum Latinorum*, 81, par. 2, 132).

9. *AAS* 78 (1986), 809–900.

been exercised in every place and at every time, indeed in every individual'. This is an action which, to be sure, is intimately 'linked with the mystery of the incarnation and the redemption' (53). That is to say, the universal activity of the Spirit is inseparably connected with what the Son of God did for all human beings by taking on the human condition, by dying and rising from the dead, and by sending the gift of the Holy Spirit from the Father.

The first papal encyclical to be dedicated to the Holy Spirit since Leo XIII's *Divinum Illud* ('that divine [office]') of 1897, *Dominum et Vivificantem* firmly recognized that the activity of the Spirit takes place in the whole world, but the main scope of the document remained within Christianity. The Pope wished to complete his teaching on the Trinity, with this encyclical of 1986 finishing the trilogy begun with *Redemptor Hominis* of 1979 (on the Son) and *Dives in Misericordia* (1980) (on the Father). Even more, as he explained in the introduction, he aimed to do something for the unity of Christendom (no. 2). The encyclical introduced new terminology into official teaching by twelve times calling the Holy Spirit 'the Self-communication of God'. Over lunch a few years later I thanked the Pope for adopting that term, which has a fairly rich background in modern German theology, both Catholic and Protestant. 'I didn't take it from Karl Rahner', he said with a smile, obviously thinking that as a Jesuit I had that Jesuit theologian in mind. He then explained his intention: 'I wanted to use some fresh language that might help build bridges with Orthodox Christians'. He thought of the difficulties that Greek, Russian, and other Orthodox Christians have with the way in which Catholics talk (or fail to talk) about the Holy Spirit's place in the eternal life and historical mission of the tripersonal God. Sensitive to the complaints from the Orthodox about Catholics making the Holy Spirit subsidiary within the Trinity, the Pope stressed the importance of the Spirit and, in particular, reached out to the Orthodox with some new language. His encyclical letter was nothing less than a heartfelt prayer for the love, unity, and peace that the Holy Spirit wishes to bring to separated Christians and their world.

Writing three years before European Communist regimes across Europe 'officially' fell in 1989, through his encyclical the Pope looked ahead in the hope of healing an ancient rift and promoting vigorous collaboration between Catholics and Orthodox in building a more Christian Europe. Sadly that was not going to happen. Ugly religious clashes were to occur in what was then the USSR, and around 200,000 people died in the break-up of Yugoslavia—a conflict partly fuelled by hostility between Catholics, Muslims, and Serbian Orthodox.

While the main scope of *Dominum et Vivificantem* pre-empted paying much attention to the Spirit operating in the wider world of other religions and cultures, a little later in 1986 the Pope addressed that theme. In a remarkable address to the aboriginal peoples of Australia, John Paul II spoke of the mysterious presence and activity of the divine Spirit in their culture and religion: 'for thousands of years you have lived in this land and fashioned a culture that endures to this day. And during all this time, the Spirit of God has been with you. Your "Dreaming", which influences your lives so strongly . . . is *your own way of touching the mystery of God's Spirit* in you and in creation'. The Pope added: 'the silence of the bush taught you a quietness of soul that put you in touch with *another world, the world of God's Spirit'.*[10] In this address delivered at Blatherskite Park (Alice Springs) to the largest gathering of the aboriginal peoples that has ever taken place since they first came 40,000 years ago to Australia, John Paul II used their language: above all, the motif of 'Dreaming' and the 'Dreamtime legends' which 'speak powerfully of the great mysteries of human life, its frailty, its need for help, its closeness to spiritual powers, and the value of the human person'.

Gestures and a Third Encyclical

Constantly reaching out to Jews, Muslims, and followers of other religions also characterized the work of John Paul II in implementing the call to dialogue and collaboration issued by *Nostra Aetate, Ad Gentes,* and *Gaudium et Spes.* Along with his addresses and writings, gestures played a major and often unprecedented role. On 19 August 1985, at the invitation of King Hassan II of Morocco, John Paul II spoke in Casablanca to over 100,000 young Muslims on the religious

---

10. 'Address to Aborigines and Torres Strait Islanders of Australia', 29 November 1986, *AAS* 79 (1987), 973–9, at 973–5. 'The Dreaming' or time of creation lays down for indigenous Australians patterns of life and spirituality involving sacred places, animals, plants, the birth of their children, and much else besides.

and moral values common to Islam and Christianity.[11] Since the days when Muhammad launched Islam more than 1,300 years ago, no pope has ever been invited by any Muslim leader to do anything like that. On 13 April 1986, John Paul II visited the main synagogue in Rome. He was probably the first pope to enter and pray in a synagogue since the early days of Christianity. Later that same year, as we saw above, he went with the heads or representatives of the world's religions to pray for peace in Assisi.

On 7 April 1994, the Pope hosted a Holocaust memorial concert in the Vatican. The Royal Philharmonic Orchestra came from London and was conducted by Gilbert Levine, an American Jew who had served as conductor of the Krakow Philharmonic. John Paul II sat in the Paul VI Audience Hall alongside the chief rabbi of Rome, Elio Toaff, who attended with his congregation and with 200 Holocaust survivors from twelve different countries. For the Jubilee Year of 2000, the Pope wanted to make a pilgrimage not only to Jerusalem but also to Ur (now in Iraq) and Mount Sinai (now in Egypt) to honour, respectively, Abraham and Moses. The government of Egypt welcomed him to Mount Sinai, but the government of Iraq refused the permission. John Paul II, during a ceremony in the Vatican, made a 'virtual' visit to the home of Abraham and Sarah. On 6 May 2001, on a visit to Syria the Pope prayed in a mosque in Damascus and so became the first pope ever to visit and pray in a mosque.

Along with these meetings and gestures, through his writing John Paul II also continued to lead the way in interfaith dialogue and thinking. In 1990 he issued another encyclical letter, *Redemptoris Missio* (the mission of the Redeemer),[12] in which he insisted that, while manifested 'in a special way in the Church and her members', the Spirit's 'presence and activity' are, nevertheless, 'universal'. He understood

---

11. For the entire text of this address, see *AAS* 78 (1986), 93–104; G. O'Collins, D. Kendall, and J. LaBelle (eds), *John Paul II: A Reader* (Mahwah, NJ: Paulist Press, 2007), 148–58.

12. *Redemptoris Missio*, *AAS* 83 (1991), 249–340; see William R. Burrows (ed.), *Redemption and Dialogue: Reading Redemptoris Missio and Dialogue and Proclamation* (Maryknoll, NY: Orbis, 1993), a work in collaboration that reflects on the encyclical in the light of the document, *Dialogue and Proclamation*, issued jointly in 1991 by the Pontifical Council for Interreligious Dialogue and the Congregation for the Evangelization of Peoples. See also Peter John McGregor, 'The Universal Work of the Holy Spirit in the Missiology of Pope John Paul II', *Irish Theological Quarterly* 77 (2012), 83–98.

What John Paul II taught can be summed up as an invitation to reflect on the cultural and religious values of peoples and to search for signs of the active presence of the Spirit in those values. The Second Vatican Council followed the example of Pope John XXIII by scrutinizing and interpreting 'the signs of the times' (GS 4). John Paul II went further by encouraging Catholics and others to open their eyes to the signs of the Holy Spirit present in the cultures and religions of our times. A meeting of Asian bishops, held in Rome in May 1998, took up that invitation and looked for the signs of the Spirit's presence and activity in the religious and cultural values of Asia. In the apostolic exhortation published after that synod, the bishops had much to report about the Spirit's presence in such Asian values as 'love of silence and contemplation, simplicity, harmony, non-violence, respect for life, compassion for all things, closeness to nature, filial piety towards parents, elders, and ancestors, and a highly developed sense of community' (Ecclesia in Asia, 6).[14]

Finally, John Paul II took up a mandate expressed by Nostra Aetate, Ad Gentes, and Gaudium et Spes by promoting solidarity and cooperation between all religions in their common responsibility for human welfare. This was also a major contribution to ecumenical and interfaith dialogue. In a letter dated 10 September 1992, encouraging a day of prayer for world peace, he stressed the need for believers of all kinds to remedy the situation of extreme economic and social differences between the rich countries of the north and the poor countries of the south.[15] His 1995 encyclical on the value and inviolability of human life, Evangelium Vitae (the gospel of life), called for 'the concerted efforts' of all 'those who believe in the value of life'. They must defend and promote together human life as 'everyone's task and responsibility', a common service shared by Christians and 'followers of other religions' (91).[16] This sense of making a common cause with all religious believers, 'men and women without distinction' who strive together to build 'a civilization of love, founded upon the universal

14. The text of this post-synodal exhortation is found in Peter Phan (ed.), The Asian Synod: Texts and Commentaries (Maryknoll, NY: Orbis, 2002).
15. This letter, addressed to Cardinal Edward Cassidy on the occasion of the sixth anniversary of the 1986 day of prayer at Assisi and written in French, is found on the Vatican website.
16. Evangelium Vitae, AAS 82 (1995), 401–522.

values of peace, justice, solidarity, and freedom', introduced the chapter on 'the service of human promotion' in *Ecclesia in Asia* (32–41).

Working together for true human development and justice in
human affairs, and especially support for the poor and oppressed, was
a major theme in Vatican II, above all in *Gaudium et Spes*. John Paul II
heard and practised the call to collaborate with those of other living
faiths (and with all people of 'good will') in furthering the common
good of all humanity.

Participated Mediation

This chapter has highlighted the teaching of John Paul II on the
universal activity of the Holy Spirit, a teaching that reached a climax
in his 1990 encyclical *Redemptoris Missio*. But that same encyclical also
took official teaching further on two related issues: (a) in its teaching
on 'The Kingdom of God' as distinct but not separate from the Church
(12–20); and (b) by indicating that Christ's universal mediation of
salvation and revelation allows for 'participated mediations' (5). Back
in Chapter 3, we saw how *Lumen Gentium* anticipated the longer
exposition that would be made by John Paul II about the Church
serving the kingdom, from which it remains inseparable. But theme
(b) breaks new ground. Let me explain.

The Pope, after establishing clearly in the same article that 'the salvific
universality' of Christ goes hand in hand with his universal role in
revelation, quoted the classic New Testament text on this mediation:
'there is one God, and there is one mediator between God and human
beings, the man Christ Jesus who gave himself as a ransom for all'
(1 Tim. 2: 5–6). At once the Pope commented negatively and positively
on the text: first, 'no one, therefore, can enter into communion
with God except through Christ, by the working of the Holy Spirit';
and, then, 'Christ's one, universal mediation' is positively 'the way
established by God himself'. Hence, while allowing that 'participated
forms of mediation of different kinds and degrees are not excluded', the
Pope insisted that such participated forms 'acquire meaning and value
only from Christ's own mediation' (*Redemptoris Missio*, 5).

The immediate context in the encyclical shows that the Pope had in
mind the mediation of both revelation and redemption. Hence any
figures in 'other' faiths who might exemplify 'participated forms of

mediation' could be understood to mediate, in different 'degrees', the truth of revelation and the grace of redemption. John Paul II did not specify who such figures could be, what roles they play in their particular religious tradition, or whether they belong to the founding generation(s) or turn up repeatedly in later generations. By speaking of 'different kinds and degrees', he envisaged a very considerable variety in which other mediators might exercise or fail to exercise such participated forms of mediation.

John Paul II, without saying so, respected the social and traditional nature of cultures and religions, through which, as he put it later in *Redemptoris Missio*, salvation is 'made concretely available' to those brought up in 'other religious traditions' (10). In all those various traditions, different 'kinds' of people and in 'different degrees' can mediate to others something of the truth and saving grace of God made available through Christ and the Holy Spirit. Many centuries ago, St Augustine of Hippo (d.430) wrote of such 'hidden saints' and 'prophets' among the Gentiles (*Contra Faustum*, 19. 2; *De catechizandis rudibus*, 22. 40). He declared roundly that 'prophecy was extended to all nations' (*In Ioannem*, 9. 9).

These other 'mediators', whatever their office and position in the various religious traditions, can in some degree and measure 'participate' or really share in the revealing and saving mediation of Christ. The papal language points to something intrinsic, akin to the sharing in 'the mystery of redemption' that belongs to all human beings from the first moment of their existence (*Redemptor Hominis*, 13). While all people, through the mysterious activity of the Holy Spirit, share, in differing but real degrees, in Christ who is the Light of the world and the Life of the world, leaders and functionaries of different religious traditions, despite all their deficiencies and failures, can share in mediating the light and life of Christ. Their participated mediation acquires any 'meaning and value' it may enjoy 'only from Christ's own mediation'.

This chapter has sampled some of the major ways in which Pope John Paul II implemented and carried further the teaching of Vatican II on other religious traditions. Let me turn now to Jacques Dupuis, a major figure in the theological reception of that teaching.

NINE

Jacques Dupuis' Contribution to Interreligious Dialogue

It need not be denied that the eternal Logos could manifest itself to other peoples through other religious symbols.

Avery Dulles, *Models of Revelation*

From the 1990s not only repeated encouragement from Pope John Paul II but also current world events put the theology of religions and interreligious dialogue among the top priorities for responsible Catholic and other Christian leaders, thinkers, and activists. It was in this dramatic context that Jacques Dupuis (1923–2004) of the Gregorian University (Rome) took his work on Christian faith and the 'religious others' to a climax by publishing two books.[1]

In late 1997 Dupuis brought out *Toward a Christian Theology of Religious Pluralism*, a 447-page theological reflection on Christianity and other religions.[2] Written originally in English, this book appeared almost simultaneously in French and Italian, and subsequently in Portuguese (1999) and Spanish (2000). Shortly after the book was published in October 1997, the publishing house of Queriniana (Brescia) asked Dupuis to write a shorter, more accessible version. This time Dupuis wrote in Italian, completing the manuscript on 31 March 2000, just over five months before the Congregation for the Doctrine of the Faith published the declaration *Dominus Iesus* and almost

---

1. See G. O'Collins, 'Jacques Dupuis', *New Catholic Encyclopedia Supplement 2010* (Detroit: Gale, 2010), 420–2.
2. *Toward a Christian Theology of Religious Pluralism* (Maryknoll, NY: Orbis, 1997).

a year before the Congregation issued on 27 February 2001 a 'notifica-tion' concerning *Toward a Christian Theology of Religious Pluralism*.[3] For various reasons the publication of Dupuis' shorter work was delayed for more than a year and finally appeared in the autumn of 2001. A full year later, English, French, and Spanish translations were published.[4]

The literature and documentation on *Toward a Christian Theology* are vast. An article written by Dupuis himself that appeared in *Louvain Studies* took into account, for example, twenty reviews that had appeared in English and twenty-seven in French.[5] Some of these, such as the assessment by Terrence Merrigan in *Louvain Studies*, entered into critical dialogue with Dupuis in a way that was admirable; others, such as an equally long piece in *Revue thomiste*, seemed an odd going back to a dead past. In all, there have been over 100 reviews in English, French, German, Italian, Portuguese, and other languages, as well as articles and chapters in books dedicated in whole or in part to a critical evaluation of his views.[6] Clearly Dupuis addressed a central question: how can Christians profess and proclaim faith in Jesus Christ as the one redeemer of all humankind, and at the same time recognize the Spirit at work in the world's religions and cultures—as was done by John Paul II? From a Christian perspective, what is the place in God's providence of the other religions, some of which pre-date the birth of Christ, and what beneficial impact can they have towards the salvation of their adherents? As revealer and redeemer, Jesus is unique and universal, but in practice the visible paths to salvation have remained

3. The notification said that the book contained 'notable ambiguities and difficulties on important points, which could lead a reader to erroneous or harmful positions'. But Dupuis was not asked to change a single line in the book. For the full text of the notification, see *AAS* 94 (2002), 141–5; trans. *Origins* 30, no. 38 (8 March 2001) 605–8.

4. *Il cristianesimo e le religioni: Dallo scontro all'incontro* (Brescia: Queriniana, 2001); *Christianity and the Religions: From Confrontation to Dialogue* (Maryknoll, NY: Orbis, 2002); *Le rencontre du christianisme et des religions: De la confrontation au dialogue* (Paris: Cerf, 2002); *El cristianismo y las religiones: Del desencuentro al diálogo* (Santander: Sal Terrae, 2002).

5. J. Dupuis, '"The Truth Will Make You Free": The Theology of Religious Pluralism Revisited', *Louvain Studies* 24 (1999), 211–63.

6. For a bibliography on *Toward a Christian Theology*, see Daniel Kendall and Gerald O'Collins (eds), *In Many and Diverse Ways: In Honor of Jacques Dupuis* (Maryknoll, NY: Orbis, 2003), 270–81. The discussion continues: see e.g. Mara Brecht, 'The Humanity of Christ: Jacques Dupuis' Christology and Religious Pluralism', *Horizons* 35 (2008), 54–71; T. Merrigan, 'The Appeal to Yves Congar in Recent Catholic Theology of Religions: The Case of Jacques Dupuis', in Gabriel Flynn (ed.), *Yves Congar: Theologian of the Church* (Louvain: Peeters Press, 2005), 427–57.

many. What might the various religious traditions mean in the divine plan to save the whole of humanity?

In this chapter I first summarize the content of *Christianity and the Religions* and indicate terminological and substantial issues that Dupuis took up in the two books. As he himself explained, the second more accessible book omits much scholarly debate with other authors and reduces footnotes to a minimum. But Dupuis also aimed at avoiding some earlier ambiguities, using further data from Christian revelation and tradition to back up his positions, and clarifying those positions more successfully.[7] In the second book, he faced the same basic questions: (a) can the adherents of the other religions be saved? (b) If one answers yes, do the elements of truth and grace found in these religions mean that their adherents can be saved, not despite, but through these elements? (c) If one again answers yes, do these religions enjoy a positive meaning in God's one plan of salvation for all human beings—or in the language of the Letter to the Ephesians—in the one 'recapitulation' of all things in Christ (Eph. 1: 10)? In responding affirmatively to all these questions, *Christianity and the Religions* sums up Dupuis' position by introducing a new expression 'inclusive pluralism', which is explained in the ten chapters of the book.

Dupuis begins with three chapters that summarize (a) the attitude of Jesus and the first Christians towards those who do not belong to 'the people of God', (b) the teaching of Vatican II, Paul VI, and John Paul II, (c) as well as major theological views in the field of the theology of religions. The other seven chapters treat themes that expound Dupuis' own 'inclusive pluralism'. The Bible recalls how God established saving covenants with 'other' peoples, who can therefore also be called 'peoples of God' (Chapter 4). The 'many and various ways' (Heb. 1: 1) through which the divine revelation has come may be understood to have prompted wider religious traditions (Chapter 5).[8] The Logos has acted and acts salvifically in ways that go 'beyond' the created humanity of Christ, although always with reference to the humanity it has assumed (Chapter 6). Other religions are 'participated mediations' in

---

7. Dupuis, *Christianity and the Religions*, 262.
8. Dupuis' appeal to Hebrews to underpin a 'wider' view of revelation could be further supported by also recalling the 'wider' view of faith found in Heb. 11 (see Chapter 5 in this present book). The list of outstanding examples of faith is not confined to Abraham, Sarah, and subsequent members of the 'people of God'.

the 'one mediation' of Christ (Chapter 7). While not separated from the kingdom of God, the Church is not identical with it (Chapter 8). Interreligious dialogue proves mutually enriching (Chapter 9), and, in particular, shared prayer should be fostered (Chapter 10). As before, a Trinitarian Christology (one that involves not only the Son but also the Father and the Holy Spirit) constantly supports the position of Dupuis, even if in *Christianity and the Religions* he sums up his theology of religions as 'inclusive pluralism'.

When evaluating the views of Dupuis expounded in the two books and how they receive and develop the teaching of Vatican II, one might sort out the issues that have emerged into terminological and substantial ones. Terms such as 'distinguish', 'separate', 'absolute', 'definitive', 'complementary', the 'Logos' qualified in various ways, and 'pluralism' have recurred over and over again in reflection on and objections to Dupuis' books. The debate itself has essentially come down to the work of Christ, of the Holy Spirit, and of the Church for the salvation of all people. Let us look first at the terms, trying to 'watch our language' in ways that analytic philosophy rightly encourages but contemporary theology sometimes neglects.

Some Terms

Over and over again Dupuis insists that he distinguishes but does not separate various things: for instance, (a) the divine and human operations of the incarnate Son of God, and (b) distinct paths of salvation within the one plan of God to save all human beings. In using this language to make such points, he shows himself a faithful follower of the Council of Chalcedon and its vitally important language about the two natures of Christ being distinct but not separated. No critic has found a passage in Dupuis' two books (or other writings) where he moves beyond a distinction and introduces a false separation, for instance, between the incarnate Word's action within the Church and in the world at large. Some critics have alleged that he separates the Word of God and the man Jesus into two separate subjects,[9] but

---

9. This was an accusation made, for instance, in two unpublished documents from the Congregation for the Doctrine of the Faith (26 September 1998 and 27 July 1999); see Kendall and O'Collins, *In Many and Diverse Ways*, 270.

they have never produced chapter and verse to back up this accusation. What Dupuis consistently argues is that within the one person of Jesus Christ we must distinguish the operations of his (uncreated) divine nature and his (created) human nature. Here Dupuis lines up with Thomas Aquinas, who championed the oneness of Christ's person but who also recognized how Christ's 'divine nature infinitely transcends his human nature' (*Summa contra gentiles*, 4. 35. 8).

Some reviewers puzzled over Dupuis calling Christ 'universal' and 'constitutive' but not 'absolute' Saviour and Redeemer, and speaking of the whole 'Christ-event' as 'decisive' rather than 'definitive'. Dupuis disliked the inflationary use of 'absolute' and 'absolutely' that flourishes in much ordinary speech and in some theological talk. He maintained a firmly Thomistic line: only God, who is totally necessary, utterly unconditional, uncaused, and unlimited, is truly absolute. While Dupuis never wanted to reduce Christ to being one saviour among many, he remained sensitive to the limits that characterized the historical incarnation of the Son of God, the created character of the humanity he assumed, and the specific quality of his redemptive, human actions. Moreover, the incarnation itself was a free act of God's love and not unconditionally necessary. As regards the other dimension of the divine self-communication in Christ, God's self-revelation that was completed with the resurrection and the outpouring of the Holy Spirit, no one should so emphasize the 'fullness' of this revelation as to ignore what Vatican II called 'the glorious manifestation of our Lord' still to come (*DV* 4). Those who claim otherwise ignore the way the language of revelation in the New Testament is strongly angled towards the future (e.g. 1 Cor. 13: 12; 1 John 3: 2), as Avery Dulles pointed out in his *Models of Revelation*.[10] John Paul II said the same thing in his 1998 encyclical on the relationship between faith and reason, *Fides et ratio*, where he wrote of 'the fullness of truth which will appear with the final revelation of God' (2). We now 'see through a glass darkly' and not yet 'face to face'; hence it is more accurate to call the revelation completed in Jesus Christ 'decisive' rather than 'definitive', a term that could too easily suggest (wrongly) that there is nothing more to come. A knee-jerk reaction characterized some who were upset by Dupuis' refusal to speak of God's historical self-communication in Christ as 'absolute': 'he

10. A. Dulles, *Models of Revelation* (2nd edn; Maryknoll, NY: Orbis, 1992), 228–9, 240–2.

must mean that it is only relative and that there are various more or less equal saviours and revealers'. That was not what Dupuis meant: in declining to use 'absolute' and 'definitive', he stuck closely to the language of Vatican II's Constitution on Divine Revelation and that of the New Testament itself.

As regards 'complementarity' between Christianity and other religions, Dupuis never intended to claim that the revelation which reached its fullness in Christ needs to be 'filled' out by other religious traditions. Rather he used that term to indicate how some elements of the divine mystery can be vividly conveyed by the practices and sacred writings found beyond Christianity. In prayerful and respectful dialogue with other traditions, Christians may 'hear' something which enriches them spiritually. They can receive as well as give, as the closing message of the 1977 international bishops' synod on catechetics recalled (5).[11] Nevertheless, to express the unique fullness of the divine self-revelation in Christ, it may have been better for Dupuis to have characterized from the outset the kind of complementarity he had in mind. In *Christianity and the Religions* he called the complementarity 'asymmetrical', an adjective which brings out the Christian belief that in Jesus Christ the divine revelation enjoys a unique fullness and suffers from no void to be filled up by other revelations and traditions.

In *Toward a Christian Theology* Dupuis distinguished the Logos *asarkos* (the Word of God in himself and not, or not yet, incarnated) from the Logos *ensarkos* (the Word precisely as incarnated). Dupuis was surprised to find this distinction leading a few readers to conclude that he was 'doubling' the Logos as if he were holding that there were four persons in God! To avoid such odd misunderstandings, in *Christianity and the Religions* he dropped the terms *asarkos* and *ensarkos*. However, he continued to distinguish between the Word of God *in se* or as such and the Word of God precisely as incarnated. We must make such terminological, 'reduplicative' distinctions. Otherwise, we will finish up joining some critics in such a strange statement as 'the Word of God as such is the Word incarnate'. Those who fail 'to watch their language' and use this kind of expression unwittingly attribute an eternal, real (and not just intentional) existence to the human being created and simultaneously assumed by the Word of God at a certain point in the

---

11. On this synod, see Chapter 7 above.

history of the world. They also appear to cast doubt upon the loving freedom of the Word of God in becoming incarnate for our salvation. The divine Word was under no compulsion to 'become flesh and dwell among us'. We return below to the need to introduce 'reduplicative' expressions, if one is to avoid such gross mistakes.

Finally, the word 'pluralism' obviously acted as a red rag to certain readers. Some linked it at once to such 'pluralists' as John Hick, who simply put Christ on a par with other religious founders or else allege that he differs from them only in degree but not in kind.[12] But 'pluralism' means a range of things: above all, 'pluralism de facto' (which recognizes the fact of different religions) and 'pluralism *de iure*' (which endorses pluralism on the basis of some principle). Now the latter pluralism in principle may take a soft, Hickian form: in principle, all major religions have equal authority and efficacy, and hence in principle are equally valid, separate paths to salvation. But pluralism *de iure* or pluralism in principle may take another form as when the Congregation of the Doctrine of the Faith's declaration *Dominus Iesus*, published in September 2000, followed the lead of John Paul II in his 1990 encyclical *Redemptoris Missio* and acknowledged how God becomes present to peoples through 'the spiritual riches' that their religions essentially embody and express (8). 'The presence and activity of the Spirit' touch not only individuals but also 'cultures and religions' (12); the 'elements of religiosity' found in diverse 'religious traditions' come 'from God' (21). Now, granted that God never acts merely 'in fact' but always 'in and on principle', such statements from *Dominus Iesus* about (a) the Spirit's activity in various religious traditions and about (b) all that comes from God to the religions necessarily implied some kind of religious 'pluralism' which exists in principle. I use this example from an unexpected source, *Dominus Iesus*, to illustrate how one needs to differentiate sharply between the 'pluralists' and 'pluralism'. Then one should scrutinize carefully the kind of 'pluralism' that Dupuis or anyone else endorses. Knee-jerk reactions to terminology are totally out of place here. The careful statement of what he meant by 'inclusive pluralism' in

12. See J. Hick, *The Metaphor of God Incarnate* (London: SCM Press, 1993); Stephen T. Davis, 'John Hick on Incarnation and Trinity', in S. T. Davis, D. Kendall, and G. O'Collins (eds.), *The Trinity: An Interdisciplinary Symposium on the Trinity* (Oxford: Oxford University Press, 1999), 251–72; and G. O'Collins, 'The Incarnation Under Fire', *Gregorianum* 76 (1995), 263–80.

while the human acts of the Word's whole historical story enjoy an
ever-present efficacy, the universal divine operations are not cancelled
or restricted by his assumption of a human existence that has now been
glorified through the resurrection. Both before and after the incarnation the Word of God remains divinely present and active everywhere, and has not been somehow 'eclipsed' by the assumption of a
human nature. This vision of the Logos's activity draws support from
the way some major exegetes understand John 1: 9 ('the true Light that
enlightens everyone coming into this world'), from the writings on the
Logos by Justin Martyr, Irenaeus, Clement of Alexandria, and Athanasius, and from such modern theologians as Avery Dulles. In fact,
Dulles anticipated the conclusion that Dupuis wished to draw from
the universal activity of the Logos:

It need not be denied that the eternal Logos could manifest itself to other
peoples through other religious symbols . . . In continuity with a long Christian tradition of the Logos theology that goes back as far as Justin Martyr . . . it
may be held that the divine person who appears in Jesus is not exhausted by
that historical appearance. The symbols and myths of other religions may
point to the one who Christians recognize as the Christ.[16]

To such a position Dupuis wanted to add two points. (a) First, he
repeated over and over again that the Word of God who continues to
be universally operative is personally identical with Jesus of Nazareth.
One must distinguish between the divine and human actions, but
never between two personal agents. (b) Second, along with all the
distinctions to be made, there is only one divine plan of salvation. All
people are called to share finally in the one divine life of the Trinity,
through the gracious activity (both human and divine) of the incarnate
Son of God and the divine activity of the Holy Spirit. I could not
understand how some readers of Dupuis' *Toward a Christian Theology*
(including those at the Congregation for the Doctrine of the Faith who
wrote the so far two unpublished documents of September 1998 and
July 1999) could miss his insistence that the divine plan of salvation
through Christ and his Spirit remains undivided and not multiple.
Dupuis excluded any talk of two 'economies' of salvation: either in
the form of an alleged Pneumatocentric plan of salvation separated

16. Dulles, *Models of Revelation*, 190; cited Dupuis, *Toward a Christian Theology*, 243, and
Dupuis, *Christianity and the Religions*, 124.

from a Christocentric one, or in the form of an economy of salvation in and through the Word as such that is separated from an economy of salvation in and through the incarnate Word (and the Holy Spirit).

(2) Mention of the Spirit leads us to a second major issue. On the one hand, the Holy Spirit was poured out at Pentecost to give life to the Church in her mission to preach to all people the good news of Christ crucified and risen for human salvation. Dupuis valued as much as the Second Vatican Council the ongoing power of the Spirit, working in and through the glorified Christ, both in the life of the Church (*LG* 3–4) and in the whole world (*GS* 22). But, on the other hand, he also emphasized that the action of the Spirit is not confined to acting in and through the risen humanity of Christ. 'Before' the incarnation, the Spirit acted in a revelatory and salvific fashion (*AG* 4). With the resurrection and Pentecost, the Spirit, while working in total communion with the glorified Christ, does not lose its universal, divine activity, so as to exercise its mission *ad extra* only through the mediation of Jesus' risen humanity. To allege that the Spirit's revelatory and saving action takes place exclusively through Christ's glorified humanity means maintaining a kind of Christomonism that Eastern Christians have often rightly denounced. If the visible incarnation did not mean the suppression of the divine powers of the Word, a fortiori the invisible, non-incarnate mission on which the Holy Spirit was and is engaged 'after the incarnation and Pentecost' did not entail limiting the divine nature and operations of the Spirit. What Dupuis wrote about the universal mission of the divine Spirit filled out nicely what John Paul II taught about the Spirit operating beyond the visible Church and enriching the world's cultures and religions.

This activity of the Spirit reaches and enriches the members of various religions in and through their religious life and practice. Normally there is no other way possible, since that is where Hindus, Buddhists, Muslims, and others live and worship. Since these religions contain elements of truth and goodness (*NA* 2) and since the Spirit of God is mysteriously but powerfully present to them, adherents of these religions can reach salvation by following the ways proposed to them. In some sense their religions are ways of salvation for them. In a guarded fashion, the International Theological Commission reached this conclusion in its 1997 document on 'Christianity and the Religions': 'because of such explicit recognition of the presence of Christ's

Spirit in the religions,[17] one cannot exclude the possibility that these [religions] *as such* exercise a certain salvific function' (84; italics mine). The document went on to allow cautiously that the religions can be 'a means which helps their followers to salvation' (86).

(3) Dupuis adds four qualifications to this picture. (a) First, over and over again he relates the ways of salvation proposed by other religious traditions to 'the event of Jesus Christ': that is to say, Dupuis never forgets the mysterious but real relationship of these 'ways' to the incarnation, life, death, resurrection, present activity, and future coming of Christ. (b) Second, all this happens as foreseen and intended by God. Granted that under God the various religions have or can have a positive role for the salvation of their adherents, there is only one, divine master-plan for saving the entire world, a whole in which we can distinguish different parts or paths: namely, the paths proposed by different religious traditions. In that picture it is God the Father who seeks out human beings and saves them, through his incarnate Word and his Spirit. It is improper, or at best secondary, to speak of people being effectively saved through any religious traditions. In his replies to the Congregation for the Doctrine of the Faith, Dupuis appealed here to the Council of Trent, which called God the Father 'the efficient cause' of justification and salvation (DzH 1529; ND 1932). (c) Third, Dupuis highlighted the *final* causality in the divine plan for salvation. In that one master-plan, all things, all cultures, and all religions converge towards the coming reign of God and the omega-point, the risen and glorious Son of God.[18] (d) Fourth, Dupuis repeatedly acknowledged that the fullness of the means of salvation is found only in the Christian Church. But what then is the role of the Church for the salvation of those who, while not baptized, go to God after a life spent practising their religious faith?

Most theologians remain grateful that the Second Vatican Council never repeated the old slogan 'outside the Church no salvation'—a slogan that many explained (or should one say explained away?) by talking of people being saved through 'implicitly desiring' to belong to the Church by an 'implicit baptism of desire'. The Council used

---

17. The reference is to John Paul II's *Redemptoris Missio*, 55.
18. Dupuis, *Toward a Christian Theology*, 389–90; Dupuis, *Christianity and the Religions*, 194.

rather, as we saw (Chapter 3 above), the language of all people, under the headship of Christ, being 'ordered' or 'oriented' towards the Church (*LG* 15–16).[19] What then is the necessity of the Church for the salvation of all human beings?

First, one should follow Dupuis (and before him John Paul II in *Redemptoris Missio*) in recognizing that the reign of God is the decisive point of reference. The Church exists for the kingdom and at its service, and not vice versa. Second, one should join Dupuis in acknowledging that the official magisterium of the Catholic Church from the time of Vatican II has been more cautious and less precise about the Church's role in bringing saving grace to those who are not baptized Christians (e.g. *Redemptoris Missio*, 9–10); the mysterious nature of God's plan to save all must be respected.

Third, the Church mediates grace to its members principally, although not exclusively, through the proclamation of the word and the administration of the sacraments, the centre of which is the Eucharist. The Church intercedes for 'the others'. Here Dupuis recalled that the Eucharistic prayers distinguish between (a) the invocation of the Holy Spirit to maintain the unity of the faithful and (b) liturgical intercessions 'for others' (intercessions that do not take the form of an *epiclesis*). The 'law of praying' should encourage theologians not to blur the distinction between the Church's role for the salvation of her members and for the salvation of 'the others'.[20] Here, however, I would take a more robust view of the function of the prayers made by the Church for the world through Christ the high priest (Chapter 7 above). Dupuis was right to distinguish what the Church does for her members from what it does for others. Yet that should not bring us to play down the force of the prayers of the faithful, directed through Christ and for the salvation of the whole world.

At a special audience on 6 April 2001, to commemorate 450 years of the Gregorian University's existence, John Paul II highlighted the importance of interreligious dialogue in today's world where members of different cultures and religions so often live side by side. Jacques Dupuis, as a systematic theologian who spent nearly forty years of his life in India, continues to offer a shining example of one who

---

19. On this, see Dupuis, *Toward a Christian Theology*, 347–56; Dupuis, *Christianity and the Religions*, 208–10.
20. Dupuis, *Christianity and the Religions*, 210–12.

supported such a dialogue, not only through his *Toward a Christian Theology of Religious Pluralism* and *Christianity and the Religions* but also through other publications and activities. His theology of the religions converged with the official teaching and actions of John Paul II and provided it with a massive theological underpinning.

TEN

Final Perspectives

The question of Christian identity in a world of plural perspectives
and convictions cannot be answered in clichés about the tolerant co-
existence of different opinions. It is rather that the nature of our
conviction as Christians puts us irrevocably in a certain place, which
is both promising and deeply risky, the place where we are called to
show utter commitment to the God who is revealed to us in Jesus
and to all those to whom his invitation is addressed. Our very
identity obliges us to active faithfulness of a double kind.

Archbishop Rowan Williams, Address to the Porto Alegre General Assembly
of the WCC (2006)

In his opening address to the Second Vatican Council (11 October
1962), John XXIII (pope 1958–63) expressed his dreams for what he
had set in train by calling an ecumenical council. Among other things,
he hoped for a fresh 'formation of consciences' and what he called 'a
new order of personal relations'.[1] In various ways the collective conscience of the Catholic Church was to undergo a sea change in its
perspectives on other living faiths—not only towards Judaism but also
towards Buddhism, Hinduism, Islam, and other world religions. After
the debates that led to *Nostra Aetate* and its promulgation, not to mention
further texts of Vatican II, things could never be the same again. In the
'new order of personal relations' with the 'religious others', there could
be no going back to a suspicious and often hostile past.

Understanding 'the other' inevitably involves understanding God;
discovering and engaging with 'the other' always mean discovering
and engaging with God. Seeking to glimpse how God operates in

---

1. *AAS* 54 (1962), 785–95; trans. *Catholic Mind* 60 (December 1962), 48–52, at 50, 52.

gospel are certainly not incompatible. Mission and dialogue, while distinguishable, condition each other reciprocally.

In his role as an official consultant to the Pontifical Council for Interreligious Dialogue, Jacques Dupuis played a major role in drafting *Dialogue and Proclamation*, published on 19 May 1991.[3] The full title of this forty-page document ran: *Dialogue and Proclamation: Reflections and Orientations on Interreligious Dialogue and the Proclamation of the Gospel of Jesus Christ.*[4] While proposing 'an open and positive approach to other religious traditions', this text could not 'overlook the contradictions that may exist between them [those other traditions] and Christian revelation'. Where 'necessary', one should recognize that 'there is incompatibility between some fundamental elements of the Christian religion and some aspects of such traditions' (ND 1060). This means that, 'while entering with an open mind into dialogue with the followers of other religious traditions, Christians may also have to challenge them in a peaceful spirit with regard to the content of their belief'. Nevertheless, Christians 'must allow themselves to be questioned. Notwithstanding the fullness of God's revelation in Jesus Christ, the way Christians sometimes understand their religion and practice may be in need of purification' (ND 1061).[5] Through such mutual questioning and challenges, Christians and 'the others' can 'deepen their religious commitment', 'respond with increasing sincerity to God's personal call', and undergo 'a deeper conversion towards God' (ND 1063).

After describing how interreligious dialogue should draw out the best in each other, the document pressed on to maintain firmly that interreligious dialogue and mission, as 'authentic elements of the Church's evangelising mission', are not only 'legitimate' but also 'necessary'. While 'intimately related', both 'activities remain distinct' (ND 1064). Dialogue does not 'replace proclamation' (ND 1065), and proclamation remains driven by 'a deep love for the Lord Jesus' and 'the

---

3. On this document, see J. Dupuis, 'A Theological Commentary: Dialogue and Proclamation', in William Burrows (ed.), *Redemption and Dialogue* (Maryknoll, NY: Orbis, 1993), 119–58.
4. The complete text is found in the Pontifical Council for Interreligious Dialogue, *Bulletin* 77/26 (1991/2), 210–50.
5. A major purpose of Vatican II was nothing less than purifying the ways in which Catholics had been understanding and practising their faith (Ch. 7 above).

Select Bibliography

Alberigo, G. and Komonchak, J. A. (eds), *History of Vatican II*, 5 vols (Maryknoll, NY: Orbis, 1995–2006).

Anderson, G. A. and Stransky, T. F. (eds), *The Lordship of Jesus Christ and Religious Pluralism* (Maryknoll, NY: Orbis, 1981).

Barker, G. A. and Gregg, S. E. (eds), *Jesus Beyond Christianity* (Oxford: Oxford University Press, 2010).

Becker, K.-J. and Morali, I. (eds), *Catholic Engagement with World Religions* (Maryknoll, NY: Orbis, 2010).

Bristow, E. J. (ed.), *No Religion is an Island: The Nostra Aetate Dialogues* (New York: Fordham University Press, 1998).

Brown, S. E. (ed.), *Meeting in Faith: Twenty Years of Christian-Muslim Conversations Sponsored by the World Council of Churches* (Geneva: WCC, 1989).

Burrell, D., *Faith and Freedom: An Interfaith Perspective* (Oxford: Blackwell, 2004).

Charlesworth, M., *Religious Inventions: Four Essays* (Cambridge: Cambridge University Press, 1997).

Clooney, F. X., *Comparative Theology: Deep Learning Across Religious Borders* (Malden, MA: Blackwell, 2010).

Cornille, C. and Willis, G. (eds), *The World Market and Interreligious Dialogue* (Eugene, OR: Cascade, 2011).

D'Costa, G., *Christianity and World Religions: Disputed Questions in the Theology of Religions* (Chichester: Wiley-Blackwell, 2009).

Dupuis, J., *Toward a Christian Theology of Religious Pluralism* (Maryknoll, NY: Orbis, 1997).

Dupuis, J., *Christianity and the Religions: From Confrontation to Dialogue* (Maryknoll, NY: Orbis, 2002).

Faggioli, M., 'Concilio Vaticano II: bollettino bibliografico', *Cristianesimo nella Storia* 24 (2003), 335–60; 26 (2005), 743–67.

Faggioli, M., 'Council Vatican II: Bibliographical Overview', *Cristianesimo nella Storia* 29 (2008), 567–610; 32 (2011), 755–91.

Faggioli, M., *Vatican II. The Battle for Meaning* (Mahwah, NJ: Paulist Press, 2012).

Faggioli, M. and Turbanti, G., *Il concilio inedito. Fonti del Vaticano II* (Bologna: Il Mulino, 2001).

Flynn, G. and Murray, P. (eds), *Ressourcement: A Movement for Renewal in Twentieth-Century Catholic Theology* (Oxford: Oxford University Press, 2012).

Gäde, G., *Christus in den Religionen: Der christliche Glaube und die Wahrheit der Religionen* (Paderborn: Ferdinand Schöningh, 2003).

Geffré, C., *De Babel à Pentecôte: Essais de Théologie Interreligieuse* (Paris: Cerf, 2006).

Gioia, F. (ed.), *Pontifical Council for Interreligious Dialogue: The Official Teaching of the Catholic Church (1963–1995)* (Boston: Pauline Books, 1997).

Heft, J. L. (ed.), *Catholicism and Interreligious Dialogue* (New York: Oxford University Press, 2012).

Henry, A.-M. (ed.), *Les Relations de l'Église avec les Religions non Chrétiennes* (Paris: Cerf, 1966).

Hewer, C. T. R., *Understanding Islam: The First Ten Steps* (London: SCM Press, 2006).

Hünermann, P. and Hilberath, B. J. (eds), *Herders Theologischer Kommentar zum Zweiten Vatikanischen Konzil*, 5 vols (Freiburg im Breisgau: Herder, 2004–6).

Jones, L. (ed.), *Encyclopedia of Religion*, 15 vols (Detroit: Macmillan, 2005).

Juergensmeyer, M. (ed.), *The Oxford Handbook of Global Religions* (Oxford: Oxford University Press, 2006).

Kendall, D. and O'Collins, G. (eds), *In Many and Diverse Ways: In Honor of Jacques Dupuis* (Maryknoll, NY: Orbis, 2003).

Latourelle, R. (ed.), *Vatican II: Assessments and Perspectives*, 3 vols (Mahwah, NJ: Paulist Press, 1988–9).

Miller, J. H. (ed.), *Vatican II: An Interfaith Appraisal* (Notre Dame, IN: University of Notre Dame Press, 1966).

O'Collins, G., *Salvation for All: God's Other Peoples* (Oxford: Oxford University Press, 2008).

Race, A. and Hedges, P. M. (eds), *Christian Approaches to Other Faiths* (London: SCM Press, 2009).

Rahner, K., *Theological Investigations*, 23 vols (London: Darton, Longman & Todd, 1961–92); essays concerned with other faiths are found in vols 5, 12, 14, 16, 17, and 18.

Rahner, K., *Foundations of Christian Faith: An Introduction to the Idea of Christianity*, trans. W. V. Dych (New York: Seabury Press, 1978).

Ratzinger, J., *Truth and Tolerance: Christian Belief and World Religions*, trans. H. Taylor (San Francisco: Ignatius Press, 2004).

Ruokanen, M., *The Catholic Doctrine of Non-Christian Religions According to the Second Vatican Council* (Leiden: E. J. Brill, 1992).

Sesboüé, B., *Hors de l'Eglise pas de salut: Histoire d'une formule et problèmes d'interprétation* (Paris: Desclée, 2004).

Sullivan, F. A., *Salvation Outside the Church?* (New York: Paulist Press, 1992).

Vorgrimler, H. (ed.), *Commentary on the Documents of Vatican II*, 5 vols (London: Burns & Oates, 1967–9).

Waldenfels, H., *Jesus Christ and the Religions: An Essay in the Theology of Religions* (Milwaukee, WI: Marquette University Press, 2009).

Index of Biblical References

Index of Names

Adam, A. 64n.
Adolphus, L. 61n.
Ahn, G. 85n.
Alberigo, G. 61n., 85n., 109n.,
    129n., 144n.
Alexander VIII, Pope 41
Alfaro, J. 170
Ambrose of Milan, St 26, 125n., 172n.
Ambrosiaster 172n.
Anatolios, K. 20n., 21n.
Anawati, G. C. 101n.
Anderson, J. B. 110n.
Anselm of Canterbury, St 15
Anzir, King 23–4, 58
Aquinas, St Thomas 23, 25–6, 75,
    76, 172n.
    on Christ as head 73, 157
    on Christ's humanity 185, 189–91
    on images and shadows 12–14
    on salvation outside the
        Church 27–31, 32, 50, 55
Aratus of Soli 9
Arinze, F. 167
Arnauld, A. 41
Athanasius of Alexandria, St 6n., 20–1,
    129n., 192
Augustine of Hippo, St 12, 15, 75, 110
    on divine beauty 75, 136
    on Gentile prophets 180
    on no salvation outside the
        Church 22, 26, 32–3, 40
    on psalms 65–6
    on self-questioning 89
    on the true Light 21
Averroes 27

Avicenna 27

Balthasar, H. U. von 36n.
Barsotti, D. 84
Barth, M. 4n., 158n.
Bascour, H. 35n.
Basil of Caesarea, St 129n.
Bay, M. de ('Baius') 40
Bea, A. 50.
Beauduin, L. 62
Bechert, H. 96n.
Becker, E. 92–3
Becker, K.-J. 71n., 72n
Bellarmine, St Robert 37n., 49
Benedict XVI, Pope
    see Ratzinger, J.
Bernanos, G. 98
Berryman, P. 172n.
Bettenson, H. 6n., 31n.
Biechler, J. E. 35n.
Blanke, H. 4n., 158n.
Bloom, A. 44n.
Boersma, H. 54n.
Bonaventure, St 25n.
Bond, H. L. 35n.
Boniface VIII, Pope 31–2,
    41, 46
Bonner, A. 34n.
Boulding, M. C. 13n., 110n.
Bourke, D. 56n.
Brecht, M. 182n.
Brechter, H. S. 109, 110, 144
Bruemmer, V. 164n.
Buddha 19, 58, 98
Bultmann, R. 107